EDI: The Competitive Edge

EDI: The Competitive Edge

Phyllis K. Sokol

Intertext Publications
McGraw-Hill Book Company
New York, N.Y.

To Scott, Bruce, and Eric with all my love

"No matter how long you have gone on a wrong road, turn back."

Turkish proverb

Library of Congress Catalog Card Number 88-82421

10 9 8 7 6 5 4 3 2 1

ISBN 0-07-059511-9

Intertext Publications/Multiscience Press, Inc.
One Lincoln Plaza
New York, NY 10023

McGraw-Hill Book Company
1221 Avenue of the Americas
New York, NY 10020

Composed in Ventura Publisher by Context, Inc.

Contents

Acknowledgments

I would like to give special thanks to Glen Dubois, Chuck Kosy, Jim Oravec, and Bill Plumb for sharing with me their in-depth knowledge of their respective industries; to Lou Spreitzer for his encouragement over the last five years and for critiqueing these chapters; to Michael LaBush for his patience and support; to Myrna Tortorello for being my sister; and to all of the following friends and colleagues for being so generous with their time and knowledge in support of this project: Robert Bone, Sue Coburn, Garlon Crossno, Sheila Feinstein, Dave Goad, Bob Grau, Ed Guilbert, Randy Homes, George Klima, Bob Mercer, Ralph Notto, Randy Patterson, Charles Richards, David Rogers, Tom Sample, Jim Stechshulte, Bruce Siecker, Ph.D., and Tom Warner.

Preface

By every indicator, EDI, electronic data interchange to accomplish business transactions by transmitting and receiving machine readable data between trading partner companies, is taking the business community by storm.

From a very small user base only a short three years ago, projections are that for each of the next three years, the number of companies who have implemented EDI in at least one functional business area will double. By 1993, 70% of all U.S. companies will be making significant use of EDI.

Those that implement early will realize a competitive edge over their more traditional competitors. They will develop closer working relationships with their customer and supplier trading partners and they will be poised to take advantage of such benefits as reduced inventory and safety stock requirements, more efficient handling and crediting of customer payments, reduced processing error rates, and elimination of many manual, people intensive tasks throughout their organization.

Already, in some industries EDI has gained such widespread usage that it is a prerequisite of doing business. For companies in those industries, not using EDI puts them at a marked competitive disadvantage. In several other industries, the same is rapidly becoming the case.

Because of its inter-company aspects, electronic data interchange has been assumed to be a data processing and communications project and has been assigned to programmers, analysts, and communication specialists.

This is not the case. While computers and software programs are needed to support EDI and communication of business transactions, EDI is really a new way of conducting business. As such, it should be the province of functional business managers with strong support from their top level managers to evaluate potential benefits of EDI, develop new business procedures for the electronic environment and develop business specifications for system enhancements and development.

This book is intended as a handbook for functional business managers. Its focus is on business issues, integration of applications, cost/benefit analysis, and planning and implementation of EDI. Also included are chapters on the automotive, drug/pharmaceutical, and retail/grocery industries to be used as examples of various economic situations, business problems, and EDI and other related technologies being employed to solve those problems.

In order to write this book I have drawn from my educational and work experience. As data processing manager of a corporate EDI project I designed and developed the software needed to process, translate, and control EDI transactions for a trading community of almost two hundred trading partners. As active member of the ANSI X12 committee since 1983, I participated in the maintenance and public relations subcommittees, and several task groups. As design consultant and sales support with two EDI third party service providers, I designed the EDI management software necessary to translate and track EDI data going through the EDI host system. And, as an independent consultant I made contributions to the EDI planning and implementation projects of several major corporations.

All of the above has given me the corporate perspective that, I hope, will make this book valuable to you, the functional business manager, in evaluating the potential benefits of EDI and identifying the critical steps required to implement EDI within your organization.

Phyllis K. Sokol

Chapter

1

Setting the Stage for EDI

Objectives

- Demonstrate how the current competitive environment has increased the need to cut costs throughout the company.
- Show how just-in-time (JIT) manufacturing schedules can cut internal costs, but can be maintained only with JIT throughout the company.
- Explain how intra-company messaging capabilities to disseminate information throughout the organization have become much more sophisticated than inter-company messaging capabilities.
- Describe the inherent problems in paper-based business documents; how companies have sought improvements for these problems in the past and how EDI promises to be the solution for the future.

Major U.S. industries are looking for cost cutting measures to make them competitive with foreign suppliers. Some are moving to offshore locations where labor rates can be as low as one-fifth of domestic rates. Others are merging to take advantage of economics of scale and to secure lower prices and more favorable delivery schedules by becoming major customers to their suppliers.

A brief glimpse at some major U. S. industries shows –

THE ELECTRONICS INDUSTRY, reaching over $40 billion in sales in 1987 with an increase in current dollars of 8% over 1986, is experiencing a very tight market. Price competition is strong with both domestic and foreign companies as customer demand has become increasingly responsive to price. Cost cutting is industry-wide, with many companies instituting supplier management programs and phasing in JIT manufacturing schedules.

THE AUTOMOTIVE INDUSTRY is continuing to experience a shift in market share from American to foreign producers, prompting the possible shutdowns of manufacturing and assembly plants. Cost savings through JIT and quality improvement are major goals of the industry.

THE TEXTILE/APPAREL INDUSTRY is experiencing the same loss in market share for American apparel manufacturers with imports now accounting for half of U.S. apparel sales. Employment in this highly labor intensive industry declines each year with production workers constituting 85% of the workforce. The major goal of the industry is to reduce the amount of time it takes to get garments on the shelf for a retailer's order. In order to do this, closer relationships between customer and supplier are needed with rapid communication between the trading partners.

THE STEEL INDUSTRY is experiencing declining shipments, weakening prices, and labor turmoil. It has had losses for six consecutive years because of declining automobile production and a weak oil market. Aside from this, large producers are losing market position to emerging small mills, which operate with lower production costs.

THE PHARMACEUTICAL INDUSTRY is one in which manufacturing companies are amongst the most profitable companies in the United States; realizing 25% profit and wholesalers are amongst the least profitable with after tax profit margin under 1%. The number of pharmaceutical wholesalers is declining due to mergers designed to take advantage of economies of scale. In addition, new technology such as EDI is being employed in order to streamline procedures and reduce internal costs.

Today –

- Foreign products are eating into market share traditionally held by American products.
- Eroding profit margins are cutting into the expected profits.
- Extremely inelastic demands for our products are causing a large downward swing in demand as a reaction to a small increase in price.
- Wholesalers/distributors are experiencing severe competition, which forces them to work on very slim profit margins.
- American salaries are much higher than foreign labor rates.

In light of the current economic environment, what are the paths open to our corporations that will enable them to improve productivity and customer service and increase net profit margin?

How can they use their assets more efficiently, reduce labor and product costs, eliminate time lags, and provide value added services to their trading partners?

Many of the guidelines that were espoused several years ago for a healthy and thriving business have been adjusted or even reversed in the economic business climate today.

Years ago economists believed that large bank balances and sizable inventory levels were signs of a healthy and profitable business.

Today we know that the key to a profitable business is to have all your assets working for you.

The trend has been for

FINANCIAL MANAGERS to maintain bank balances only large enough to cover current commitments and invest other cash assets.

PLANT MANAGERS to store only enough parts inventory to satisfy current manufacturing requirements, with additional parts ordered for a specified delivery schedule as needed.

FUNCTIONAL BUSINESS MANAGERS to streamline business procedures so staff is used to accomplish activities requiring human judgment, while rote operations are handled faster and more efficiently by automated procedures and computerized systems.

ADMINISTRATORS to take advantage of the databases of information available to them locally on a microcomputer by developing reports that show past and current activity, and which help them to forecast future trends and product demands.

MARKETING AND CUSTOMER SERVICE MANAGERS to seek ways of becoming more responsive to customer requests and to fill orders faster and more accurately.

Many manufacturing companies are taking their lead from the Japanese and instituting just-in-time (JIT) manufacturing.

Traditionally, companies retained high levels of inventory, in part to protect against poor product quality, supplier delinquencies and faulty order entry. They even planned manufacturing steps to further build inventories of component parts prior to assembling the complete product.

Watching old films showing automobile assembly lines, one would see hundreds of fender assemblies moving down the conveyor belt, only to be stored until needed in another assembly operation.

However, maintaining a large inventory requires excessive storage capacity, excessive handling of stored product and the tying up of large quantities of capital.

The underlying philosophy of JIT manufacturing is for parts and components to be on time, of 100% quality and at the best price. Additionally, manufacturing steps are arranged so that each operation produces only what is necessary to satisfy the demands of the next step.

In several industries today, with automotive the most noteworthy, the major OEMs are placing increased pressure on their suppliers to support the JIT demands of product quality and delivery schedules.

At the same time they are drastically reducing their supplier base. The assumption is that those suppliers that can support the demands will get even more business and will have an even closer relationship than before – the ultimate competitive edge.

This is working to change the traditional customer- supplier relationship from one that has been predictable and somewhat adversarial, with each party trying to impose requirements on the other to the greatest extent possible, to one that is based on cooperation and mutual respect.

The "I've got to have it by...." and "You can't possibly get it until...." syndrome that has been evident in trading relationships in the past has not been conducive to cooperative inter-company relationships.

However, in order to effect the timely receipt and processing of orders and shipments of goods, data transfer must also be handled just in time. This means that the manufacturers are requiring their suppliers to support system technologies that they are currently not familiar with and are, therefore, unable to support.

However, the suppliers usually find that they have little leverage to effect similar changes with their own suppliers.

Let's take a look at how business systems and data handling have progressed within companies.

In many companies, processing of business transactions has progressed from a manual to a computerized effort. Data, which was stored in simple sequentially organized files, can be found today in relational, randomly accessed databases.

The more sophisticated companies have internal computer applications to handle most of their business processes.

With the advent of large memory and data storage capacity in microcomputers, processing has moved from a centralized mainframe computer run by a technical staff of computer operators and programmers to localized microcomputers with user friendly computer programs run by functional business managers.

Because of increased computerization and local processing, there has been a growing need for an intra-company messaging capability to disseminate information, to eliminate reentry of data and to provide an audit trail of intra-company activity.

What then is the inter-company messaging environment?

Standard business transactions, usually in the form of a paper document, telephone call or facsimile cover all aspects of inter-company relationships. Included are pre-purchasing and purchasing transactions, billing, invoicing and payment transactions, shipping and distribution transactions, financial transactions and various inquiry and response transactions.

Considering that inter-company transactions are the lifeblood of a company, their structure and handling have remained virtually static until fairly recently.

The majority of companies still deal in the traditional paper-based trade documents, accept lag time of up to several days while they are in transit via regular mail, then interpret and key-enter the printed data into a computer system.

A small but growing number of companies have developed electronic inter-company trade arrangements with major trading partners. Often these have been based on a proprietary system offered by the initiating company.

In many trading relationships one of the partners more often the customer, has a good deal more clout than the other. A major customer may dictate how it wants business to be conducted and may even sweeten the pot by promising a closer trading relationship or a competitive edge to its supplier. Sometimes a major supplier can exert similar pressure on its customers.

Additionally, a handful of industries have developed electronic trade arrangements, which key companies in the industry have adopted.

Because of the tremendous need to streamline inter-company business transactions and also as a result of very real benefits derived from those that have adopted electronic trade, many companies and industries are currently investigating and implementing similar arrangements.

Until recently, unless faced with a specific business reason for implementing EDI, few companies did. The EDI climate has been changing so that in the past year the feeling is growing that

- Electronic interchange is the wave of the future.
- EDI will soon be a necessity in order to trade in some industries.
- Unless a company is doing EDI in a few years, it will be at a marked competitive disadvantage.

This mood is evidenced by the throngs of interested people attending EDI trade shows (over 2000 at the 1987 annual EDI forum sponsored by the EDIA – formerly TDCC), the ANSI X12 and other standards committee meetings, and EDI presentations at industry trade shows.

The interest is high; however, the overwhelming majority of companies still support traditional paper-based business transactions. Current EDI activity has hardly reached “tip of the iceberg” level.

Let’s take a look at the problems inherent in traditional paper transactions.

First, they are slow. They require a substantial amount of handling time, mail time, interpretation, key-entry, and processing at both the sending and receiving sites.

Second, if manually prepared, they may contain inaccurate or incomplete information. If key-data entry is performed, errors may be introduced at the receiver’s location. Processing incorrect data or introducing errors in the data can result in high costs to a company.

Third, handling of paper is very labor intensive, especially interpreting the printed and written information and key-entering it. All three characteristics make paper an expensive medium to deal in.

Some see electronic trade as the answer to all three problems. However, it's certainly not the first possible solution tried.

There have been several interim solutions implemented by companies to alleviate one or more of the problems. For example, companies have increased the speed at which business documents reach them by:

- Reducing the time spent in transit in the mail system by getting local post office boxes, and setting up lockboxes and accounts in local banks.
- Processing incoming transactions in disbursed locations, often local to trading partner locations.

They have increased the speed at which paper transactions are handled and processed by:

- Eliminating separate enveloping of computer generated documents.
- Developing menu driven key-entry systems with on-line edits for completeness and correctness.
- Developing proprietary computer systems to handle transactions and communications at the trading partner site.

Companies have tried to eliminate many of the inaccuracies associated with reading, interpreting, and key- entry of incoming information by:

- Developing preprinted forms to provide a common, recognizable format.
- Developing on-line edits in key-entry operations to catch both the errors introduced during key-entry and those sent incorrectly.
- Using product codes to describe a product and maintaining alias tables, which describe the same product by various different code sets.
- Developing proprietary systems that support certain functions such as inventory inquiry or ordering in a user friendly series of menus and preformatted screens with internal edits and automatic transmission to the recipient.

Finally, companies have tried to make the handling of transactions less labor intensive by:

- Developing computer applications to replace manual processes.
- Eliminating key-entry operations by developing a link between inquiry and ordering systems, and the internal order entry/processing system.
- Automating reconciliation procedures.

Each interim solution represents an improvement over the manual processing of paper-based transactions. The logical end point would be to generate a file of data by an application formatted so that, once received, it could be fed into and automatically processed and acted upon by a receiving computer application.

This, in fact, is what electronic data interchange (EDI) promises when companies are poised to benefit by having a satisfactory communications capability and computer application.

Even then there are issues to be considered, changes to be instituted, and money to be spent before EDI becomes a reality.

Chapters 4 and 5 discuss all of the business issues a functional manager needs to consider:

- How to evaluate readiness and potential benefits.
- Which staff members need to get involved and at what stages.
- What tasks need to be accomplished in order to effect an EDI implementation and roll it out to the majority of his/her trading partners.

Chapters 6, 7 and 8 spotlight certain industries that have instituted, or are in the process of instituting, EDI. These chapters are not meant to be anecdotal, but rather are meant to investigate the specific business needs present in each industry, problems that needed to be corrected, what, if any, solutions were tried prior to EDI, and finally how EDI is working for the buyers, suppliers, and wholesalers/distributors in the industry.

Business managers may notice similarities between the situations discussed here and those they encounter in their own business environment. These parallels may then be used to help managers formulate a plan for entry into the EDI arena and to anticipate trading partner and intra-company attitudes.

Finally, Chapter 9 discusses EDI futures.

Summary

This opening chapter has sought to lay the framework for implementing EDI in the corporation today in response to a company's need to remain competitive in the world market and to maintain market share and profit margins in the domestic market.

The number of companies showing an interest in EDI has been growing rapidly as shown by the mandate to thousands of automotive trading partners to do EDI in order to support JIT manufacturing schedules and to hundreds of mass merchandiser vendors to do EDI in order to remain a viable vendor.

The pressure is on. However, most companies are not familiar with EDI or its communication and computer hardware and software requirements. EDI is an important step aimed at eliminating the problems inherent in traditional paper-based business transactions. Interim solutions have attempted to move transactions faster, improve their accuracy, and decrease their labor-intensive handling. EDI promises to dramatically improve the transaction of inter-company business and, by transmitting data electronically, eliminate paper and key-entry tasks.

Chapter

2

Opportunities for EDI

Objectives

- Provide a working definition of EDI.
- Provide a common knowledge base of EDI by giving an overview of electronic trade between a buyer and a seller company.
- Demonstrate the major benefits of EDI in the corporation.
- Explain what types of business environments are particularly applicable for attaining benefits from EDI.
- Trace the growth of EDI through the use of proprietary company standards, industry specific standards, and finally to a generic, cross-industry standard.

In the never-ending quest for the competitive edge and increased market share and net profits, electronic data interchange (EDI) is viewed as a panacea for all ills. It is certainly not that. EDI is not a cure-all for poor internal systems or inefficient business procedures. However, in the environment of electronic trade, companies have the opportunity of reducing the flow of paper with its inherent error rate, shortening the sales-purchase-pay cycle substantially, and improving business efficiency by more effective use of data.

Understanding What EDI Is (and Isn't)

Electronic data interchange (EDI) is the INTER-COMPANY COMPUTER-TO-COMPUTER communication of STANDARD BUSINESS TRANSACTIONS in a STANDARD FORMAT that permits the receiver to perform the intended transaction.

Inter-Company

Inter-company specifically refers to the electronic transmission of data between companies. This implies that the trading partner companies must have common communications capabilities. As this is not always the case, the companies involved can either purchase communication hardware and software, as required, or seek the services of a third-party service provider to act as the buffer between themselves and their trading partners. It is rather unusual for a project to span company boundaries as this one does. Consequently, the project requires a great deal of coordination of activity and involves representatives from trading partner firms and possibly third party service providers.

Computer to Computer

Not only are data traveling between companies, but they are, in fact, traveling from computer to computer between computer applications. The computer applications are assumed to be in place at both the sender and receiver locations prior to the implementation of EDI. Today the sender application generates a paper-based transaction and mails it to the receiver. The receiver key enters the data and processes it by running the receiver application.

In the EDI environment the sending application generates the business transaction, transmits it to the receiver, and the receiver uses the data as input to the receiving application. See Figure 2-1 for the paper and electronic data flows, using the purchase order as sample document. This places a good deal of responsibility on the sending application to generate a complete and accurate business transaction and on the receiving application to interpret and use the data received. While paper-based business transactions have been somewhat free-form in nature, sometimes requiring human interven-

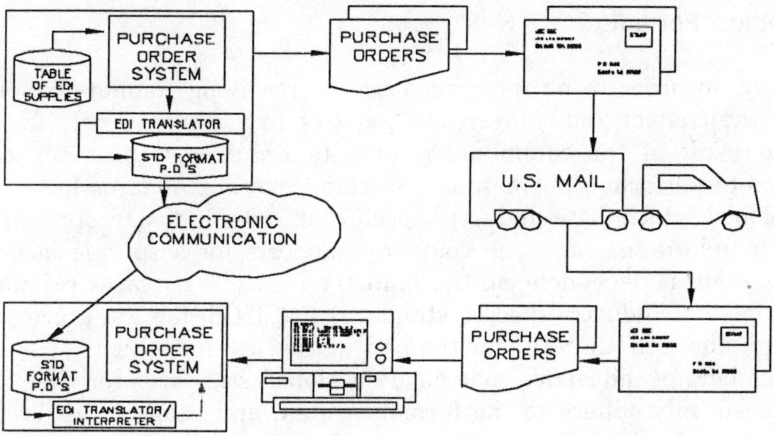

Figure 2-1 Paper and EDI data flows.

tion to complete or correct them prior to processing, machine-readable transactions cannot be interpreted correctly by the receiving computer application if they contain any ambiguities or errors. Rejected transactions become exceptions. Exceptions must be handled by hand, which eliminates many of the benefits of transmitting them electronically. Trading partners must agree beforehand on the form and content of business transactions in order to have a successful EDI implementation.

Standard Business Transactions

It must be clear that EDI does not refer to the transmission of electronic mail or other free-form messaging capabilities. The data referred to here are intended to permit the receiver to perform a standard business transaction, e.g., enter and process an order or bill a customer. Again, cooperation between trading partners is an essential component. The sender of data, as the partner that generates the transaction, determines the data availability. The receiver, as the processor of the transaction, determines the data requirements. Situations arise where the sending application must be enhanced to provide additional data or where the receiving application is not prepared to use all data fields that it potentially can receive.

Standard Format

Finally, in order to be recognized by the receiving computer application, the transmitted transactions must be in a standard data format. As a result of the commonality of data requirements among companies to perform a business transaction, several standards have been developed which have industry-specific or cross-industry application. The standard that any one company supports for a specific business transaction is dependent on the industry in which it trades primarily. Examples of industry-specific standards are UCS, for the grocery industry, and ORDERNET, for the pharmaceutical industry.

Members of industries that have developed standards for their own use need only adhere to the format, syntax, and usage rules for that format to begin trading electronically with any of their trading partners in that industry.

With the widespread acceptance of the American National Standards Institute (ANSI) X12 standard business transactions as a cross-industry standard, many industries new to the EDI arena are supporting it for use by their members. While the standard defines the data format, the individual industries are developing guidelines for usage and interpretation of the data fields.

Members of these industries, including electrical, chemical, metals, paper, office products, apparel, and others must adhere to the ANSI X12 format and syntax rules, as well as follow guidelines for usage of their industry to trade with others in the same industry.

Companies wishing to support the ANSI X12 standard that are in industries not yet supporting a standard or not yet developing guidelines for usage, as well as companies trading cross-industry using the ANSI X12 standard, must adhere to the ANSI X12 format and syntax rules, and develop their own guidelines for usage with their trading partners. As more and more companies, supporting industry guidelines, start trading electronically with partners supporting other industry guidelines, the potential for conflict in data usage will grow. A great deal of cooperation and coordination will be required to insure that trading partners can interpret data received correctly.

Different standards may be supported for different business transactions and for trading partners in other industries. Since the standard format is meant to serve only as a communications medium, no change of the internal application is required in order to implement EDI. Instead, a piece of software must be developed by both the sender and receiver, which acts as an application link between the internal application and the standard format. The sending application still generates the data for the paper-based transaction. However, rather than print it, the data necessary for the standard format of the transaction is mapped into the appropriate fields. The transactions are communicated to the receiving party. They are fed directly into the receiver's application link software, which maps the standard data fields into the input format required by the receiver's application software.

How Does It Work?

The concept is simple. Transmit machine-readable data between trading partners' computers. Figure 2-2 represents the interchange of electronic data. It shows two trading partners, in this case a buyer and a seller, and an EDI data stream transmitted from the buyer's computer to the seller's computer. Let's suppose the data stream is a group of purchase orders.

The buying company generates the transactions in its "gateway application," purchasing, as it always did. However, instead of using the purchase order data to develop the traditional paper transaction, it passes the data through an "application link" piece of software that

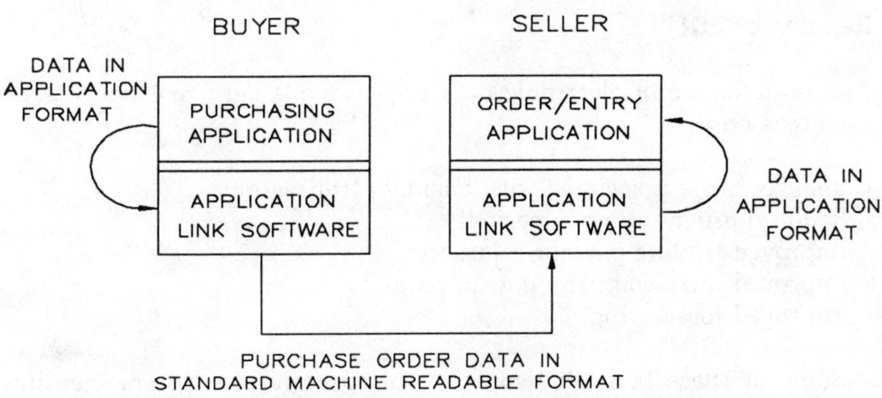

Figure 2-2 Overview of EDI.

maps it into a standard machine-readable data format. That format is then transmitted to the seller's site, where it is passed through the seller's "application link" which maps it to the internal format expected by the seller's order/entry "gateway application. Order/entry processes it just as it would any incoming purchase order.

The important aspects to note are:

- Ideally there is a gateway computer application in place at each end of the trading pair.
- Existing applications rarely, if ever, generate standard data format or expect standard data format as input. Therefore, the application link software is a necessity to bridge the gap between application format and the standard data format.
- Today several software developers are offering EDI front or back ends to their application software packages. These preclude the need for application link software by performing the interpreting and mapping functions between the ANSI X12 standard format and the internal format.
- The standard format was developed as a communications medium. Use of a standard is agreed to by both trading partners, who also agree to support the standard syntax and usage rules in order to insure that the receiving computer application can interpret the incoming data correctly and process the transaction properly.

Benefits of EDI

The interchange of electronic data does provide very real benefits in the areas of:

- Reduced costs associated with business transactions.
- Reduced order-cycle-pay period.
- Improved trading partner relationships.
- Improved intra-company flow of data.
- Improved forecasting.

Some of these benefits happen as a direct result of implementing EDI, while others are derived from making effective use of EDI data.

Let's take a closer look at each of the potential benefits.

- REDUCED COSTS ASSOCIATED WITH HANDLING OF BUSINESS TRANSACTIONS. With EDI, you eliminate key data entry and errors introduced by the receiver during that activity. Also eliminated are manual sorting, matching, filing, reconciling, and mailing tasks.

- REDUCED COSTS FOR MATERIALS AND SERVICES TO SUPPORT PAPER TRANSACTIONS. Upon implementing EDI you will decrease costs for paper, envelopes, and mailing materials as well as for telephone and courier services used to support transmission of orders and paper documents. Additionally, you will free up storage space for paper and material supplies and, eventually, for filing of paper transactions.

- REDUCED ORDER CYCLE-PAY PERIOD. By eliminating use of regular mail and by decreasing the time needed to process an order transaction, product can be shipped and received sooner. Therefore, the buying company need not order new product as soon and can lower its level of inventory safety stock.

  The selling company not only ships sooner, but can invoice sooner as well. By receiving an electronic invoice in a timely manner, the buyer has the opportunity of taking advantage of discount terms offered, thereby paying less for product. The seller, in turn, can receive payments sooner, improving its cash position and allowing it to pay less for its supplies by also taking advantage of discount terms.

- IMPROVED TRADING PARTNER RELATIONS. In order to successfully transmit, interpret, and process transmissions automatically, a good deal of trading partner cooperation is required. With each party counting on the other to either provide accurate data or to process and act on data received, it is important to make agreements in the following areas prior to implementing electronic trade.

  - Developing business procedures.
  - Defining data requirements and usage.
  - Communications methods, line speeds, and "operational windows" (period of time during which data can be sent).
  - Setting up testing schedules prior to implementing electronic trade.

  Also, by receiving more accurate and complete data and by eliminating key entry errors on the receiving end, suppliers can be assured of making more accurate and timely shipments to their customers, as well as eliminating the need for charges associated with return shipments of incorrect product.

With this higher level of customer service, the supplier can look forward to more and larger orders from its regular customers and attracting a larger customer base.

- IMPROVED INTRA-COMPANY FLOW OF DATA. With the generation and receipt of more accurate business transactions, the opportunity exists to glean information from all EDI transactions, and to develop and maintain a complete audit trail of that activity.

  By disseminating that data to managers within the company, possibly in an on-line inquiry and reporting system, you provide the wherewithal to develop forecasts for future business opportunities, track vendor performance, evaluate cost savings, justify additional EDI activity, improve marketing strategies, and improve management control.

  Auditors, natural opponents to a system perceived to offer less control and tracking features than the current paper environment, will become proponents of EDI with major improvements in these areas.

- IMPROVED PLANNING AND FORECASTING. In an electronic environment, rapid receipt of accurate and complete business transactions is the norm. Orders can be processed quickly and shipments can be scheduled accurately. Companies can plan more accurately for receipt of goods as well as scheduling assembly line manufacturing tasks. Down time during the manufacturing cycle can be virtually eliminated, thereby reducing operations costs.

  In the area of cash management, managers can plan cash flow more precisely by receiving and making payments sooner than before. As more business is converted to EDI, the cash position improves as assets are freed up from reduced safety stock and storage space requirements.

The Fertile Business Environment for EDI

There are certain business situations that are particularly applicable to EDI, such as:

- THE COMPANY THAT BUYS OR SELLS LARGE VOLUMES OF STOCK ITEMS. For example, the purchasing department of a manufacturing company orders raw materials and component parts to support its manufacturing activities.

- THE COMPANY THAT BUYS OR SELLS A PRODUCT THAT CAN BE DESCRIBED BY A PRODUCT CODE AND IS QUICKLY CONSUMED. Tremendous numbers of purchase orders and invoices characterize the grocery industry and drug industry. Buyers and sellers in these industries were among the pioneers in EDI.

- THE PRODUCT REQUIRES CAREFUL TRACKING AND REPORTING. Food, drug, and chemical companies are some of those on whom strict tracking and reporting requirements are imposed. By maintaining manufacturing information and combining it with EDI ordering information, a complete audit log of who received what product can greatly facilitate recall, and provide accurate, complete tracking.

- THE BUSINESS TRANSACTION REPRESENTS A TREMENDOUS AMOUNT OF PAPERWORK. Shipping documents fall into this category of transaction.

- THE COMPANY OR INDUSTRY FINDS ITSELF IN A VERY COMPETITIVE MARKET. A highly competitive market is characterized as being price sensitive; i.e., a small price increase will result in substantially lower sales. Revenue can be increased only by increasing the number of items sold. As the EDI environment provides the opportunity for a company to offer better customer service in the areas of order and inventory information and more timely order processing, sales can be expected to increase while costs decrease. Both increase of sales and decrease of costs will tend to increase profits.

- THERE IS A REQUIREMENT FOR RAPID PROCESSING AND DELIVERY OF GOODS. Here, the electronic environment is a virtual necessity.

Manufacturing companies supporting JIT manufacturing schedules are pressuring their suppliers to accept orders electronically and report their intention to ship via an electronic advanced shipping notice. EDI may not only be a convenience in this situation, but, with strong customer pressure as is the case in the automotive industry, may be a necessity for the supplying company to remain a viable vendor.

Manufacturing companies often combine vendor management activities (reducing the number of vendors and developing closer ties and larger commitments to those remaining) with EDI implementation.

On the other hand, sporadic or one time ordering situations are not compatible with EDI. Likewise, transactions dealing with custom product are likely to require manufacturing specifications, graphics, blueprints, and narrative comments accompanying the request for quote and ordering transactions. These would be difficult or impossible to handle in an electronic environment with today's technology.

A noticeable exception is the metals industry, represented by aluminum and steel, which have attempted to quantify and codify all manufacturing specification parameters associated with their products.

A computer system receiving such a purchase order would have to be extremely "smart" in order to interpret and act upon such complex incoming data.

Growth of Electronic Trade

It is interesting to look back at the first attempts at trading in an electronic environment, to follow the evolution thus far, and from that, to predict the directions and activity we expect of EDI in the future.

EDI was introduced as a medium of trade initially by two types of companies, one, a major supplier, the other a major customer. Each offered to its trading partners a system supporting its own proprietary company format. Both did it to improve their own business situations and both had the clout to influence their trading partners because their business represented a major portion of the trading partner's business.

Let's look a little more closely to discover what each stood to gain from use of the proprietary system, and how the trading partners fared.

The MAJOR SUPPLIER offers a proprietary ordering system, as shown in Figure 2-3, to its large customers and may even throw in hardware and software. Usually this company has a centralized order/entry function, so all orders come in through the one gateway system.

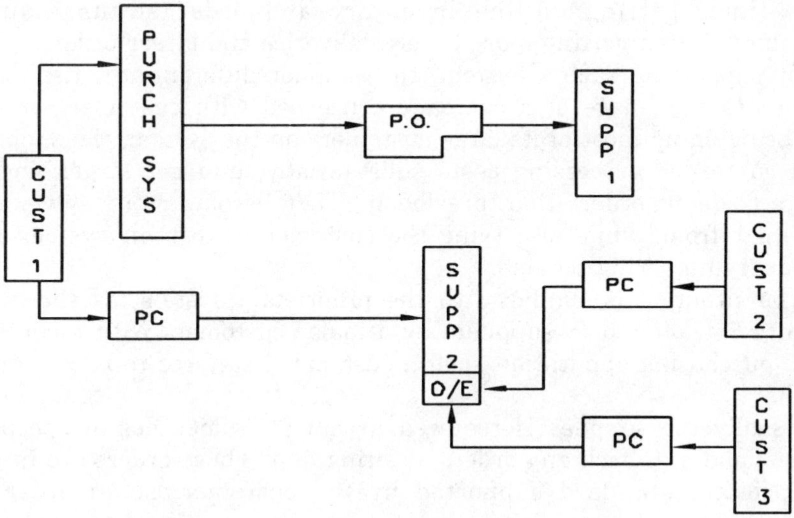

Figure 2-3 Supplier proprietary company standard.

A typical proprietary ordering system is usually interactive at the customer site and generates the internal order format required by the supplier's order processing system. Sometimes the system requires input of a particular purchase order format rather than key entry onto a screen. In that case the supplier gives documentation explaining the format requirements to its customers, who are expected to generate and transmit the appropriate file to him.

However, the customer may deal with several major suppliers. If each "offers" a proprietary system, the customer soon has a half-dozen microcomputers with as many different menu systems, product numbering schemes, order formats, and communications requirements. Soon the convenience of each becomes a large hassle.

Also, while all of the systems direct order information to the suppliers, none direct any data into the customer inventory systems or other internal applications. In order for customers to maintain order data, they have to turn around and key enter it into their own internal systems.

In return for use of the system, the customer is promised better service to give it the competitive edge with its competitors.

In fact, the customer does realize benefits from use of the system, sometimes getting on-line inventory and order status inquiry capability; often getting more timely deliveries and larger orders.

By supporting such a system, the supplier differentiates itself and promotes the image of a company concerned with customer service. By bringing up most of its large customers on the system, the supplier can cut order processing costs substantially, and get larger and/or more frequent orders than previously. They become more convenient to order from, while also tying the customer in to their system and product numbering scheme.

The situation is similar with the proprietary system, as shown in Figure 2-4, offered to suppliers by a major customer. With a centralized purchasing application such a customer is a force to be reckoned with.

Usually the supplier is required to call in (sometimes at specified times) and pull back any orders awaiting him. Those orders are in the proprietary standard supported by the customer, so in order to process them, the supplier must interpret the incoming data, reformat it or key-enter it into his existing order/entry application, and then process it as any other order.

Since the pressure is coming from the customer side, with promises of giving favored suppliers the competitive edge, there is rarely a need to offer hardware or software to convince suppliers to use the system.

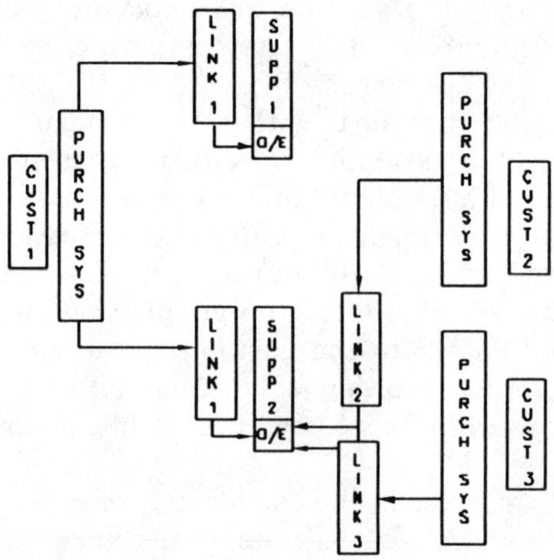

Figure 2-4 Customer proprietary standard.

In fact, the customer often increases the amount of business it does with suppliers on its system and may even use this opportunity to decrease its supplier base.

However, the supplier may have several major customers and may have to accommodate each by accepting orders in its proprietary standard format, by calling and retrieving orders in a specified method and at predetermined times, and by accepting its unique product numbering scheme.

For each different format it brings in-house, the supplier must develop a software link to reformat it into the internal format required by its order/entry application. All in all, this may represent a substantial amount of software development and maintenance and may be seen as returning fewer benefits to the supplier than it does to the customers.

Proprietary company systems, in general, offer greater benefits to the initiator of the system than they do to the trading partners.

Industry-specific standard format, on the other hand, was not developed by any individual company, but rather from input of many buyers and sellers in the industry and usually with an active trade organization sponsoring or supporting the effort.

With broad participation in their development, transaction formats should contain the functionality needed by all companies in the industry. Additionally, the requirements for the suggested or required method of communication must be developed with the industry companies in mind, so they must work for all sizes and sophistication of participating industry members.

An industry format is based on the homogeneous data requirements needed to perform business transactions within that industry. Different industries have developed very different types of standards and methods of communications.

For example, the pharmaceutical/drug industry, spearheaded by the distributors and the National Wholesale Druggists Association (NWDA), developed a fixed length standard format in the late 1970's for the purchase order transaction. At that time the NWDA endorsed one third party provider through which all transactions would flow. Communication protocol and line speed were left to the discretion of the participants and the third party.

Later, this industry developed formats for additional transactions, most notably, some that never before existed in paper form. Chapter 6 spotlights this industry and describes its business conditions, competitive environment, and proprietary and industry EDI activities.

Another example, the grocery industry, led by the major grocery manufacturers, retailers, and brokers, and Uniform Communications Council (UCC), developed a variable length standard for purchase orders, invoices, and various other transactions. They were also active in developing a standard for public warehouse documents called WINS, and used some transportation documents which had already been developed by TDCC. The preferred communication method was direct, with trading partners using Bisynchronous 2780/3780 protocol at 2400 baud.

The grocery industry is another that will be handled in depth, as part of Chapter 8 on the retail industry. It will be interesting to note how these two industries have progressed in EDI considering how different their early decisions and development were.

However, you will see that the benefit of developing an industrywide EDI capability, as illustrated in Figure 2-5, is that any industry member wishing to trade electronically with others in the industry can do so by developing one software link between its own application and the prescribed standard.

Potentially, the full trading community of manufacturers, distributors/wholesalers, and retailers can implement EDI using the

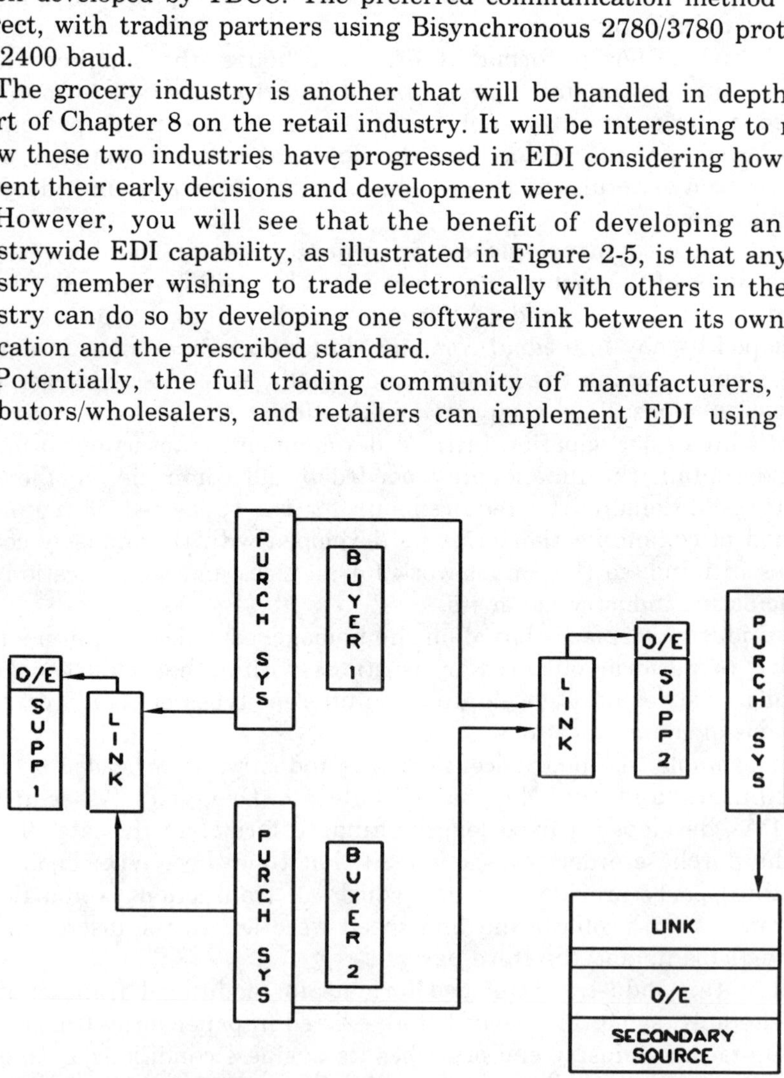

Figure 2-5 Industry specific standard.

same standards. As benefits of EDI accrue in direct proportion to the amount of business carried on electronically, this scenario provides potentially very high benefits.

The next step in the logical progression from company standard to intra-industry standard was to inter-industry standard. What was needed was a generic standard, based on the homogeneity of business transactions across industry lines, which would support multi-industry electronic trade.

American National Standards Institute (ANSI) became the sponsoring standards organization with the ASC (Accredited Standards Committee) X12 committee getting the mandate to develop variable length data formats for standard business transactions that would have inter-industry application.

The ASC X12 committee, accredited in 1980, has as its members representatives from many buyer and seller companies as well as third party providers in EDI.

Because inter-industry application normally requires more functionality than would be needed by any one industry, the ANSI X12 transactions tend to be more complex than an industry specific or company proprietary standard. Additionally, there may be more different types of transactions than any particular company or industry has need for.

However, companies often find that they have trading partners in several different industries. By supporting the generic ANSI X12 standard, a company can trade electronically in those industries by developing only one software link between its application and the standard, as shown in Figure 2-6.

Most industries that are investigating EDI, which have not already developed an industry specific standard, are today supporting the ANSI X12 standard.

Some examples of industries and corresponding trade organizations currently supporting X12 are:

Automotive	AIAG
Retail	NRMA, VICS
Chemical	CIDX
Electrical	EDX
Metals	Aluminum Association and AISI
Paper	API
Office Products	NOPA, WSA

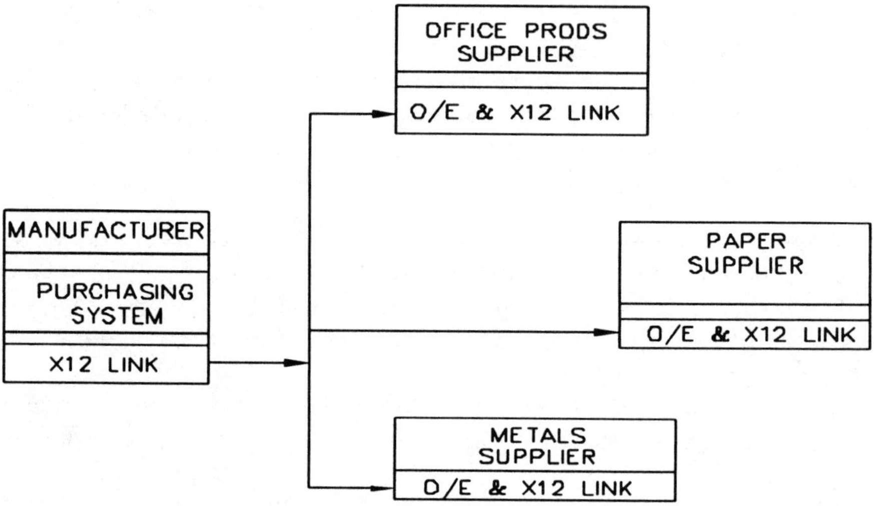

Figure 2-6 Generic cross industry standard.

Of these, the automotive industry will be examined more closely in Chapter 7.

Narrative-Style Messaging Capabilities

Narrative or free-form messaging communicated electronically via electronic mail and facsimile has existed as an inter-company messaging capability for many years. However, the free-form format requires a human interface at each end. While it does save time, being independent of mail service, it cannot be handled automatically. It is important to note, though, that EDI is only the inter-company messaging component of the total messaging capability required in business.

Electronic mail could be a very efficient method of handling the intra-company messaging requirements. With a link between intra- and inter-company messaging, an EDI transaction could be generated out of an electronic-mail message or a narrative-style message or report out of an EDI transaction. In this way, the flow of accurate and timely data would be uninterrupted.

Is Now the Time for EDI?

There is tremendous interest in EDI today as evidenced by the large numbers of company representatives participating in standards organizations, trade shows, and EDI classes and seminars.

The number of publications specializing in EDI has grown from none a year ago to at least a dozen today. See Appendix A for a list of these publications. Aside from these, many computer, purchasing, business, and industry magazines regularly feature articles on the benefits of electronic trade.

Whether or not EDI is right for you depends on many factors, including your business environment, the potential benefits and costs, and your corporate readiness.

Understanding the business and technical issues, analyzing the potential in your functional business areas, and planning and implementing are what this book is about.

Summary

This chapter has provided the background knowledge of what EDI is, how it has developed, and how it can benefit the corporation.

Electronic data interchange makes possible transaction of business by transmitting machine readable data from one computer to another. It permits companies to save both time and money because the data is transmitted rapidly, requires no key data entry, and has been generated accurately by an application program. Additionally it greatly reduces the order cycle/pay period, which in turn allows a company to reduce its inventory levels and improve cash flow.

By examining the types of business environments that provide fertile ground for electronic trade, we can understand why certain companies and industries implemented EDI years ago, and can anticipate the interest of others in the same or similar situations.

Chapter

3

Are You Ready For EDI?

Assuming that EDI can be beneficial in many business situations, the question is, are you ready to implement EDI and take advantage of the benefits it has to offer?

This chapter will deal with:

- Why and how EDI is introduced into a company.
- Inter-corporate interfaces in different types of companies.
- Levels of readiness.
- Distributed vs. centralized processing in a business area.
- Flow of data through internal systems.
- Communications, computer, and software requirements of EDI.

Typically, EDI is introduced at the operational management level of a business area. The idea may stem from internal inefficiencies or external pressure from trading partners with whom the firm does business.

Very little computational and communications capability is needed to physically accomplish EDI. The minimum requirements for a company's entry into the EDI arena are:

- A computer installed in-house (micro, mini, or mainframe).
- A communications capability to the outside with at least asynchronous error-detecting protocol.

However, a company on this level would gain few benefits from EDI. In order to attain benefits, the sending and receiving companies must have:

- A computer application to generate/interpret business transactions.
- Application link software to map data fields between the internal application format and the EDI standard data format.

Additionally, for maximum benefits from EDI with minimum setup costs, a company should have either centralized processing in the business area or distributed processing with identical application software in all distributed locations.

Following is a historical view of why and how processing within companies has changed between centralized and disbursed, and how that affects their readiness to implement and take advantage of EDI.

Starting with manual procedures, business was handled on a localized basis. In a small company there may have been staff that handled all transaction requirements such as receiving and processing a purchase order, checking inventory levels, directing shipment of goods, acknowledging receipt of the purchase order and intention to ship to the customer, purchasing replenishment stock or parts to manufacture product, sending invoices, and receiving invoices and reconciling them to the purchase orders sent.

Larger companies had segregated staff so that different transactions were handled by different personnel. To the extent that the company had only one location, information was accessible to anyone who needed it, although often hidden by an intricate filing scheme.

As computers became popular, information (soon to be referred to as data) was "filed" or stored in centralized files on a central mainframe computer. However, access was removed from the user, with jobs scheduled and run by a centralized or corporate operations staff. Printed output of the systems executed had to be disseminated to the user community.

To alleviate the remote access problem and to allow users to execute jobs on request, terminals were attached to the growing mainframes. However, while allowing remote job entry, and often printout of job reports, the terminal had no computing capability of its own.

With the growth of the microcomputer and with the extensive amount of memory and computing capability available at the user site, processing quickly became disbursed. Local files replaced corporate databases of information. Systems were much more user friendly, usually menu driven; able to be managed by even the computer neophyte. The trend was for local departments to buy or develop software for their own use, with little regard for intracorporate processing or data access needs.

Many companies have this disbursed environment today and have lost the corporate perspective for their functional business areas. Some, though, have gone one step farther, having corporate mainframe computers with microcomputer terminals at disbursed locations. They are bridging the gap between corporate data storage and remote access and computational ability.

In this situation, some companies have provided directives to their various locations of which application products should be purchased, or have developed an application system which is then distributed for use to the various functional locations.

These companies are poised to attain maximum benefits of EDI while minimizing initial costs. They need only develop the software required for one "EDI gateway" in order to implement EDI for one business area throughout the company.

The focus is generally on one or more functional business areas. Let's compare the requirements to implement EDI in a company with disbursed processing, as shown in Figure 3-1, as opposed to one with centralized processing, as shown in Figure 3-2.

Disbursed Processing

The disbursed processing case might be a corporation with separate autonomous divisions, each having several sites. See Figure 3-1. Each location might have its own functional business areas, computer center, and applications. Each would probably deal as a separate unit with its suppliers, even if it had many suppliers in common with other divisions of the company.

The number of purchasing departments in this corporation would be one for each location within a division. Each might have developed its own procedures, possibly ranging from manual to sophisticated computer applications.

If this corporation wanted to implement EDI in the purchasing area, clearly they would have to provide the interface between the current procedures and systems and the new EDI procedures and systems for each purchasing department. That effort would include:

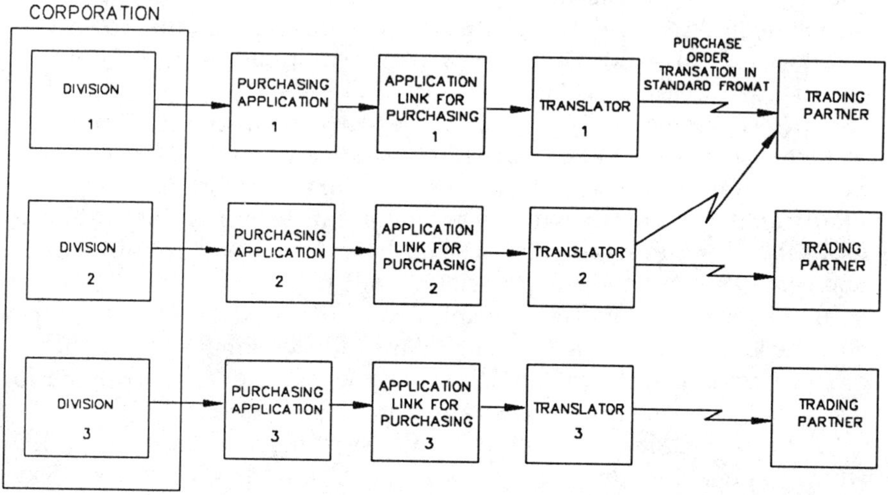

Figure 3-1 Disbursed processing.

- Developing a new data flow path for the EDI environment.
- Linking the existing application to a fixed field length file by developing application link software.
- Translating the fixed field-length file to a standard format by developing or purchasing translation software.
- Possibly purchasing communication hardware or software.

Considering the large initial outlay for any one purchasing department, benefits would be limited to business emanating from only that one department/division. Additionally, while the corporation as a whole might purchase a significant amount from a supplier, any one department of the corporation would likely not be considered a major customer. With little business between the parties, the supplier may not find the prospect of implementing EDI with this company as attractive.

To implement EDI in all of the divisions would require development of multiple application links and purchase or development of multiple translators.

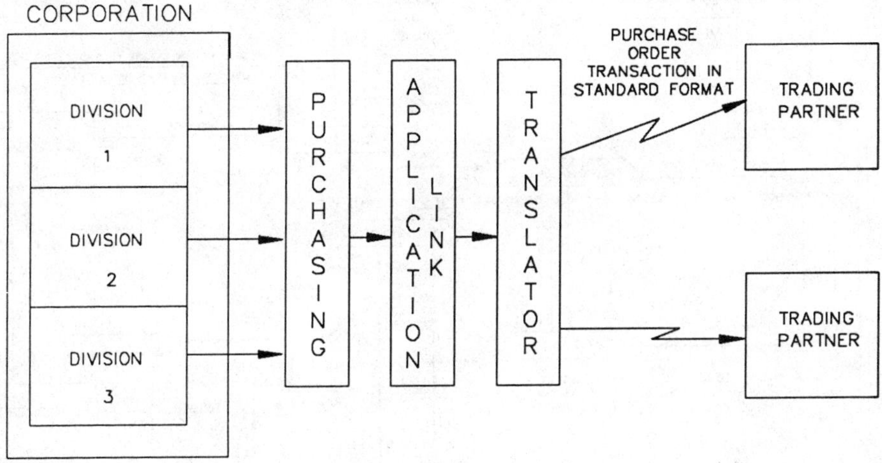

Figure 3-2 Centralized processing.

Centralized Processing

Looking at a centrally organized situation in Figure 3-2, there would be only one purchasing department for the whole corporation. If the EDI gateway had been established here with application and translation software, the initial expenditures would have provided the means to handle all of the corporation's purchasing. With the same outlay, the potential benefits would be much greater.

In evaluating a functional business area for potential EDI benefits, a company sometimes finds that it is not yet poised to attain those benefits. One of the reasons may be that its processing is too disbursed. Initial costs would be much too high to justify the attainable benefits. Such a company might choose to reorganize and centralize some processing or to adopt identical application software at the various computer sites prior to implementing EDI.

Let's examine the inter-company interfaces in various types of companies: manufacturer, distributor, financial institution. Within each type there are several business areas that can generate or receive

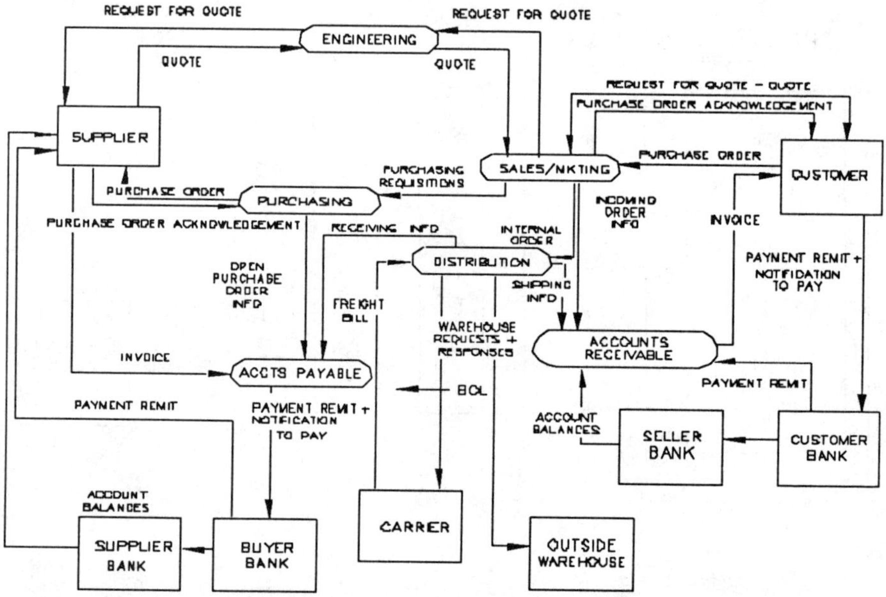

Figure 3-3 EDI for the manufacturer.

business transactions to/from trading partners. Which areas are they, what transactions do they handle, and how will the current business environment be affected by EDI?

EDI In a Manufacturing Company

Figure 3-3 represents a manufacturing company. The outside entities or trading partners of the company, customers, suppliers, financial institutions, and public warehouses are represented by squares. The functional business areas are represented by ovals. Transactions to/from trading partners are shown along arrows. Currently these are paper-based or telephoned transactions, but potentially each could be an EDI transaction.

The same ordering and paying transactions occur with directions reversed between a company and its suppliers and the same company and its customers. They flow between the customer's purchasing area and the supplier's sales/marketing area and between the customer's accounts payable area and the supplier's accounts receivable area. They are:

- Pre-ordering transactions of request for quote, quotes, inventory, availability inquiry.
- Ordering transactions of purchase order, purchase order acknowledgment, purchase order change, purchase order change acknowledgment, order status inquiry.
- Billing transaction of invoice.
- Payment transaction of payment remittance.
- Additionally, shipping transactions flow between the manufacturer's distribution area and its carriers, and shipment and inventory transactions flow between the distribution area and an outside warehouse.

EDI In a Distributor/Wholesaler Company

Figure 3-4 shows the outside entities, functional business areas, and transactions flowing for a distributor/wholesaler type of company.

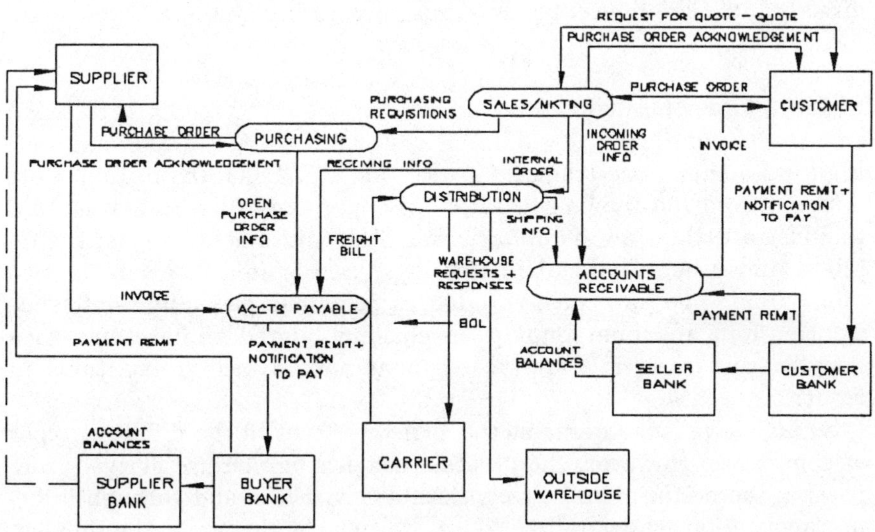

Figure 3-4 EDI for the wholesaler.

Note that all of the gateway business areas, those dealing with outside entities, are the same, except, in this case we haven't shown the outside warehouse.

The same information flow is required to effect business transactions here as in the case of the manufacturer, as the company also deals with customers, suppliers, carriers, and banks.

EDI potential may differ in certain areas based on the size and sophistication of the trading partner base and on the need to provide customer service. To the extent that the distributor's customer base is comprised of small retail stores and individuals, EDI potential is rather limited because these customers will probably not be prepared to support the electronic interchange of data.

However, some retail stores, large chain stores, and mass merchandisers will readily see the benefits of EDI and offer excellent EDI potential. For these customers, a distributor may offer an on-line inquiry and ordering system sometimes with capability of entering sales and inventory information. As discussed above, this provides a good deal of customer service by allowing inquiries into inventory and sometimes shipment status, and supports electronic ordering. Also, it discourages changing supply source as it ties the customer to the distributor's system. While not, technically speaking, EDI because it is interactive, it provides the distributor with electronic data which goes directly into the order/entry and order processing systems.

EDI In a Financial Institution

Figure 3-5 shows the transaction flow for a financial institution. Customers have been shown separately as buyer and seller companies just to illustrate the flow of information. Also illustrated are bank suppliers and other financial institutions. EDI potential exists in two main areas: one as a pass-through of customer payment remittance information, and one sending purchasing related transactions to a supplier and receiving acknowledgment and invoice transactions in return.

So far we've looked only at the EDI interfaces in the different types of companies. However, the greatest benefits of EDI are derived from passing the accurate and timely data received into and through internal applications. Looking at Figure 3-6 which illustrates the application environment of the manufacturing company, let's examine the

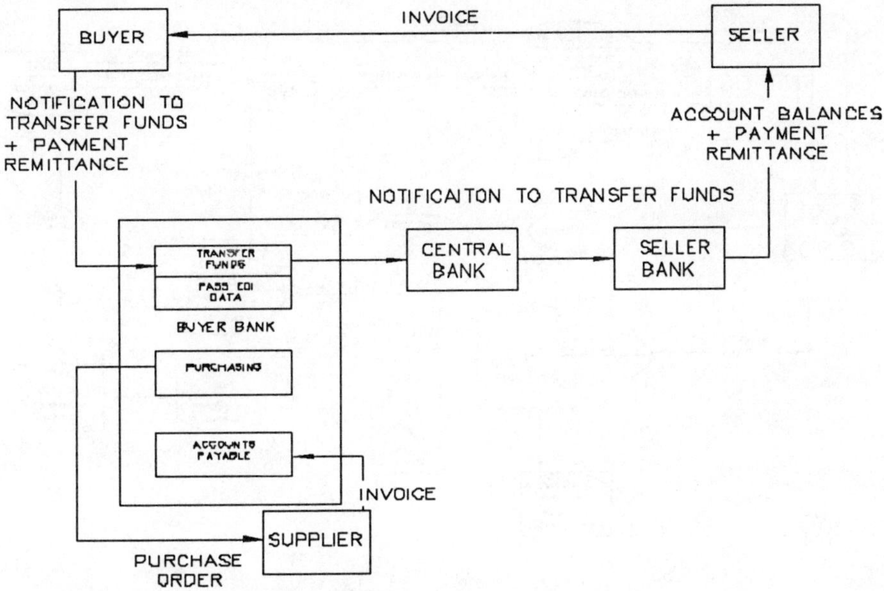

Figure 3-5 Transaction flow of a financial institution.

data needs of the applications and see how EDI data can be used directly, eliminating the need to do any additional data entry.

Starting with a request for quote (RFQ) received from a customer, which could be for stock or custom product, the response to a stock item RFQ can be generated out of the order entry application and transmitted to the sender. However, with an RFQ for custom product, the data must be passed to the engineering department, where it is evaluated, manufacturing specifications developed, and a response finally generated. This is a difficult area in which to implement completely automatic response to EDI data because:

- Such a request would usually be accompanied by drawings and other textual information.
- This company might have to send RFQ's out in turn to potential suppliers of raw materials and component parts.
- It would generate a quote in terms of price and manufacturing/delivery schedule.

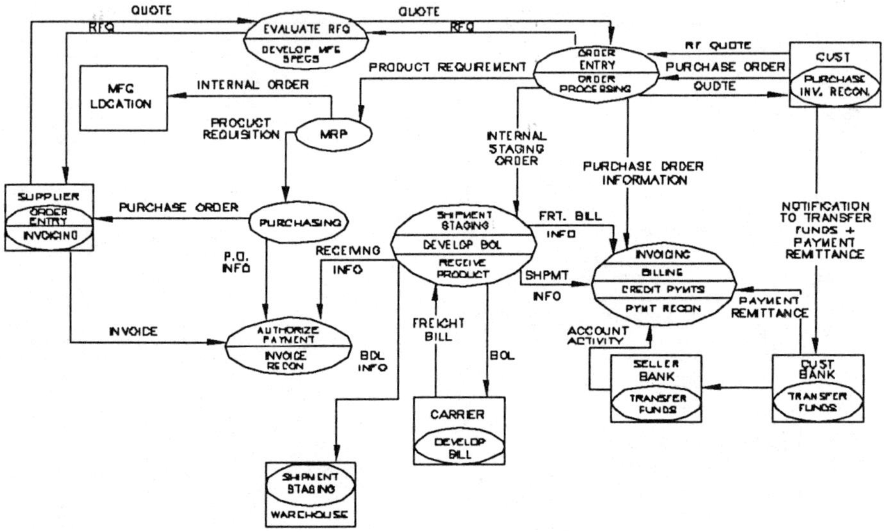

Figure 3-6 Internal applications of a manufacturing company.

In this figure, we are showing integrated order entry, order processing, and MRP (Materials Requirements Planning) systems. This is quite a sophisticated shop, which could benefit greatly from EDI. Let's look at the paths. The purchase order is received into the sales/marketing areas order/entry application.

Customer information is updated as needed, credit is checked, and the transaction is passed on to the order processing system.

The order processing system evaluates the order as being for stock or custom. If from stock it checks current inventory and marks the order as fillable from stock or in need of manufacture or assembly.

If available in stock it generates an internal staging order and directs it to the warehouse for shipment staging. If out-of-stock, it calls the MRP system to check product structure and parts inventory and then generates an internal order which it directs to a manufacture/assembly location.

Order processing also identifies the need to acknowledge the order and generates the acknowledgment, in large part from the original purchase order data.

Finally, the system maintains record of all open purchase orders. This information is accessed by the invoicing application to generate the invoice and by the payment reconciliation application in order to reconcile incoming payments prior to crediting them to internal accounts.

With integrated internal applications, a company is poised to attain maximum potential benefits from EDI. All that is needed is to assure that the data flowing through those systems is accurate and timely. In fact, it is not uncommon for the receiver of data to introduce errors during interpolation or key entry, and errors are very costly to handle.

By making the gateway application able to accept machine readable data, we are linking incoming purchase order data through the order entry and order processing systems, through the material requirements system, and finally through the purchasing system for raw materials and parts for the manufactured products ordered. This will cause a purchase order to be sent to the vendor with no additional key entry or human intervention. Once the order processing system has determined how much of the order can be filled with existing inventory, it generates an internal order to the shipment staging application at the warehouse and passes the open purchase order information to the invoicing application to develop the initial invoice.

The internal order that flows into the warehouse for stock items can be used to generate pick instructions for the warehouseman. Any deviations between the internal order and the actual shipped order must be noted and saved by the warehouse for the invoicing application as it provides the information with which to generate a corrected invoice from the initial invoice. It is the warehouse also that deals with carriers to ship orders. If there is an internal application available to generate a bill of lading that reflects the actual order awaiting shipment, that transaction is transmitted electronically in machine readable form to the carrier who rates the shipment and returns the freight bill.

Freight charges in that bill are the last piece of information needed to generate the final invoice.

So, aside from some adjustments to the internal order that must be key entered, probably at the warehouse site, there is no other need for key-entry or paper through the entire order, ship and invoice cycle.

In trading with suppliers, the company sends purchase orders generated from corporate or MRP requisitions and eventually receives the invoice into its accounts payable area. Once received, that invoice must be reconciled against the open purchase orders and receiving documents of incoming product.

Reconciliation tasks are notoriously wasteful in both time and effort. However, with the open purchase orders maintained in data format with shipping information available from barcoded labels on shipping cartons, and invoices received in data format, the three parts of the reconciliation triangle are available for automated reconciliation. All those items that have been invoiced correctly can be automatically authorized for payment with only exceptions kicking out to be handled by staff.

Potentially even payments can be handled in an automated fashion by authorizing payment through a financial institution and having them transfer funds to the seller's account, often through an intermediary or central bank facility.

When evaluating your company's EDI potential, think about the internal applications or lack of them that exists in your company's current business environment. Your goal must be to provide a full messaging capability, both inter- and intra-company.

The distributor has many of the same applications as the manufacturer. Orders come in for stock items only and the order processing system must examine current inventory levels and pass an internal order to the warehouse. The flow of data through internal systems is similar as is the potential for EDI traffic. Again, it depends on the level of customer whether EDI is feasible in that direction. However, transactions between a distributor and its suppliers offers great benefits to the company, especially if the purchasing application is centralized.

Many distributors and mass merchandisers realize that the invoice reconciliation process takes an inordinate amount of time and manpower, so they want to receive machine readable invoices from their suppliers and automate the reconciliation process.

Again, internal applications are the key to using the accurate and timely EDI data received from trading partners.

Components Of An EDI Implementation

There are three main requirements for an EDI implementation:

- Inter-company communication capability.
- A computer.

• Application link and translation software.

Following is an examination of each component with minimum requirements, benefits, shortcomings, and buy/lease/develop possibilities of each.

Communications

Communication of data between two points is governed by software on the sending and receiving sides called the communication protocol.

The protocol is programmed to recognize which party is the controlling one (usually the sender), examine data that has been received, and acknowledge its receipt prior to calling for more data (usually in a unit called blocks). If the protocol is error detecting, it will call for a resend of data in the form of a negative acknowledgment (a NAK) if it ascertains that the data received is not identical to the data sent. It will call for a send of the next block in the form of an acknowledgment (ACK) if the data received is identical to the data sent.

Note that the protocol makes no value judgments on the data itself, just checks that data received is identical to data sent.

The minimum communication requirement for EDI should be an error-detecting protocol which ensures integrity of the data received by detecting error introduced during transmission.

There are error-detecting protocols that are asynchronous as well as bisynchronous. Traditionally, mainframe computers have utilized bisynchronous protocols while microcomputers use asynchronous protocols. Today, there are both kinds for any size computer. However, bisynchronous protocols can typically handle transmission of data at faster line speeds (baud rates) from 2400-9600 bits per second (where one character is equal to 8 bits) while asynchronous protocols handle from 300-4800 bits per second.

When dealing in an inter-company environment, compatibility of communication capability between the companies is more important than which communication protocol to use. Anticipating EDI volumes can help to choose a line speed.

Not all asynchronous or bisynchronous protocols are compatible with one another, so the protocol to be used for transmission of data between trading partners must be evaluated for each trading partnership.

Often companies realize that they do not currently support and do not wish to support the variety of communication protocols needed to trade electronically with several trading partners. They may opt to effect transmission through an intermediary company known as a "third-party provider of EDI services."

This type of company offers access to each trading partner through a variety of different communication protocols and line speeds. Figure 3-7 illustrates how each partner arranges the best communication scenario of protocol and line speed between itself and the third party, freeing it up from the compatibility issue with its trading partners.

Also related to communication is the number of hours per day and days per week that transmissions will be supported between trading partners. This is known as the "operational window." As opposed to mail service, which arrives ready or not, the receiving company must be ready to receive data in the EDI environment or the transmission will be unsuccessful. Typically, trading partners agree on acceptable hours and days. Sometimes industry groups define acceptable protocols, line speeds, and operational windows.

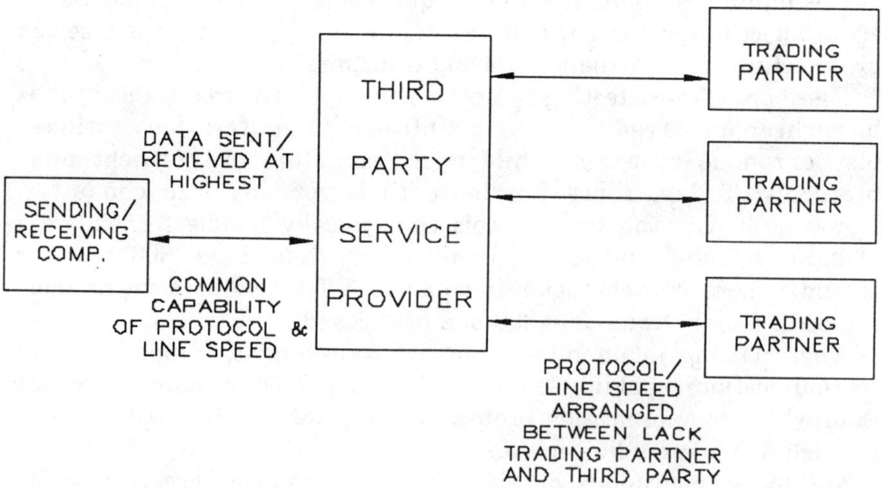

Figure 3-7 Communications arrangements between lack trading partner and third party service provider.

Third-party providers can alleviate a company's burden of being available to receive transmissions during hours or days that it might not ordinarily be operational. Third parties are normally open for transmissions 24 hours a day and 7 days a week, and maintain an electronic mailbox for each customer to which all incoming data is routed awaiting retrieval by the recipient.

The benefits and costs involved in using a third-party will be discussed in a later chapter that will also examine the criteria for selecting a third party and the other services they offer.

Computer Requirements for EDI

There are various hardware (computer) and software (application programs) solutions for an EDI implementation within a company. This section will examine micro, mini, and mainframe computers, and evaluate the benefits and shortcomings of using each.

The microcomputer is the least expensive but usually slowest of the three choices. This is a possible solution for one of three types of companies.

1. The company that has no computer today, but needs to satisfy the minimum requirements for doing EDI would use the micro as a standalone computer.
2. The company that already has a micro and wishes to utilize it for EDI.
3. The company that has a mini or mainframe computer, but wishes to use a micro as a front end to it.

If a company already has a gateway application on the micro or larger computer, it would need to be modified by an application link program to generate the data format required by the micro translator software instead of the print format for the paper document it is most likely generating currently. From this data format, the micro translation software would map the data fields to an EDI standard format, generate the standard file, and then transmit it.

If a gateway application does not currently exist, the company might want to purchase translation software with menu-driven entry screens and possibly application functionality. In this case, data entry would be accomplished interactively by completing pre- formatted screen layouts. Transactions would be interpreted and outputs would be generated on paper with micro, standalone software.

For a small, non-computer oriented company, a microcomputer may be the best EDI solution, as it can contain all of the required application link, translation, and communication software at a reasonable price with capability of entering outgoing data interactively and printing incoming data.

The standalone micro setup is also relatively inexpensive and easy to start up, and it is portable to the user location. Software products for the micro are also fairly inexpensive and typically are user-friendly with menu systems and pre-formatted screens designed for data input.

However, data entry is slow and cumbersome. There is little reduction in the number of errors introduced, as the user is generally not computer-wise. Also, the system is relatively slow, so it cannot handle large volumes of data and, while the transmission protocol is generally included in the software product, it can only support one transmission protocol. Finally, it usually cannot be bridged to existing applications.

The microcomputer can also be used as a front end to a mainframe or minicomputer. In this case, the micro translation software would need to be able to accept an input file downloaded from the mini or mainframe application and generate an output file which could be uploaded..

While the front end micro solution is user friendly and fairly inexpensive, many of the same benefits exist for a micro front end and it provides the additional benefits of being able to support higher volumes of EDI activity and eliminate the need for key entry of data.

Even when companies have mini or mainframe computers and application programs, they sometimes choose the front end micro solution for the short term as theyanticipate few EDI trading partners and little EDI activity.

With both application and EDI translation on the mini or mainframe computer, integration can be accomplished. Data would flow directly between applications with no need to up- or download data files.

With mini or mainframe software, the need for key entry is eliminated. It can support multiple transmission protocols, and can handle large EDI volumes. Examining the cost side, it is relatively expensive to either develop or buy an EDI translation product. Development requires extensive work and quite a bit of expertise in the standard. Such a product is not as user friendly or portable to the user location as its micro counterpart. It may also be harder to test and modify, and, while it can be integrated with internal applications, that job usually requires a good deal of work and data processing staff time.

In short, expenses and work are substantially higher for this solution, but so are potential benefits.

EDI Software

There are two processing steps generally required to link an existing internal computer application to a machine readable data format.

Sometimes, one piece of software can do both. Often two are needed: one to map the application fields taken from either key entered data input or from existing data files into a pre-defined fixed field length data format, and a second that accepts the fixed format as input and translates it into the variable length standard format. Figure 3-8 shows the functions performed by the internal application, the application link software, and the translation software for the outgoing stream.

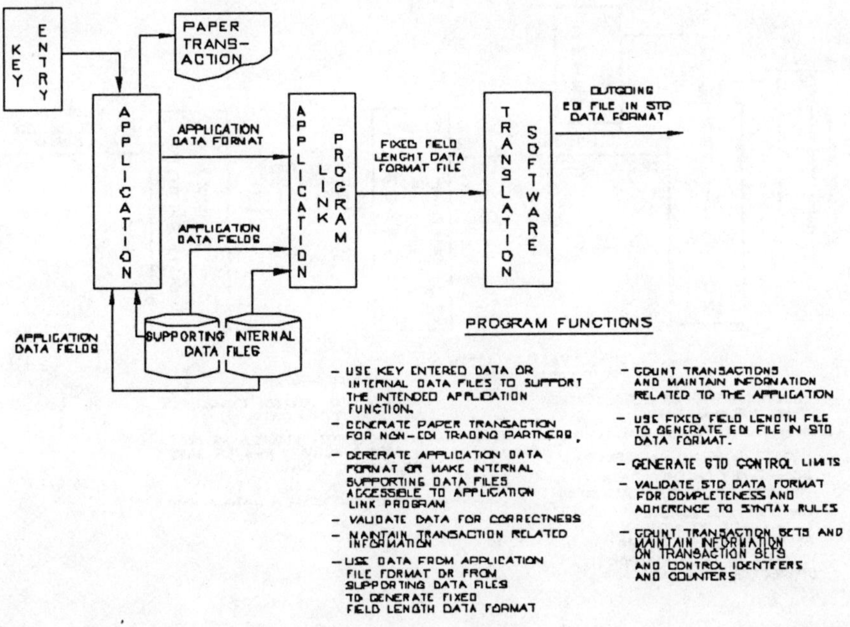

Figure 3-8 Outgoing EDI transmission.

For incoming data this procedure happens in reverse as shown in Figure 3-9. The translation software accepts the EDI standard format and translates it into the fixed format; then the application link software maps the fixed fields into the data format required as input by the application program.

Software products available for micro almost always need or generate a specific predefined fixed file. Sometimes, though, they have application functionality besides just translation procedure in them. If they do not, the company must either develop the application software link between the existing application and the product, or use the product as a standalone and print the output.

Usually, mini and mainframe products allow the user to predefine his internal application format to the translator, the product then translates between the standard and the predefined application format, eliminating the need for application link software.

Even with this capability, internal development is often required to develop an application format from the many different files in various file types (e.g., sequential, randomly accessed database).

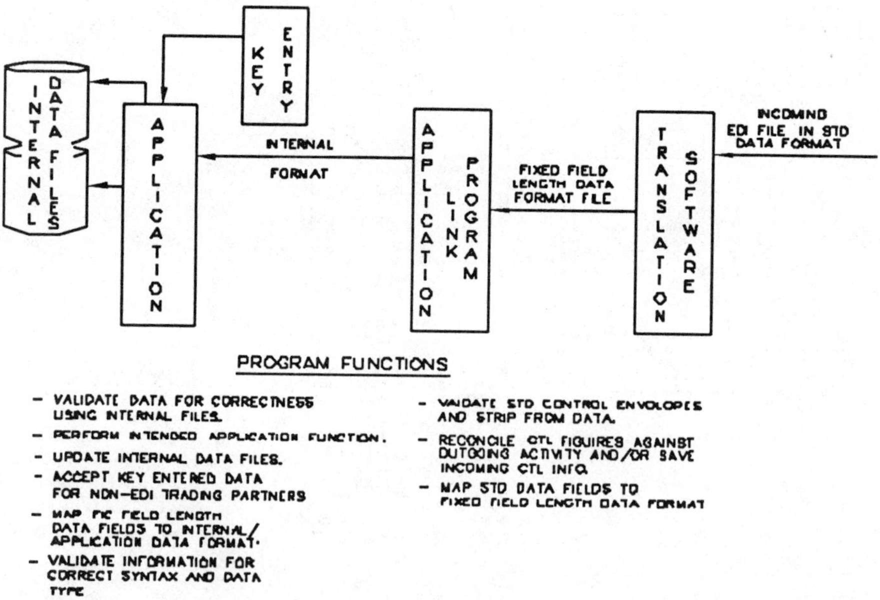

Figure 3-9 Incoming EDI transmission.

An example would be a purchasing application that draws vendor information from a corporate vendor file, product information from a catalog database and order quantity information from a keyed inventory file in order to develop its printed purchase order. The purchasing application, then, does not actually produce an EDI-usable internal application format prior to generating the paper purchase order. A company with this application would be required to either develop the specific internal format required by a translator product, develop its own application format and define it to the product, or modify the product to accept input from a variety of files as required to complete the data requirements for an EDI transaction.

One of the main selling points of buying a translation product and minimizing or eliminating internal development is that it distances the company from the need to deal directly with the standard.

The tradeoffs of development to purchase are:

Development	**Purchase**
Product handles all company requirements.	Product may have to be modified to handle company requirements (sometimes not possible).
Development must be scheduled according to priority of project.	Product already exists and is programmed to accept or generate standard.
Staff must have expertise in standard syntax and data requirements.	Company need only produce fixed field length file.
Company must maintain product as standard changes.	Product and standard format are maintained by developing company.
Price of development is an internal cost to user.	Price of product is paid to outside vendor.

A product may also be purchased as an interim solution so that EDI can be up and running long before internal development is complete for the full-fledged corporate EDI capability or for limited use when the product handles only a few of the many possible EDI transactions that the company expects to support in the long run.

See Appendix B for a list of available EDI translation products for micro, mini, and mainframe computers.

Summary

This chapter has explored the parameters that determine a company's readiness to implement and attain benefits from EDI and has traced the flow of data in various types of companies.

Is EDI being considered because of outside pressure from trading partners or because of internal inefficiencies? Is the company being forced into EDI or is it planning for the transition into electronic trade?

In either case the manager needs to evaluate the readiness of his business area in terms of internal applications, business procedures, and communication capability, to determine how best to implement EDI.

Chapter

4

Business Issues

This chapter will discuss the business issues that must be resolved and sometimes agreed to by trading partners in order to implement EDI. Topics included are:

- Impact on the business area.
- Standard support.
- Security.
- Third party or communication direct decision.
- Business agreements between trading partners.

Impact On the Business Area

As was mentioned, EDI is usually implemented in a particular business area, so the major impact on the company is the revised data/paper flow and the change in job tasks and expertise required by the staff.

The transaction of inter-company business is currently dependent on sending and receiving paper-based business documents which are designed to contain all the information required by the receiver to accomplish the business transaction. However, in practice, information may be lacking or incorrect, necessitating a good deal of interpretation and handling on the receiving end prior to actually processing and acting on the transaction. Sometimes, errors are even introduced into the data at the receiver site.

In the current paper-based business environment, when a business transaction is received it must be:

- Opened and prepared for processing.
- Read and interpreted.
- Completed/corrected as needed.

If a gateway computer application exists it can then be:

- Key entered into the computer system.
- Edited for correctness and completeness.
- Evaluated and passed to the computer application for processing.

In the EDI environment, the manual handling, interpreting, and correcting steps are eliminated. In its place we introduce the requirement to translate the incoming standard format into a predefined fixed field length file. Translation functions include mapping of data fields and evaluating data for adherence to the standard syntax rules. The fixed file may be the internal application format required by the gateway application or it may be a fixed file predefined by the translation software, which still has to be mapped by an application link piece of software into the internal format.

The fixed file can then be immediately directed to the application if that system has already been enhanced to accept it. Most likely the system is now expecting input of interpreted and corrected transactions through key data entry. In order to accept electronic data, the application must be able to accept a data file and do more extensive editing and validating of incoming data fields.

Once past the evaluation step, the processing application program should not be impacted at all by the EDI data. It should be totally transparent to the program what route the data took, manual key entry or input of machine readable data.

Looking at the other direction, sending business documents to a trading partner, a company would have a gateway computer system to generate the print format of a business document and then print it, place it in an envelope, and mail it.

In the EDI environment again, the printing and handling steps are eliminated. However, the computer application must be able to generate an acceptable data format instead of the print format. Often the system was designed to read corporate files and pick up supporting information to complete the paper transaction. With EDI, basic transaction information and supporting information must be included in the output data format.

The application must be programmed to generate a file that contains all the information needed to produce a standard data format file for transmission to a trading partner. That file may be the format required by the translation product or it may be a different fixed length file. If so, an application link piece of software would have to be developed to map the fixed file into the format required by the translator.

Generating and sending a transaction is, in general, easier than receiving, interpreting, and acting on a transaction. You can see how EDI can virtually eliminate the need for inter-company paper to effect business transactions. However, more extensive and smarter computer applications must be put in place to replace the evaluations and decisions currently handled by people.

Because of the elimination of paper, the reduced need for clerical personnel, and the increased need for computer-wise users, you can begin to see some of the places from which internal objections for the proposed system would arise. These objections must be answered in order to effect a successful EDI implementation. In Chapter 5 on planning we will discuss internal barriers to entry in more detail.

Standard Support

Until recently, one of the main stumbling blocks which faced a company considering implementing EDI was the lack of an accepted standard data format. Aside from the standards that had been developed to fill industry-specific and proprietary company needs, there was no generic standard.

Considering the receiving computer system's need to understand the machine-readable data it receives, not only does the format have to exist, but data usage must be agreed to by the trading partners prior to any electronic transmission of transactions.

Which standard any particular company should support in its EDI activity is a question of great importance and is dependent on industry affiliation and which standard its trading partners are supporting.

For companies in those industry groups having industry-specific standards, new EDI trading partners will normally choose to accept and use the existing standard. Some examples of industry standards are:

ORDERNET – for the Pharmaceutical industry.
UCS – for the Grocery industry.
EAGLE – for the Hardlines industry.

A company from one of these industries that is implementing EDI today can take advantage of the existing EDI trading community in its industry and have many potential trading partners immediately upon implementing the standard.

However, until recently, companies in industry groups with no industry standard had no generally accepted standard to support. The emergence of the American National Standards Institute (ANSI) X12 standard with cross-industry application has been the biggest boon to EDI. Today, there is a ground swell of acceptance for this standard from many different industry groups, many of which have become active in its development and monitor its progress.

Because of the widespread acceptance of this standard we will take the time here to examine it a little more closely and to give an idea of what is involved in supporting it. We will look at the various components of the standard such as the transaction set, standard syntax, and transmission control envelopes.

The standard has been developed, using a transactions set, the electronic representation of a paper-based business document, as the basic building unit. Included in a transaction set are all of the data requirements needed by the receiver to transact the indicated business transaction; data fields, individual items of information, are grouped into segments, which, in turn are the building blocks of transactions.

Because business transactions are fairly homogeneous over industries, one transaction set can be defined to handle data requirements for all industries. However, because business systems vary over companies and industries, the standard transaction set must also have a great deal of flexibility. The way that flexibility is insured is to define fields generically and provide qualifier codes to indicate how the data is to be interpreted. If one were to examine the ANSI X12 standard, looking for a field in which to put ship to name or bill to name in a purchase order, one would find only a *name* field preceded by a qualifier code. The appropriate qualifier code to represent ship to name is SH, as found in the list of valid qualifier codes.

The receiver then interprets SH as: The following name and address should be interpreted as SHIP TO information.

You would think that in order to include the amount of functionality required to support multiple industries while providing flexibility, the standard would most likely be more complex than any one company or industry would require. In fact, that is exactly the case.

Because of this complexity, individual companies and industry groups have analyzed their data requirements by examining their current paper-based transactions and have defined "the subset" of the standard that they intend to support. This allows the company to support the standard while at the same time limiting their exposure.

Each transaction, in its ANSI X12 transaction set diagram, is defined as having a transaction header and trailer, and header, detail, and summary areas, as has its paper counterpart. Figure 4-1 demonstrates the electronic form of an X12 transaction set as related to the paper document.

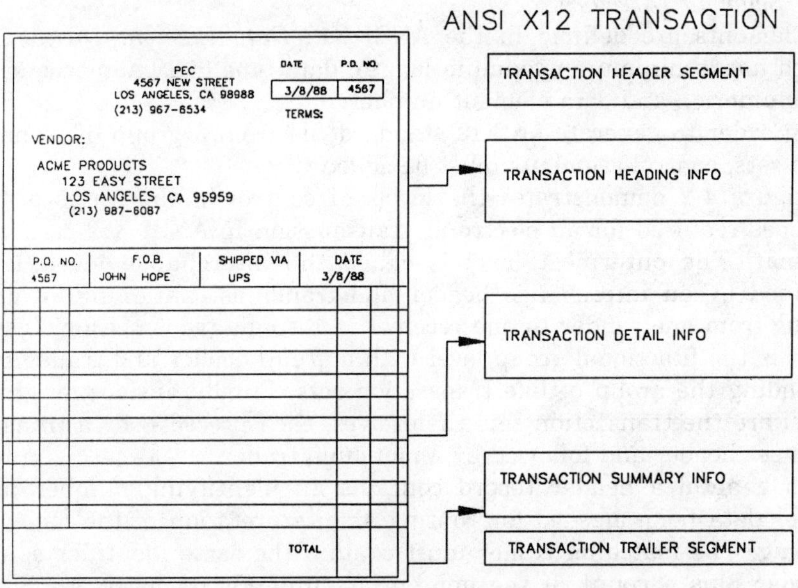

Figure 4-1 The electronic form of an X12 transaction set.

Header information is defined as relating to the entire transaction. It may be overridden by detail information. The detail area is the same as the line item area of the paper transaction. The summary area is similar to the total line of a paper transaction, but additionally contains summary information which may be used for control to assure that a complete transaction was received and that it had not been tampered with.

Each transaction is defined in an ANSI X12 transaction set diagram as a series of segments within each of the three areas, a segment being a group of related data fields. Segments are designated as mandatory or optional, can be repeated up to a maximum number of times, and must be used in the specified order for the transaction set. The same segments are used in many different transaction sets.

All valid segments are defined in the ANSI X12 *Segment Directory*, data elements in the *Data Element Dictionary*.

Just as transactions are composed of segments, segments are composed of data elements, whose usage designator may be mandatory, optional, or conditional. Conditional elements must be used in conjunction with one or more other specified elements as noted in the X12 *Segment Directory*.

Elements are defined in the ANSI X12 *Data Element Dictionary*. Each has a minimum/maximum length, data type (e.g., numeric or alphanumeric), and data element number.

In order to generate an X12 standard file from a group of transaction sets, control segments must be added.

Figure 4-2 demonstrates the levels of control in the series of envelopes required for an electronic transmission in ANSI X12 standard format. The outermost level is called the interchange level. It is defined by an interchange header and trailer as containing all data going from one sender to one receiver in a single transmission. Inside that is the functional group level with a group header and trailer surrounding the group of like transaction sets. Finally, inside the group level are the transaction sets themselves, each preceded by a transaction set header and followed by a matching trailer.

In general a header record contains an identifying number plus other data fields needed for routing or interpretation of the data following. The matching trailer must contain the same identifier as the header plus a count of the appropriate unit for its level. An interchange trailer contains the count of the number of functional groups contained in the interchange. A group trailer contains the number of

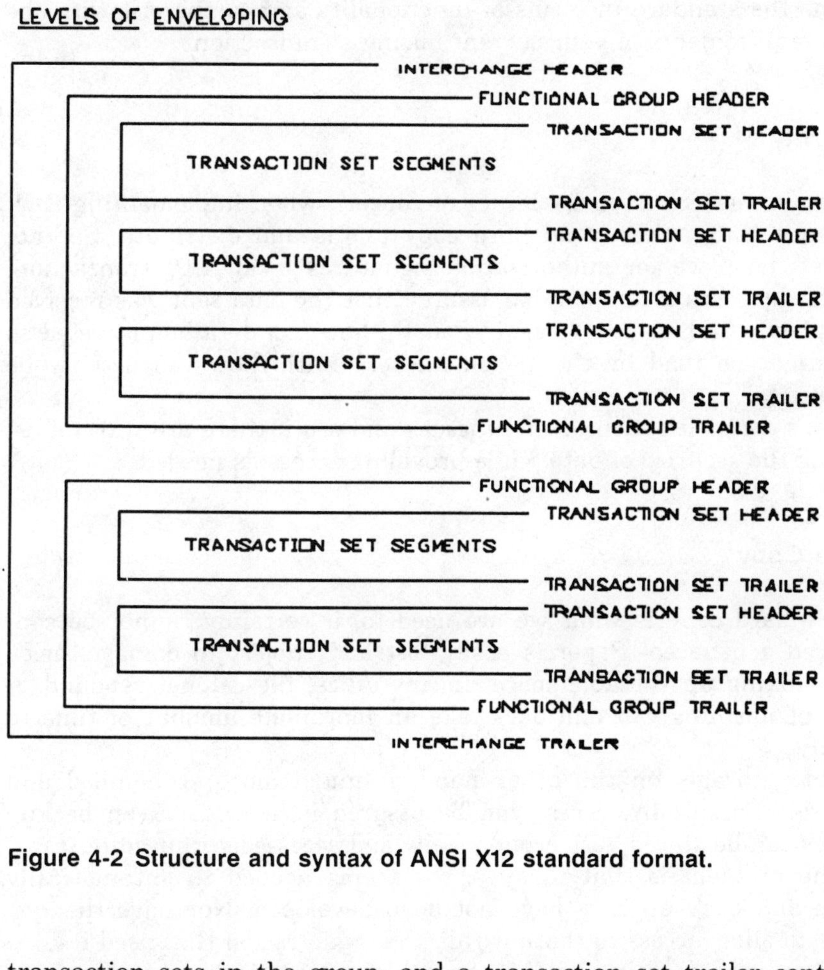

Figure 4-2 Structure and syntax of ANSI X12 standard format.

transaction sets in the group, and a transaction set trailer contains the number of segments contained in the transaction set.

These levels of control on a file are new to the EDI environment. Internal files have no need for control as they remain in place. With transmission of data, it is necessary for the receiver to be able to verify that a complete transmission was received. Without control envelopes the receiver has no way of knowing what the sender sent.

As the manager investigates the requirements for implementing EDI, one of the most important aspects is the choice of a standard to support.

In order to evaluate the different possibilities, it is necessary to examine the standard in terms of functionality and compare it with the data requirements of your current business transactions.

Security

There are several security issues of concern when implementing EDI. For one thing, there's no hard copy to file and distribute. Second, there's no place for authorization signatures in an EDI transaction. Third, how can a company be assured that the data sent was received completely and exactly as sent? Fourth, how can data be protected so it cannot be read by the casual hacker? Fifth, how can activity be tracked?

Let's deal with each of these issues and see if there are ways of assuring the security of data while providing access as needed.

Hard Copy

While hard copy is what we are used to, it certainly cannot be considered a panacea. Paper is easily lost and subject to damage, aside from taking up valuable space. In any office, file cabinets abound. A case of misfiling can and does take an inordinate amount of time to rectify.

Data storage, on the other hand, is much more economical and secure. Potentially, access can be assured in seconds. Even backup copies can be stored very economically and accessed within minutes.

The problem is that today, the systems needed to automatically store and back up data have not been developed. Nor have the systems to allow access to those within the organization that need it.

When implementing EDI, if these systems are incorporated as part of the initial system design, you will be providing greatly enhanced security and control over whatever was possible in the paper-based environment.

The dissemination of information throughout your organization can do more toward improving business procedures, productivity, and customer service than any other single change.

Since EDI data is machine readable, access is most effectively offered in an online mode on formatted screens. Print copy can also be offered as needed.

Not only can individual transactions be easily accessed, but historical or cumulative data, based on flexible parameters is just as easily available.

For example, data to show:

- All purchase orders from a specific customer for the following dates from xx/xx/xx to yy/yy/yy.
- All undelivered orders from a specific vendor.
- All shipments that missed their delivery schedule by more that 24 hours.
- Any purchase order sent within the last three months that required a back order of a particular product.

You can have the data at your fingertips to evaluate vendors and shipping companies, and to track customer business. Any of this data can be printed on request.

So, in fact, this aspect of security can be greatly improved in the EDI environment. Getting the auditors and functional managers involved right up front to help develop business specifications for the audit and control system will improve your chances of a successful EDI implementation.

Authorization and Limited Access

How can the authorization or limited access aspect of security be handled with EDI? Currently, paper is sent confidentially to only those authorized to see it. Signatures are obtained as needed and are recognizable as correct.

The same degrees of security are readily available with EDI, but in order to attain them, system changes or new systems must be put into place.

The authorization issue can be handled by issuing identification codes of various levels to parties within the organization. For example, the data entry clerk can enter all product and departmental information for a purchase requisition. The purchasing staff can see that information and enter vendor and price information to generate a purchase order. Orders above a certain dollar value must be passed to a purchasing manager for authorization. He may see all of the information entered thus far, but is the only one authorized to enter the approval code as authorization for the purchase. Only the manager with the appropriate identification code can ever gain access to the authorization field so *that* code becomes the manager's signature. Alternatively or in addition, there are computer pads on which a written signature can be placed, which can then be validated by the system. An incorrect signature can cause the system to drop while at the same time logging the unauthorized attempt in a complete log of all activity on the system.

Tracking Data

With the transmission of data, there is a good deal of discomfort as to how to track what has happened to the data once it has left your shop. In fact, EDI data are a good deal more secure and faster than paper transactions traveling via mail service.

The receipt of data identical to that sent can be guaranteed by the error-detecting communication protocol. Data is transmitted via telephone line with the protocol software on one end taking control of the transmission and sending a block of data, and the protocol on the other end acknowledging receipt of identical data or negatively acknowledging receipt and calling for a resend of the block that varies in any way from the original. A predetermined number of negative acknowledgements (NAKS) will cause the line to drop. When the sender fails to get a successful end-of-transmission message from the protocol software, he knows that he must resend the data. When the receiver fails to get successful end of transmission, he should purge the data already received and expect a resend of the full data file.

In this way, the sender knows that if the transmission was completed successfully, the receiver received data identical to those sent.

Once the data have been successfully received, the recipient trading partner evaluates the transmission for completeness and adherence to standard syntax.

As described in Chapter 3, the standard is based on a series of control envelopes, each of which contains a header preceding the block of data to which it pertains and a trailer following it. The receiver verifies that he has received a complete unit by ascertaining that the control number in the header and trailer match. He then counts the appropriate unit for that level and verifies it against the count in the trailer. If they are the same, he has received the complete unit. Figure 4-3 illustrates the control envelopes with the data fields needed for this process.

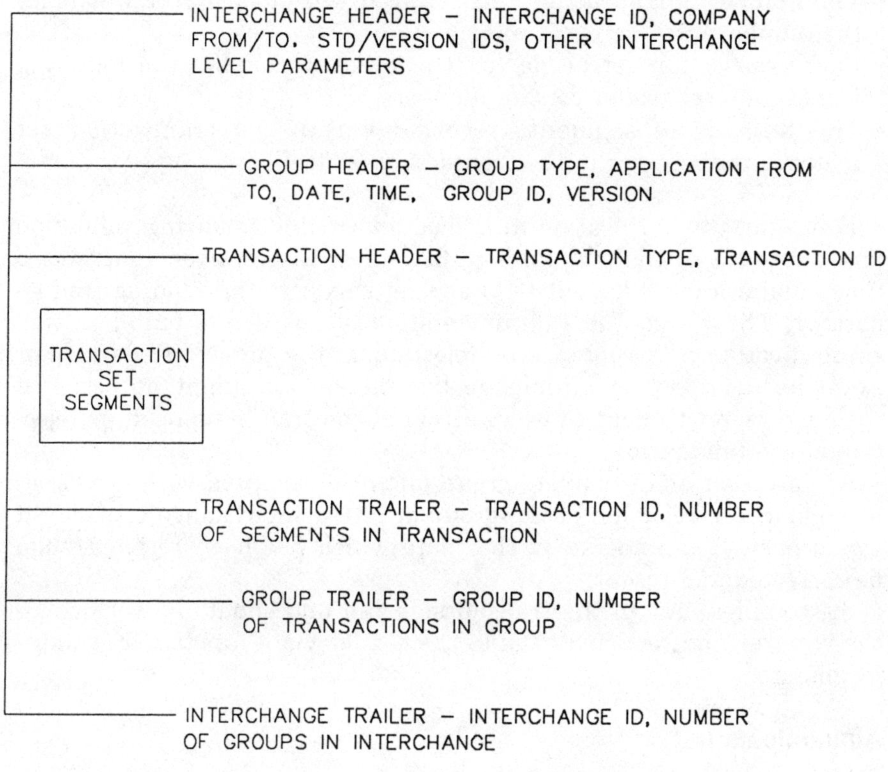

Figure 4-3 Tracking data.

In order to verify completeness of the full transmission, the receiver must verify for each interchange group within the transmission that:

- The interchange header control number matches the interchange trailer control number.
- The number of functional groups received matches the number in the interchange trailer.

- Each functional group header control number matches the following group trailer control number.
- The number of transaction sets received within each group matches the number in the group trailer.
- Each transaction set header control number matches the following transaction set trailer control number.
- The number of segments received within the transaction set matches the number in the transaction set trailer.

Following the verification described above, and following validation for adherence to the standard syntax rules, the receiver generates a functional acknowledgment (FA) and returns it to the sending trading partner. The FA contains documentation of any errors found as well as notification of acceptance or rejection at the pre-agreed level. For example, incorrect or incomplete transaction set might be accepted with errors, or it might cause rejection of the transaction set, or rejection of the full group.

An incorrect or incomplete group might be accepted with errors, or it might cause rejection of the group or of the interchange of which it was a part. It is understood that data which has been rejected must be corrected and resent.

So, completeness of the transmission can and should be verified by the receiver and reported back to the sender via a functional acknowledgment.

Authentication

When data security is of prime concern, as in financial transactions, there is an additional level of security that can be used to ensure that any tampering with transmitted data can be detected by the receiver. The method that provides this security is called authentication.

Immediately prior to transmission, there is a MAC – Macro Authentication Code – computed by performing certain multiple computations on the original data, initiated by a secured authentication key. The MAC obtained is appended to the original data and is transmitted along with it.

Upon receiving the data, the receiver performs the same computations using the same authentication key. If the data received is identical to that sent, the same MAC is computed at the receiving site. Any difference in MAC shows that the data has been tampered with.

You can see that the security of this method rests on the security of the authentication key at either end of the transmission. Ideally, the responsibility for maintaining each key is divided, with at least two people knowing only a portion of the key, each not knowing the other parts. Additionally, the key must be updated regularly.

As any key is only valid between a specified trading partnership, the business of key management – i.e., the generation and transmission of authentication key parts to the necessary parties – will be a very important component of this security system.

Because authentication is a very cumbersome procedure, it will probably not gain support in corporations unless it is dictated as a requirement by the receiving trading partner. The financial community and the government have intimated that authentication may become a requirement in the future, but, so far, have done little in this area.

Encryption

It is interesting to note that, while authentication provides a means to detect tampering, it does not camouflage the data in any way.

In order to make transmitted data indecipherable to the casual inquiry it must be scrambled. The scrambling technique is called encryption. Again, the sender employs a key to encrypt the data and the receiver must employ the same key to decrypt the data.

To ensure total security – i.e., encryption and authentication – the data must be authenticated first and then the full stream excluding the outside envelope, which identifies the sender and receivers must be encrypted.

Just a note on how authentication and encryption would be handled if a third party were being used as an intermediary between trading partners. With authentication, there would be no impact on the third party. They just pass the data along as usual. Authentication remains the sole responsibility of the trading partners.

Transmission of encrypted data may cause some procedural changes in the normal processing a third party. Usually, at least some cursory validation is performed when the third party receives EDI data. However, since encrypted data would be indecipherable, validation would not be possible, Also, if a third party normally billing by number of segments, an arrangement of counting by average number of characters per segment would have to be substituted.

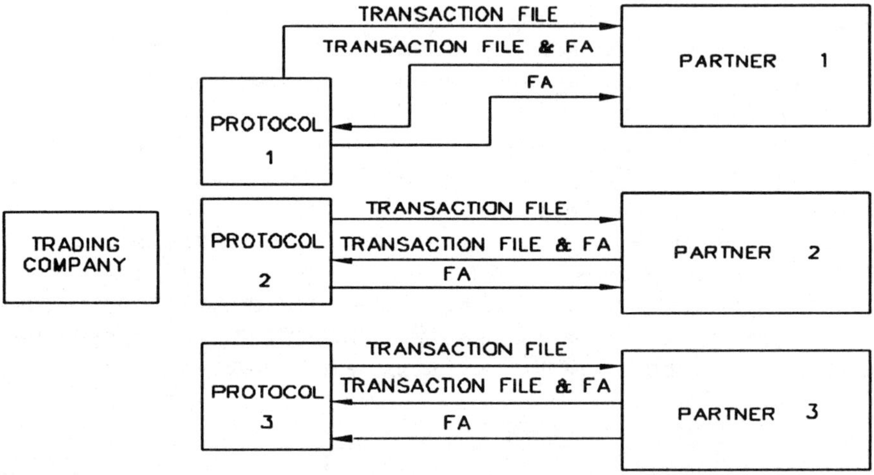

Figure 4-4 EDI direct to trading partners.

Third Party or Direct

One of the major considerations when implementing EDI in-house is whether to transmit data directly with each trading partner or to go through a third party. Your decision will determine the amount of in-house support this project will require, not only during the implementation period, but on an ongoing basis as well.

Figure 4-4 illustrates EDI handled directly with three trading partners. For each trading partner, a communication capability and an "operational window" (hours when transmissions can be sent) must be agreed upon. In addition, the company initiating the communication must generate separate EDI files and transmit the data directly to each trading partner. If the company sent data to and received data from each trading partner only once each day, it would need to handle between 6 and 12 transmissions daily. For each trading partner, it would:

- Send a data transmission.
- Receive a data transmission and a functional acknowledgment for the transmission sent earlier in the day, possibly in one data stream.
- Return a functional acknowledgment for data received from the trading partner. Note: You might save this transmission and send the functional acknowledgment along with tomorrow's transmission. Usually you guarantee return of a functional acknowledgment within 24 hours of receipt of data.

To complicate the issue, there may be transmissions that do not complete successfully and have to be retransmitted. Also, data may be ready to be sent and have to be held because of a busy line or because the recipient is not prepared to receive at that time.

So, potentially, this company would have to support three different communication capabilities and perform or accept up to 12 transmission sessions daily. All of this for only three trading partners. Quite an overhead of equipment and personnel for only limited EDI activity.

On the other hand, Figure 4-5 illustrates EDI through a third party with electronic mailboxes. In this instance, the initiating company prepares a transmission file of data to be routed to three of his trad-

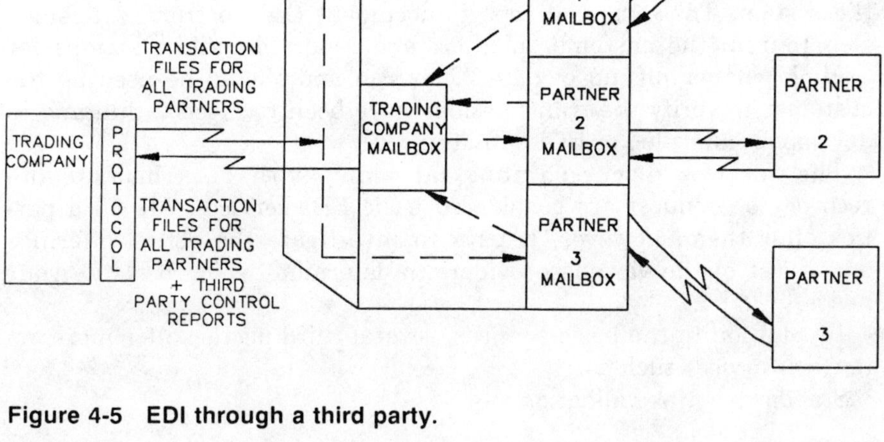

Figure 4-5 EDI through a third party.

ing partners and transmits it in one session to the third party. During the same transmission session, it retrieves from its mailbox all data and functional acknowledgments received for him and routed to his mailbox, and all system reports generated since the last mailbox pull. Not only can all activity be limited to one or two transmissions daily, but it only requires one communication capability, usually the most cost effective the company has available in-house, and can be effected at the company's convenience regardless of when trading partners choose to send or retrieve their own data.

Each trading partner realizes the same convenience by dealing with a third party. However, if one chooses not to become a third-party customer, then that company must be prepared to receive data from the third party via outdial as soon as it is received. Also, it will not get the activity reports available only to customers.

The tradeoff for all this convenience is, of course, third-party charges for the various EDI services. It would certainly pay to evaluate the impact on your operations and user departments that would be caused by various levels of EDI activity and compare that to the charges you would incur by transmitting through a third party. A more in-depth discussion of the role of the third party follows.

Role of the Third Party

The third party provides several important services. In its role of communication intermediary, it allows a company to trade electronically with many trading partners by developing only one communication procedure. Additionally, it provides an electronic mailbox into which it deposits all incoming customer data and control reports generated by the system. These control reports document the electronic transmission to/from the customer mailbox and report date/time stamps for trading partner pickup of data. They can and should be used by the customer to verify the transmissions have been received in full and to develop an audit log of EDI activity.

The services discussed thus far along with data backup and recovery on request are considered basic EDI services. All third parties offer them; however, it pays to investigate the actual offerings and prices of the various providers to determine which best fits your needs.

In addition to the basic services, several third parties offer more extensive services such as:

- Standard syntax validation.

- Translation.
- Links to intra-company messaging products.
- Sale of communication protocol and translation software products.
- Enhanced routing.
- Trading partner marketing programs.

Each is worth discussing as it may prove useful to you in developing your EDI implementation plans.

Standard Syntax Validation

Ideally, when data is transmitted you will immediately map it into an internal format and feed it directly into a computer application program. It may be preferable to have the syntax validated prior to bringing the data in-house, which will ensure that data received is, at least, syntactically correct. The alternative would be to incorporate the logic for the syntax checking into the module that does the mapping. However, programming such a module requires expertise in the standard that your staff may not currently have and that you do not want to develop.

When generating EDI data, you should automatically validate as you generate each transaction. Some companies, however, request that the third party perform validation on data it is transmitting to a trading partner as a test of its own internal program. Usually this would only be requested for a short time until the internal system has "proven out" and is considered correct.

Translation

As we discussed previously, application programs never automatically generate or accept data files in standard format. This means that translation to/from standard format is a necessity in all EDI implementations. It can either be performed in-house by translation software that was either developed or purchased or it can be performed in-network (i.e., in the third party data center). If translation is performed in-network, the usual scenario is for the third party to define a fixed field length file that it will translate to/from the standard format. If a company opts to purchase in-network translation services, it need only develop application link software to generate or accept that fixed field length format by mapping it to/from its internal application format. Not only does it take less expertise in the standard to develop this simpler mapping module, it also insulates the user from changes to the standard.

Sometimes, a third party will allow its customer to predefine a file of its own to the translator. In that case, the customer could transmit its internal application format directly to the third party translator, thus eliminating the need to develop the mapping module at all.

Another use of in-network translation is to eliminate the need to support more than one standard in-house. Take the case of a company that has trading partners in two industries, each of which has developed an EDI standard. For example, the drug wholesaler who buys health and beauty aids from manufacturers who are most likely supporting the UCS standard and pharmaceuticals from drug manufacturers who are probably supporting the ORDERNET standard. The wholesaler will investigate its trading partner base and support the standard in-house that is supported by the majority of its major trading partners. In this case let's suppose that is ORDERNET. In order to deal with its health and beauty aid suppliers it would have to either develop a second translation capability in-house or purchase in-network translation services. In fact, it may be cost effective to do the latter.

Links to Intra-Company Messaging Products

EDI is the inter-company messaging component of the full messaging requirements that exist in business. There is also the need to disseminate messages intra-company, i.e., within the organization. Electronic mail has been gaining popularity in business to handle intra-company messaging requirements. It is an excellent way of passing information from one site to another to develop a complete transaction. Although electronic mail is best known for free-form messaging, the more useful application here is to have staff members complete a predefined transaction form within the mail product. Once complete, the transaction could be mapped from the screen fields to a standard X12 transaction and transmitted to a trading partner. In order to complete the link between electronic mail and EDI, a company would have had to define an electronic mail form containing all of the data fields necessary to complete a specified transaction and also to have programmed the link to map the fields from that form into an EDI transaction.

A second application for electronic mail is to disseminate information within the organization after it has been received in an EDI transaction. Again, the requirement for this application is to define the data fields needed by various staff members with the organization and to map the EDI data fields into a useful report format for on-line or paper access. Electronic mail is then the vehicle for distributing the data to the intra-company sites.

A third party that can provide this link is giving you the opportunity to make EDI an integral part of the way you conduct business by combining your intra- and inter-company messaging requirements.

Sale of Communication Protocol and Translation Software Products

In order to fulfill your communications and translation requirements for EDI, you may need to purchase software and hardware products. While these products may be purchased separately from various sources, you will find that it will greatly facilitate your implementation to purchase them from a single source.

In this way you will not only purchase products which fulfill your processing and communication needs, but will be assured that all components are compatible with one another and with the third party.

Enhanced Routing

There are several routing options that may prove useful to you such as:

- "carbon copy"
- "fax"
- "express mail."

With the carbon copy option you may specify one or many additional recipients of an EDI transaction and the copies will be distributed as EDI transactions, as requested. This may be used, for example, to send an invoice to the ordering location and a copy to the centralized accounts payable department.

With fax, express mail, and electronic mail options the third party maps the incoming data format to a print format for fax service, the print format is transmitted via facsimile machine. For express mail, it is either transmitted to a receiving print station or mailed. And for electronic mail it is transmitted to an electronic mailbox.

These options are particularly useful in trading with partners who are not capable of receiving EDI data. It provides the convenience for you to develop EDI transactions for all of your trading partners, while the third party develops the required print formats and transmits, faxes, or mails them to your trading partners.

Trading Partner Marketing Programs

EDI cannot be performed in a vacuum. It takes trading partners. In fact, benefits attributable to EDI are realized in direct proportion to the amount of business transacted electronically. In effect, more partners, more benefits.

However, there is a great deal of time and effort needed to encourage partners to implement EDI and to provide guidance for and testing with each one. While some companies have chosen to dedicate staff to the job of bringing up trading partners over months and years, most companies either cannot afford to take this route or choose not to. In either case, after bringing up the most enthusiastic partners and a few others with whom they do a major portion of their business, the project falls into a somewhat static state with little or no growth over a long period of time. This does little to encourage future EDI implementations in other divisions or business areas within the company.

The third party you choose should be prepared to pro-actively market for your trading partners. Look for commitment from them in the form of an organized marketing program. Ask for references of those marketing programs they have already run. Both parties will benefit from such programs. Additional partners for you means additional revenue for them.

A final note on third parties. Look for a company that can and will interconnect to other third parties without exhorbitant charges. While you will want to encourage your trading partners to do EDI, you will probably not want to dictate which third party they should use, just as you wouldn't want to be dictated to. There is no technological issue in interconnecting. All third parties can easily do it. The issue is a political one. By mandating that all trading partners use one third party, market share can be bought. As a prospective customer, you will want to look for the most cost-effective and convenient service with the strongest customer service and support organizations. A list of third party providers is included in Appendix C. Call several and evaluate the various offerings.

EDI and International Trade

There is excellent application for EDI in international trade because of the tremendous amount of paperwork involved and the need for careful tracking.

As in the domestic arena, standards development has been the key to successful implementation of international EDI. While there has been an acceptable standard used in the European market, it was substantially different in both structure and in usage of data from that being developed in North America by the ANSI X12 committee.

With representation of the standards organizations from the United States and Eastern and Western Europe, and a great deal of cooperation, an international version of the invoice has been developed and standard syntax has been agreed upon.

While certainly not identical to the domestic standard, the necessary interchange, group, and transaction control aspects of the ANSI X12 file structure and the header, detail, and summary sections and segment structures within a transaction have all been retained. Segment names, order within the transaction, and fields within the segments, vary. Usage designator and allowable repetitions may also vary. There are more mandatory segments in the international version.

Additionally, the European method of field usage has been retained in some cases, where the ANSI fields were unable to give the functionality that was required. For example, ANSI X12 names and addresses are traditionally structured in four separate address lines – one for name, two for additional names, three for street address, and city, state, zip. That works perfectly well for us, as all of our addresses have a fairly standard shape. However, in the European market, transactions regularly cross country boundaries where addresses take various forms. Therefore, they had developed a more flexible structure containing one long field for the full name and address. Data for each part of the address is separated by a control character known as a subelement delimiter.

See Chapter 9 on EDI futures for a closer look at the development of international standards.

While certain differences do exist, the fact is that requirements for a business transaction are fairly homogeneous between countries, just as they are between industries and companies.

How can the international standard be handled by your domestic EDI software? Assume that you are generating the invoice currently for domestic purposes. In order to add an international trading partner, these are the steps that must be accomplished:

- Enter trading partner information for the new partner in order to be able to handle communications properly and identify this trading partner as needing an international transaction.
- Add the definition for the international version of the transaction to your current software.

If your translator was developed in-house you will need to know the following transaction set information in order to map your data fields to the appropriate standard fields and to generate a syntactically correct transaction set:

- Segments within the transaction set.
- The data elements of which they are comprised, their order, looping, maximum counts, and usage designators.

If your software was purchased, you will need to find out if the software supports this international transaction. You may need to notify the company from which you purchased the product that you want to support the international version of a particular transaction. The developer will have to send you the transaction tables and programming logic necessary to generate the standard. You will need to have available all of the data required to generate the international standard out of your gateway application, or you will need to enhance the current application to make them available.

The same steps are required if you are the receiver of the international transaction. Instead of generating it, you would need to validate and interpret the incoming data. When mapping the fields to your internal format, you may find that you need to enhance the current application to accept pieces of information that were not received in the domestic version.

Several companies are currently involved in a pilot program using the international invoice. Work on other transactions will be done as companies expand their plans to implement EDI for other areas of international trade. Having completed the invoice, we know that data requirements between countries are similar enough to be supported by a common format.

Payment Terms In the EDI Environment

Many years ago, payment terms were offered to the payer by the supplier, usually as an inducement to get paid sooner. Terms were arrived at by computing the opportunity value of capital at that time. Historically, terms have remained static from that time to the present, while prices, interest rates, and the like have fluctuated up and down.

Let's take a look at a common terms discount of 2% 10 net 30, meaning take a 2% discount if paid within 10 days; full payment is due within 30 days. When the invoice took three to five days to arrive, getting payment back within 10 days was not easy. The inducement, of course, was the 2% discount. However, if the invoice were to arrive within minutes, all other things being equal, might the 10-day period be shortened to 7? With the development and implementation of software to automatically reconcile the incoming invoice with the open purchase order and receiving information, might authorization to pay be accomplished within 48 hours and with electronic funds transfer might actual payment be transacted within another 24–48 hours. So payment could be made earlier in the electronic environment. However, with the traditional float period for mail and check clearance, reducing float is not a popular concept amongst payers.

As payment is usually triggered by payment terms, it would seem that there would be mutual benefit derived by renegotiating terms for the electronic environment. Buyers and sellers may want to reevaluate the opportunity cost of capital in the current business environment in order to arrive at terms that would be mutually beneficial, either by increasing the discount period from 10 days to 12 or 13 and leaving the discount the same, or increasing the discount and leaving the period the same.

The First National Bank of Chicago has developed a software product called TERMS which will compute the range of terms favorable to both the buyer and seller trading partners using user-determined values for the pertinent financial parameters of one or both parties.

Trading partners can share the benefits of EDI by trading off payment timing and price discounts. You may contact First of Chicago for information on this product.

Business Arrangements In the EDI Environment

It is important to remember that if EDI is merely imposed upon the way you currently do business, it will not deliver the expected long-range potential benefits. Yes, you will spend less on paper and envelopes, and you will certainly save mail time, but in order to reduce inventory and eliminate long and costly reconciliations, business procedures have to change. What's more, if they change in a vacuum – i.e., only within your company but without impacting the normal trading partner relationships – they will not be nearly as effective as they could have been.

Timing

For one thing, timing is an issue. Sellers must share their order/ entry processing schedules with their customers in order to give those customers the opportunity to plan their own purchasing activities to take advantage of the earliest processing time. A customer that normally sends out purchase orders to all of its vendors at 11:00 a.m. will constantly miss that day's processing of the vendor who pulls purchase orders at 10:00 daily. Even without the need to make a specific processing run, a receiving company must share information regarding its operational window, those hours per day and days per week during which it can receive transmissions. Two companies on opposite coasts will find that there are few hours in a normal work day when both are open with communications operative. They will need to agree on specific times when transmissions will be sent/received. Dealing with a third party can greatly facilitate this situation, as each party is free to send data to trading partners and to retrieve data from his mailbox at its convenience. One company need not concern itself with its trading partner's schedule.

Not only is timing important for the initial processing of a transaction, but it is just as important for acknowledgments. Acknowledging expectations are agreed to in advance by trading partners.

- What is the acceptable time frame for acknowledging receipt of a transmission?

  It should be almost immediately and can take one of two forms.

  1. Using the ANSI X12 guidelines, the receiving trading partner can immediately return a Transmission Acknowledgment, which does nothing more than warrant that the transmission has been received, but makes no value judgments on the data.
  2. He can return a Functional Acknowledgment, generated on the group level, which reports on:

     - The group level only.
     - The transactions within the group.

     or

     - The data elements and segments of each transaction in the group.

In order to develop a functional acknowledgment on the group level, the receiver need only identify a matching group header and trailer pair and verify that the correct number of transactions has been received.

In order to validate on the transactions, the receiving system must verify that, for each transaction in the group, only valid segments are contained and that the number of segments received equals the number contained in each transaction set trailer.

Complete validation of syntax and data elements includes verification of the data type, length, and requirement indicator of each data element within each segment.

By agreeing to receipt of acknowledgment data within a specified time period, the receiver makes it possible for the sender to learn of problems early and to retransmit the corrected data in a timely manner. If the data has gone through a third party, the acknowledgment will be two-fold. The third party will immediately acknowledge the receipt of the data and the eventual receiver, the trading partner will acknowledge receipt when he pulls the data from his mailbox or receives it via autodial.

Usually, within 24 hours is a practical time frame for receipt of either the transmission acknowledgment or functional acknowledgment. The preferred method is the functional acknowledgment, as it provides more in-depth information for the sender.

- How long before you should receive notification that the data is complete – i.e., that the full transmission has been received as verified by complete and accurate control envelopes on the file and by complete and syntactically correct transaction sets?

You would also want notification of any of these problems almost immediately. Considering that the data were generated by a computer application, after an initial evaluation period, both the data and the control envelopes should be complete and correct as generated. A problem at the receiving end could very well be a communications problem and should be reported early. For this reason, return of the functional acknowledgment with both receipt notification and results of the validation has been adopted by many more companies than return of the transmission acknowledgment followed closely by the functional acknowledgment. While the functional acknowledgment can preclude the need for the transmission acknowledgment, the opposite is not true.

- How long is it acceptable to wait for receipt of the transaction acknowledgment?

Here the time period is somewhat longer, usually within 48 hours from receipt. The reason is that internal processing must be complete in order to evaluate whether or not you can successfully transmit business with the data received. For example, when a purchase order is received, the initial validation will ensure that the transaction has all of the mandatory fields, that data types are correct, numeric fields are, in fact, made up of numeric characters, and that the number of segments received agrees with the number reported sent in the transaction set trailer. However, it will not determine that the product codes ordered are valid codes, that the product is in stock, or that it can be delivered on the schedule requested. That data is available only after all systems have been run, a process that may require some time. However, in order for the sender, in this case the buyer, to plan for receipt of incoming product and/or purchase from another vendor, he must wait for the transaction acknowledgment to arrive.

Trading partners must agree ahead of time on an acceptable schedule for return of each type of acknowledgment. Once agreed upon, the sender will know that his control system need only kick out exceptions, those cases where acknowledgment is not received on time or where acknowledgment shows that the transaction could not be carried out successfully. For all other cases, no intervention is necessary.

Another aspect of timing is in handling and processing change transactions. While electronic transmission of data ensures receipt almost immediately after sending, internal processes such as scheduling a manufacturing procedure, tooling for it, and accomplishing the task, take finite amounts of time. Receiving a change to a purchase order after the procedure is set up or has begun can cause a good deal of inconvenience as well loss of time and money. For this reason, companies should agree ahead of time on how long before delivery a purchase order change may be sent without incurring any additional charges.

Some companies have begun to send forecasts to their vendors electronically. The forecast may show the anticipated demand by week or month for the next year. The partners may agree that the forecast will become a purchase order at a pre-agreed number of weeks or months before the requested delivery date. This gives the vendor advance notice of an impending change in the demand for his product and permits him to make the best deal with his suppliers for component parts and raw materials and to schedule manufacture or assembly in time to fill the anticipated demand. By making a prior agreement, both parties benefit; the buyer, by making it easier for the supplier to fill orders in a timely manner, and the supplier, by contracting with his own suppliers for larger quantities at more favorable prices and delivery schedules.

Summary

In this chapter we have dealt with the most important business decisions you will need to make when considering implementation of EDI in your company. We have seen that EDI is not just put into place, but impacts your current business environment. Both procedures and staffing requirements change. In particular, new systems are often needed and existing systems must be enhanced to fulfill new requirements. Such procedures as:

- Accepting data files instead of the traditional key entry.
- Validating for adherence to standard syntax rules, and for completeness and correctness of data.
- Automatically interpreting and acting upon an electronic transaction set.
- Keeping track of EDI activity in and out of the company are requirements new to the electronic environment.

Without the existence of an acceptable standard data format, EDI could never have taken hold as it has today. However, more than one standard data format has been developed. Some were developed to support the needs of a particular company or industry group. ANSI X12 was developed to support cross-industry application. Each company should evaluate its own data needs, the industry in which it does the majority of its trade, and which standard its major trading partners are already supporting, in order to come to the decision of which one to support itself. Companies trading in multiple industries may have a need to support more than one standard.

Support of a standard means generating or accepting, interpreting, and processing data in a specified format. This process can be accomplished by developing translation software in-house, buying an already existing product for use on your computer, or sending your data through a third party's in-network translation services.

There are several security issues to be addressed in the electronic environment, such as:

- Replacing the paper (hard) copy with machine-readable data.
- Eliminating the authorization signature.
- Ensuring that the data sent was received.
- Protecting data from casual inquiry or change during transmission.
- Developing a complete audit log of activity.

It is important to address these issues from the start. A system in which no one has confidence is a little-used system. Rather than fostering a lack of security, EDI actually gives us the ability to improve security by using the accurate and timely information sent and received. Be sure that security and control measures are included in your implementation plans to encourage opponents of the new procedures to become proponents.

The decision you make, whether to use a third party as a communication intermediary or to transmit data directly with your trading partners will depend on your staff's expertise in standards and other EDI-related issues, and on your communication flexibility in supporting different protocols, line speeds, and operational windows. If you plan on trading with many EDI trading partners, you may find that supporting multiple requirements takes an inordinate amount of time and effort. Especially as you attempt to market the idea to more and more trading partners, you may experience a greater marginal amount of work involved with each ensuing one. Evaluate costs and services and compare third parties to arrive at the best decision for you. A list of third parties can be found in Appendix C.

Finally, EDI requires a close relationship with your trading partners. Unlike sending a piece of paper, electronic trade means using machine-readable data in an automated environment without the aid of human intervention to interpret or complete the transaction. Surprises are impossible to handle in this environment. Be sure to work out data requirements, processing time schedules, and change transaction processing prior to implementing EDI. You may also want to take this opportunity to reevaluate your terms discounts. Both parties may be able to benefit from a shift in the traditional terms.

Chapter

5

Planning and Implementation

In this chapter we will discuss how to best plan for EDI in your company by evaluating the potential benefits in the various business areas. We will cover the following topics.

- EDI, the inter-company project.
- Evaluating the business area.
- Cost/benefit analysis.
- Barriers to entry.
- Developing the implementation plan.
- Designing the pilot.

EDI, the Inter-Company Project

Implementing EDI takes a good deal more time and coordination than the normal internal project. When developing an intra-company system, it is fairly obvious who the major players will be. The functional business manager takes the lead role in defining the business specifications for the new system. These are passed to the MIS manager who evaluates the work required and assigns the design and development tasks to one or more data processing analysts and programmers. Communication between prospective users is usually accomplished by accessing existing data files as opposed to transmission between data centers. Once the system is programmed and tested, it is considered live and usable by the functional business area.

The implementation of EDI differs in a few important ways. First, the system requirements are based on a standard data format. Usually, the data processing staff is not familiar with this format, so either a good deal of education must precede any development work or the company must consider buying a translation product to do the job. Even in this case there is usually still some programming that must be done to link the existing application to a fixed field length interim file required as input or generated by the translation software.

Second, the system must contain various control features such as:

- It must have a tracking facility to capture the information necessary to develop and maintain a complete audit log of EDI activity.
- It must be able to generate complete standard format interchange, group, and transaction set headers and trailers for outgoing ANSI X12 data files, and to read and interpret the control envelopes on the incoming data files.
- It should contain a reconciliation routine to compare the EDI activity information that has been retained in-house with incoming third party reports and functional acknowledgments from trading partners and to develop exception reports to handle discrepancies.

Third, while internal system requirements are based on intra-company considerations, EDI requirements for transaction set data (all fields needed by the receiver of the data to accomplish the intended transaction), and for communications (both the technical aspects such as which protocol and line speeds to use and the practical aspects of when the receiving data center is operational) are inter-company in nature. That means that staff members from two different companies must come to agreements and coordinate activities and testing schedules in order to implement the project. As a rule, this introduces a great deal of complexity to the process.

In order to keep track of who is responsible for what tasks and who the counterpart is at the other company, it is necessary to assign responsibility for coordination of the project to a staff member and to require signoffs on the all tasks.

Evaluating the Business Area

As the idea for EDI most often enters the company either as a request from a trading partner (usually a customer) or as a solution to an internal inefficiency, it is most often focused on particular business transactions and in a particular business area. For example, the business manager may need to handle and process purchase orders more efficiently in response to the customer's need to receive product more quickly, as is the case with just in time manufacturing schedules, or he may need to eliminate a payment bottleneck by reducing the staff and time required to perform invoice/purchase order/receipt of goods reconciliation. In order to evaluate the costs and potential benefits of EDI then, the appropriate focus is on the functional business area. The study that needs to be performed is called a Feasibility Study and the major players in this work are, first, the functional business managers who will perform the analysis from the perspective of business needs in the EDI environment as compared to the current environment and second, data processing support staff who will evaluate the work and time required to accomplish the tasks required to implement the changes specified by the business managers.

In order to accomplish the business area analysis, keep in mind that implementing EDI provides only the direct benefit of eliminating mail time as soon, all other benefits depend on development or enhancement of internal systems and changing business procedures. Because of this fact, the first step in performing such an analysis is to carefully examine current systems and procedures and to develop a picture of the flow of data into and out of the business area.

The following steps should be performed for each business area under consideration for EDI implementation. Figure 5-1 shows the deliverables that make up the full business area Feasibility Study.

1. Develop a list of the business transactions that are currently performed in the business area and list the paper, telephone, telex, facsimile, and oral "transaction sets" (entities which contain information needed to perform a particular business function) that exist to facilitate these transactions. While a purchase order to perform the transaction of ordering would be an obvious transaction set, keep in mind that telephone inquiry is needed to complete or verify information in the transaction, system inquiries to verify incoming information against internal files, and change requests in the form of followup paper transac-

1. LIST OF CURRENT BUSINESS TRANSACTIONS.
2. ANALYSIS OF THE CURRENT GATEWAY APPLICATION.
3. REVISED DATA FLOW FOR EDI.
4. LIST OF POTENTIAL EDI TRADING PARTNERS.
5. COMPUTED INDEX OF EDI POTENTIAL.
6. BUSINESS AREA RECOMMENDATION.

Figure 5-1 Component parts of a feasibility study.

tion, telephone calls, etc. are all transaction sets needed to facilitate the "purchasing of product or services" transaction.

Be sure to note transactions that circulate only within the business area. For example, product requisitions may be sent to a buyer and then on to a manager for authorization.

Also, be sure to account for all copies of a transaction set. Often, one copy may be sent to a trading partner, a second filed in-house, and a third forwarded to another department.

2. Perform an analysis of your current "gateway" application, the one that would generate or receive EDI data. Develop a data flow diagram showing:

   - How data is currently input into the system; e.g., key entry or tape from a trading partner.
   - What manual procedures are performed from the time the paper transaction set is received in-house or generated by the application; e.g., opening or stuffing envelopes, interpreting paper transactions, answering or making telephone calls.
   - What data is required for this application and how they flow into subsequent applications.

   Make note of the number of staff you currently need to perform the manual tasks identified above and the time it takes to perform them. Get figures on the error rates you are experiencing because of such problems as:

- Incorrect interpretation of transactions received.
- Program malfunctions or inappropriate actions due to incorrect data entry.
- Incorrect or late shipments sent or received.
- Amount of returned goods sent or received.

Such figures will help you to evaluate the current costs you are experiencing.

3. Next, develop a revised data flow for the business area as it would work with EDI. Include the following:

   - Automated data entry of formatted EDI data if you are receiver of the transaction, and automated generation of a machine-readable, formatted data file to replace the paper transaction print format if you are sender.
   - Application link and translation software to map from the standard machine-readable data format to the format required by the application, or from the application format to the standard data format.
   - Control mechanisms designed to keep track of your EDI activity, either to generate or accept and reconcile standard functional acknowledgments and to read and interpret third party reports and reconcile them with your EDI transmission activity figures.
   - Consider additional functionality to give functional business managers, auditors and corporate administrators access to selected data in order to improve planning, auditing, and tracking efficiency and effectiveness..

The revised business area plan shows the long term picture, which does not preclude you from developing a phased approach to implementation. However, without the "big picture" you might very well limit future implementation plans by, e.g., missing an opportunity to plan on integrating internal systems or changing a procedure that provides an important piece of information. Furthermore, unless you evaluate several business areas within the company, you might very well miss an opportunity to integrate the systems in them. For example, by neglecting to save the appropriate open purchase order information, invoice reconciliation would be impossible.

4. Develop a list of potential trading partners with contact names and telephone numbers of functional business managers and MIS and communication support staff.

5. Compute an index of "EDI potential" by doing a cost/benefit analysis using the following equations and parameters to evaluate benefits and costs.

EDI potential = EDI benefits – EDI costs

EDI benefits = Market factors + short and long range benefits

EDI costs = Setup costs + ongoing costs

Market Factors
Ask yourself the following questions:

- Are you being pressured by major trading partners to do EDI?
- Do you need to show that you are state-of-the-art because your entire industry is starting to implement EDI?
- Do you need to cut internal costs to remain competitive?
- Do you need to improve your image by providing better and more responsive customer service?

A "yes" denotes a positive market factor, several "yesses" denote strong positive pressure. Sometimes, strong market factors can mean that you will implement EDI in spite of high costs or limited short term benefits.

Short-Term Benefits
These are derived by reducing or eliminating costs associated with manual handling and processing of transactions, labor and materials.

Investigate such costs as transaction handling, error correcting, key data entry, telephone time, and materials, and develop a matrix comparing current costs and EDI costs. Look for substantial cost savings in key data entry and error handling.

Long Range Benefits

These, as their name implies, are futures. They include such benefits as reduction of inventory, improved cash flow, improved customer service, favorable vendor status with lower prices and better delivery schedules, and overall greater business efficiency and improved information flow. In order to realize such benefits, additional software, improved business procedures, and new arrangements with trading partners will probably be necessary. However, make this an important part of the analysis, as the savings derived here will overshadow those realized in the short term.

For each category of benefits, note the current environment:

- Do you have systems in this area?
- How much manual effort is involved?
- How do the systems work?
- What problems and bottlenecks exist?

Then note how you might improve conditions by using EDI data:

- What new systems could be developed?
- How will those that already exist be improved?
- How could information be disseminated to staff within your company?
- How would use of EDI data position your company for more favorable vendor status, etc.? Try to quantify potential benefits.

Next, investigate costs. First develop an estimate for setup costs for EDI. Your internal MIS department can estimate time and effort to enhance your current application programs.

Ballpark figures for purchase of EDI products are as follows:

- Communication software $100-$500 for basic protocol software; $10,000–$20,000 for complete communication software with internal message routing capabilities and support of various protocols
- Translation software, Micro, $1000-$5000
- Mini, $9000-$11,000
- Mainframe, $18,000-$25,000

Finally, estimate ongoing costs. In order to do this you will need to estimate the number of documents you currently send/receive and then choose percentages of those figures that you expect to convert to electronic format within, e.g., one year, two years, five years.

A sample cost analysis document is included in Appendix D. This can be used as an aid in computing both one time and ongoing costs for EDI.

Use the section on analyzing the current business environment to:

- Complete the processing and handling costs you currently experience for standard business transactions used by the company.
- Estimate the costs of materials to support the current paper environment.
- Develop estimates of costs for handling errors occurring in various areas of the company. This is an important section as the greatest costs are associated with errors. Herein lies your greatest potential for savings.

In order to develop the complete picture of costs for the EDI implementation, fill in the section on one-time costs with the setup costs you anticipate for hardware and software required to implement EDI. Work through the section on ongoing transaction costs by developing the segment/character counts for a typical EDI transaction, an anticipated number of transactions and transmissions per chosen time period (week, month, year), and the number of control envelopes needed to support these transmissions.

Finally, develop an estimate of third party costs, if you plan on using one. You can use this section both to develop cost estimates and as a comparison matrix of several third parties in order to help you to evaluate services and associated costs.

With all of the analysis completed, you will be in a position to evaluate EDI potential as an index having either an upward or downward trend over various volumes of EDI activity and over varying time periods. EDI can rarely be cost justified in the short run, as setup costs may be high. Use the anticipated volumes over time to develop a trend line.

In some cases, strong market factors may outweigh all other considerations, making cost justification unnecessary.

6. Finally, develop a business area recommendation as to whether and how to proceed toward implementation. Focus on business considerations such as:

   - Is EDI viable at this time?
   - Are trading partners interested and ready to implement EDI with us?
   - What procedural changes will be needed for the new environment?
   - How will staffing requirements change?
   - What new functionality and what data requirements will systems have to support in order to transact business electronically?
   - How much funding will we need and over what time period?
   - What benefits can we reasonably expect?
   - What are the next steps?

   Appendix F contains a sample Feasibility Study worksheet for your use. Not discussed thus far, but very important in the planning stage are the corporate and employee attitudes toward an impending EDI implementation. As we will see, various members of your staff may perceive barriers to entry into the electronic trade arena. These may become real barriers unless confronted and responded to prior to implementation.

Objections Against Entry Into EDI From Within the Company

Between August 1985 and July 1986, the First National Bank of Chicago conducted an EDI management survey. They asked questions about the respondent company, its current EDI activity, if any, and the perceived barriers to entry into the EDI arena.

More than 21,000 surveys were mailed, eliciting over 1200 responses, or a return rate of about 6%.

The firms that responded ran in size from under $30 million to over $1 billion. Of those, almost 60% currently had no EDI trading partners and more than 20% had fewer than five. The responses showed that the perceived barriers to entry into EDI were, in order

- System cost.
- Security.
- Lack of standards.
- Float loss.
- Lack of training.
- Company attitude.

While none of these present real barriers to entry, they must each be addressed to reduce internal objections and smooth the way for an EDI implementation.

System Cost

THE PERCEPTION IS THAT THERE ARE EXTENSIVE UP-FRONT COSTS TO DEVELOP OR BUY SOFTWARE SYSTEMS REQUIRED TO IMPLEMENT EDI.

While it is true that the bulk of costs related to implementing EDI are front loaded, they are not prohibitive. Even a small company needing to buy a computer, translation software, and communications board and protocol software, would not find the cost of entry prohibitive. The total package would run between $3000 and $9000: from $1000–$2500 for a microcomputer, from under $1000 to about $4500 for micro-based translation software, and from $1000–$2000 for communications board and communications protocol software. With some data processing expertise in-house, the bill could even be reduced by developing a relatively simple module (to generate and/or interpret a fixed length file) to replace the translation software and use in-network translation services of a third party service provider.

A larger company, with mini or mainframe computer, may still opt to purchase or develop translation software for a micro front end and be up and running for under $4500 plus some in- house development of an application link module. On the other hand, this company may prefer to purchase a mini or mainframe translation package. The price tag of the former would be between $9000 and $11,000; for the latter, from $18,000 to $25,000. In both cases, development of application link software would still be required. In-house development of mini or mainframe software is, of course, another option. However, cost of this development would be more difficult to estimate as it would require expertise in EDI and standards issues.

While these up-front costs for software are certainly not inconsequential, they are also not prohibitive. A company that evaluated its business situation and expected to be able to realize benefits from implementing EDI would not stay out on the basis of system costs.

Security

THE PERCEPTION IS THAT THERE IS A MARKED LACK OF DATA SECURITY WITH EDI; ACCESS IS READILY AVAILABLE TO ALL, DATA CAN BE READ OR CHANGED DURING TRANSMISSION, AND NO FILE IS SAFE FROM THE PRYING EYES OF EDI TRADING PARTNERS OR OTHER CASUAL OBSERVERS.

There are several issues pertaining to security about which STAFF members may be uncomfortable. First, the perception is that data files may be more easily accessible to improper viewing than was previously possible in the paper environment, where file cabinets and offices could be locked. In actuality, security procedures can and should be put into place to restrict both inquiry and modification access to authorized personnel only. Various levels of security and data access can be built into your internal systems so that each logon ID and password is associated with only the level of access required by that person.

Secondly, there is discomfort with the idea that data could be read and possibly changed while being transmitted from one partner to another. As was discussed before, encryption (scrambling of data) can assure that data could not be read by the casual observer during transmission. Authentication would assure that if any changes were made during transmission, they would not go undetected by the receiver.

While both of these techniques are available for use, both require a good deal of management and coordination between partners to keep the current encryption or authentication keys and to decrypt and/or re-authenticate all data received. It would be a good idea to evaluate the security needed for the data you plan on transmitting electronically to see which data require these measures. In that way, you can plan to provide extra security measures for only the data that warrants it. Be sure to discuss this topic with trading partners as they will need to support the same security measures.

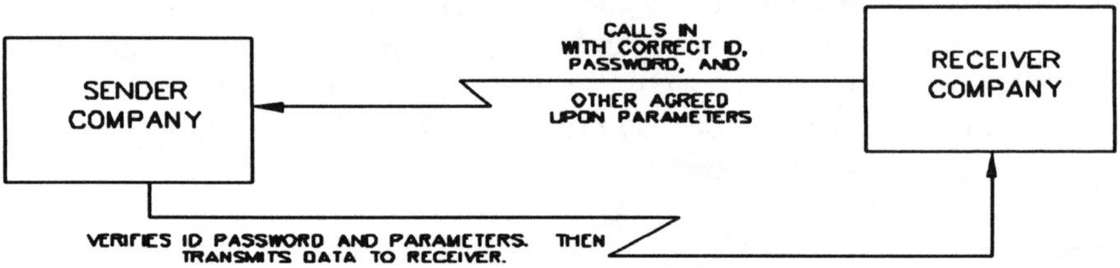

Figure 5-2 EDI as a send only facility.

Another perception causing lack of faith in the security of EDI is that a trading partner could possibly gain access to other files in your computer while it was calling in to retrieve EDI data. In fact, this fear is not based on reality, as EDI is a send only facility. As illustrated in Figure 5-2, this is the way it works. One company calls the other's data center, identifies itself, and says it is ready to receive. The other company, satisfied that the first has identified itself sufficiently well to the system, sends the data to which the receiver is entitled. Actually, there is no pulling of data at all.

Sometimes, a third party is perceived as a safety buffer between a receiver and a sender's computer. While this is not a necessary buffer as explained above, it often makes the trading partners feel that their data is more secure when using a third party.

Standards

THE PERCEPTION IS THAT IT IS TOO EARLY TO IMPLEMENT EDI BECAUSE THERE IS STILL NO STANDARD THAT HAS GATHERED BROAD ENOUGH INDUSTRY BACKING TO WARRANT THE EFFORT.

Today, the American National Standards Institute (ANSI) X12 standard, developed to support cross-industry standard business transactions, has gained broad industry support. Even as recently as three years ago, companies from only a handful of industries had evaluated the applicability of the X12 transactions for their use. In the past three years, the rolls of X12 membership have grown substantially, with representation from many new industries. Each has evaluated whether the function of X12 transactions can support that needed by its membership, and, while each new group has its fair share of maintenance requests, few of them require major changes. The basic structure and data requirements have held up remarkably well because of the natural homogeneity of business transactions in different companies, industries, and nations. Companies planning on implementing EDI and supporting the ANSI X12 standard can feel comfortable that only minor maintenance changes will be requested in the future.

Furthermore, as new industries consider implementing EDI, they are opting to support this same standard. There are no new proprietary industry standards being developed. Even companies that in the past have required their trading partners to support proprietary formats are today jumping on the X12 bandwagon.

Float Loss

THE PERCEPTION IS THAT FLOAT, THE TIME PERIOD BETWEEN WHEN A CHECK IS WRITTEN AND WHEN FUNDS ARE COLLECTED, WILL BE ELIMINATED IF EDI, IN THE FORM OF ELECTRONIC FUNDS TRANSFER, IS IMPLEMENTED.

While it is true that float will be eliminated, it is not true that vendors will have access to payments any sooner in the electronic environment. Let's take the example of a payment that must be made within 10 days of the invoice date in order to take discount terms.

In the traditional environment, the check would have to be written and mailed by day seven in order to assure receipt by day 10. The buying firm would then experience a three day float period during which the vendor would not have received the check, and an additional 2–3 day period until the check cleared. Accordingly, the buyer would not even have to maintain balances to cover the check until the 12th day.

In the EDI environment, balances may be transferred from buyer's to seller's accounts as soon as authorization to pay is received by the bank. While there would be no float period, the buying organization can authorize payment on or as of any specified date. Payment would then actually still be made on the same day. So, experiencing the loss of float would not mean experiencing a loss in cash flow.

Additionally, with EDI, the invoice can be received by the buyer on the invoice date, meaning that they would have at least three more days (traditional mail delay float) to reconcile it and authorize payment than in the traditional paper environment. With this longer period, they would more easily be able to take advantage of discount terms.

Training

THE PERCEPTION IS THAT NO ONE IN-HOUSE KNOWS ANYTHING ABOUT EDI OR DATA STANDARDS OR CAN OVERSEE THE IMPLEMENTATION EFFORT.

It is true that there is little in-house expertise on EDI in many companies. But, educational opportunities abound. Standards, organizations, industry trade groups, and functional area organizations promote many shows each year that are either entirely or partly devoted to EDI. Most invite software vendors and third party providers to display their products and services. Many have educational workshops on various topics such as planning, costs and benefits, implementation, company and industry experiences, and choosing trading partners. All have representatives of companies that have already implemented EDI and may be looking for additional trading partners.

Also, independent consultants in the field offer seminars and courses in EDI which may be scheduled in-house. Educational institutions such as the American Management Association also offer courses in EDI.

Finally, most companies have at least one trading partner that has already implemented EDI. Making contact with that partner is an excellent way to learn not only about EDI, but how it has impacted traditional business practices and how it has benefited the companies involved.

Company Attitude

THE ATTITUDE OF UPPER MANAGEMENT TOWARD ANY NEW PROJECT, TECHNOLOGY, OR PROCEDURE GREATLY IMPACTS THE ATTITUDE OF MIDDLE AND LOWER MANAGEMENT.

Without the support of upper management, EDI cannot happen. First, there will be no funding, second there will be no time allotted for it. The most successful implementations occur when there is top down pressure with specified expectations of in number of trading partners and amount of business.

It may be the job of middle management to convince upper management of the potential benefits of EDI by researching the current environment, showing today's trouble spots, and developing a revised data flow for the proposed EDI environment. Education is the surest way to success. The benefits that other companies are experiencing are the best teachers.

It may become apparent that certain attitudes toward success and productivity may need to change for the electronic environment. Take, for example, an accounts payable manager with a staff of 20 overworked invoice reconciliation clerks. This manager has high status today based on the size of his/her staff. How would the organization view this same manager with a staff of only two very productive reconciliation clerks who handle only the exceptions that kick out of the new automated invoice reconciliation application? Possibly lower, based on the number of staff, instead of higher, based on improved productivity, which illustrates one reason why EDI is not always hailed as a hero by just those staff members who could profit from it the most. Unless productivity is viewed as higher than staff count, EDI will have a tough time gaining a foothold.

You may find it useful to make note of these responses to the most commonly heard objections to EDI.

EDI Implementation Phase

The implementation phase follows the feasibility stage. Figure 5-3 shows the additional deliverables needed to develop a corporate implementation plan. In order to generate these deliverables, the following tasks need to be accomplished:

- Prioritizing the business area feasibility studies developed by the functional business managers.
- Working out data requirements, business procedures, contractual and other EDI agreements with trading partners.
- Evaluating translation software and communication options.
- Developing data processing specifications for application software.
- Choosing pilot partners.
- Developing and running the pilot program.

1. BUSINESS AREA FEASIBILITY STUDIES.
2. PRIORITIZED LIST OF BUSINESS AREAS SHOWING GOOD EDI POTENTIAL.
3. DATA REQUIREMENTS/USAGE FOR EDI ENVIRONMENT.
4. DATA PROCESSING AND COMMUNICATIONS OPTIONS, AND TECHNICAL RECOMMENDATIONS.
5. DATA PROCESSING SPECIFICATIONS FOR APPLICATION LINK SOFTWARE .
6. LEGAL AND AUDITING REQUIREMENTS.
7. LIST OF PILOT PARTNERS.
8. PILOT PROGRAM STEPS/ MILESTONES, DATES, AND RESPONSIBLE PARTIES.

Figure 5-3 Components of a corporate implementation plan.

In order to accomplish these tasks, it is necessary to expand the existing steering group of functional business managers into an implementation team with the following additional members:

- Accounting and legal representatives.
- Data processing application support staff.
- Communication support staff.
- Functional managers and data processing and communication counterparts from trading partner organizations.

Optionally, an EDI consultant can also be added to the group. If a member of the implementation team has expertise in EDI issues such as standards and industry group EDI activity, then that person may act as the consultant to the group. Otherwise, it may be helpful to include an outside consultant on the team as well.

Before examining each of the tasks mentioned above, it may be helpful to review the component parts of the feasibility study and the list of additional components in the implementation plan. See Figures 5-2 and 5-3.

Implementation phase tasks can be grouped into four categories:

- Trading partner-related.
- Data processing application support.
- Communication support.
- Full committee.

Let's examine each category in some detail.

Trading Partner-Related Tasks

Up until this point there has been little interaction between company staff members and trading partner organizations except, possibly, when compiling the list of potential EDI trading partners for the business area feasibility study. However, in order to complete the trading partner related tasks, it is necessary to establish a close working relationship with the trading partner organizations. The inclusion of functional business managers and data processing counterparts from these organizations on the implementation team will ensure that pertinent business and technical issues are discussed and resolved prior to implementation of EDI. Following are some of the important tasks in this category.

Finalizing business specifications for internal applications. The functional business managers on the EDI steering committee have recommended transmitting and receiving certain transactions and have identified the data elements available from or needed by the existing internal applications. The prospective EDI trading partners may wish to alter the list of transactions in that they may wish to receive an additional one electronically or may not be prepared to send or receive others that had been recommended.

When working with trading partners, the general rule is that the sending party provides data availability and the receiving party determines data requirements. So, this work can also reveal the absence of data fields that the receiving trading partner may consider mandatory. The sender's internal application program may have to be enhanced to provide additional data while specifications for the application link software may have to be changed to reflect the mapping between the internal system and the standard for all transaction sets that will be handled electronically. Any changes made during this exercise must be incorporated into the business specifications for internal computer applications.

Reaffirming conditions and terms for the EDI environment. While paper transactions carried with them a reaffirmation of conditions and terms in the form of small print on the back of the document, no such vehicle is available in the electronic environment. Consequently, many firms agree to reaffirm the conditions and terms in a separate contract for EDI usage or in an EDI rider to an existing contract. Either way, both parties sign and date the agreement and it remains in effect until either party wishes to change it. Often, this rider is merely a reiteration of the existing terms and conditions with only some timing expectations changed for the new environment. For example, it would no longer be necessary to provide a 10-day period for a vendor to respond to a purchase order it had received; 24 or 48 hours would be more reasonable with electronic transmission of data.

Developing the pilot program. Ideally, the pilot program should be set up with three to five trading partners and should be scheduled with a specified duration of from two to four months. Since each prospective trading partner has a good deal of internal work to do prior to the EDI implementation, he must estimate that effort in terms of man/days and elapsed calendar days in order to provide realistic dates for accomplishing each of the various pilot steps.

The pilot plan itself has a predefined structure containing all of the steps or tasks needed to set up, test, and evaluate the hardware, communications connection, software and procedures with each pilot trading partner. Each pilot step pertains to a specific activity with a specific trading partner. Each should be defined in terms of criteria for success and time period, as it is impossible to determine when and if open-ended requirements have been successfully completed. For example, "testing communications" would be too vague as a pilot step. Instead, several tests could be set up as follows:

- Each party of a trading pair must make contact with the other via telephone connection, using a specified communication protocol and line speed, and receive a "READY" through the handshake of protocols.
- Each party of a trading pair must make contact as before and transmit a predetermined data stream containing all letters, numbers, other characters, and spaces.
- The receiving party must analyze the data stream received for completeness and correctness and report the results to the other.
- Each party of a trading pair must make contact as before and send a predetermined data stream in standard format containing data in all mandatory and optional fields,
- The receiving party must analyze the standard data stream for adherence to standard syntax rules and report the results to the sender.

Milestones are defined as a group of associated pilot tasks with a specified partner. All the steps above might be associated with a milestone of "Complete communications test with trading partner A." Other examples of milestones are

- Interpret and process transaction X (e.g., purchase order) from trading partner A into receiving computer application (e.g., order entry).
- Parallel test, paper and electronic environment of transaction X processing with trading partner A.

The pilot plan is merely the list of tasks and milestones. Each should be described by the following fields

- Task/milestone name
- Task/milestone number
- Task/milestone description
- Actual completion date
- Anticipated completion date
- Party responsible for task
- Comments

It is important for some individual to be named as administrator of the pilot and be responsible for controlling and tracking the pilot tasks and maintaining the pilot plan. As each task is successfully completed, it should be reported to the pilot administrator, who records the status and date on the pilot plan. Problems encountered can be reflected as comments to the task.

At the end of the scheduled duration period, the pilot can be evaluated by the parties involved and the pilot's success/ failure determined. If successful, the milestones accomplished thus far should be converted into production mode while additional steps/phases go into or continue in pilot. All too often pilots continue forever because no criteria for success were established and no duration was set at the outset, at the end of which results would be evaluated.

Data Processing Support Tasks

The business specifications for enhancements to internal applications and development of application link software reflect the business needs for the EDI environment. Additionally, requirements may also have been requested by the accounting representative to provide adequate audit control. The data processing application specialists, who are intimately familiar with the existing computer applications, will need to evaluate them in terms of the new business requirements. They may require the advice of an EDI consultant who is familiar with standard syntax and data usage.

Initially, this group is asked to develop a time and effort estimate for enhancing existing application modules or developing new ones. They prepare a recommendation that contains these estimates along with alternative solutions such as purchase/lease of available software packages or use of third party in-network translation services as a substitute for development of the translation software.

Their recommendation is presented to the implementation team, where it is evaluated. If, after evaluating the alternatives, the decision is to proceed with internal development, the application specialists will be charged with developing programming specifications, then programming and testing the required modules. However, if the use of a third party is contemplated, they will be asked to prepare a list of third party requirements and questions. This list will become part of the "Request for Proposal" or "Request for Information" to be sent to potential third party service providers. Responses to these requirements and questions in the Request will help the implementation team to evaluate the third party candidates.

Communications Support Tasks

The communications specialists have several tasks for which they are responsible. The results of these tasks provide the basis for the communications solution they will recommend to the implementation team.

Initially, this group is called upon to evaluate the company's intra- and inter-company communications capabilities. While the focus in EDI is on the inter-company aspects of the interchange, once data has been received it often has to be disseminated to various locations through an intra-company network. Externally, there is the need to support telecommunications ports to the outside via public telephone lines with an acceptable bisynchronous or error-detecting asynchronous protocol and a line speed sufficiently fast for the anticipated volumes of data.

If the in-house communications capability is inadequate, the company is not EDI-ready from a communications point of view. The communications specialists will prepare a time and cost estimate for the additional hardware and software necessary and will need to install them prior to initial pilot testing.

They will also investigate the impact EDI will have on the operations department of the company. Using the projected data volumes and number of trading partner transmissions, they will evaluate the adequacy of the following:

- Computer storage and processing capacity.
- Number of telecommunications ports to the outside.
- Number of staff in the department.
- Operational hours per day and days per year.

Many companies find that the additional workload and responsibilities of handling and controlling multiple data transmissions from and to multiple trading partners in an EDI environment would be detrimental to the working efficiency of their operations departments. They, therefore, consider employing a third-party service as a communications intermediary.

Prior to making their recommendation to the implementation team, the communications specialists will prepare a list of pros and cons of dealing with trading partners directly or through a third party. Depending on the adequacy of the company's operations department and communications capabilities, the benefits provided by the third party will be perceived as more or less valuable to the company than the initial and ongoing costs for transmission services.

If the recommendation suggests the use of a third party, the communications specialists should include in their recommendation a list of communications requirements and questions. This list will be included in the Request for Proposal to be sent to potential third party service providers. Responses to these requirements and questions will also help the implementation team to evaluate the third party candidates.

Full Committee Tasks

While individual groups on the team make recommendations on different aspects of the EDI implementation project, the full implementation team holds meetings at which they evaluate those recommendations and make the final decisions.

Specifically, recommendations presented by the applications support group and the communications specialists are discussed in terms of costs, time and effort, and alternative solutions. If use of a third-party service provider has been recommended, a Request for Proposal/Request for Information document is generated by the group and sent to prospective third-party candidates. Included in this document are the list of functional, hardware, and software requirements and questions developed by the two technical groups. Also included are questions on:

- The third-party company and related EDI experience.
- Communications protocols and line speeds supported.
- EDI services available.
- EDI software available.
- Support.

A sample third party Request for Information is included in Appendix G.

Responses to the Requests are received by return mail and must be evaluated by the group members. The group may request that one or several candidates visit and make presentations to them prior to a final decision.

The proposed pilot program is also discussed at a full group meeting. As there is a good deal of time and effort required prior to pilot testing, it is necessary for the members to be sure that enough time has been allotted prior to the beginning of the pilot.

Members should also examine the pilot plan to verify that sufficient time has been allotted for each task/milestone for which they are responsible. Additionally, success criteria for the pilot as a whole and its duration should be discussed and agreed upon as a group.

While the pilot is administered by one member of the implementation team, it should be considered a group effort. At the end of the pilot's duration, its success or failure can be determined by evaluating the results in terms of the agreed upon criteria. A successful pilot should be converted to production mode. Lack of success is often an indication of coordination problems. In a project such as EDI, problems can surface in either the communications or data processing areas. The implementation team must evaluate the causes of failure and either make the appropriate changes and define the conditions of an extended pilot period, or agree to suspend the implementation for the time being.

Planning Summary

The EDI planning process cannot be overemphasized. Investigating the project from the corporate perspective is the first step toward incorporating electronic data interchange into the strategic plan of the organization. Each business area feasibility study brings to light another facet of the whole EDI picture and aids the development of a long-range, phased approach to implementation.

Bringing the right people together in the implementation process can mean the difference between a well planned development project and constant loose ends and back-tracking during the process. The business area perspective, application software support, communications support, legal and auditing representatives, and trading partner counterparts must all be represented in the implementation process to develop full business and technical specifications and to complete the implementation tasks.

Finally, following a predefined pilot plan takes the project from the implementation phase to production mode. In EDI, the initial pilot is just the tip of the iceberg. Trading electronically with three to five trading partners is certainly not the final goal. Building a trading community with many, and ultimately all, of the trading partners is the key to realizing the full potential benefits of EDI. By getting the necessary steps defined and completed in a timely manner during the initial pilot, a company positions itself for success during the follow-on pilots with additional trading partners.

If the EDI planning process has been handled properly, the marginal work required to add each new trading partner to the organization's EDI trading community should and will decrease over time. That, in turn, will bring the EDI goal that much closer to fruition.

Chapter

6

EDI in the Health Care Industry

The health care industry is comprised of

- Manufacturers of prescription drugs, over the counter drugs, and health and beauty aids.
- Wholesalers carrying some or all of the above in addition to some grocery, office products, and miscellaneous items.
- Hospitals.
- Drug stores and drug and retail chains.
- Drug buying groups.
- Suppliers to drug manufacturers.

Let's take a separate look at the business environment and the EDI potential that exists in each of four trading communities within this industry:

- Drug manufacturer as supplier to drug wholesalers.
- Drug manufacturer as supplier to hospitals and hospital buying groups.
- Drug manufacturer as customer to its supplier.
- Drug wholesaler as supplier to its hospital, chain store and retail customers.

Drug Manufacturer as Supplier to Drug Wholesaler

The major portion of EDI in the health care industry is found in this segment. The relationship between the drug wholesaler and manufacturer is strong, as the wholesaler serves as distributor of product to hospitals, stores, and chains. Even when prices are negotiated directly between hospitals or buying groups and manufacturers, the wholesaler is still responsible for distribution. Figure 6-1 illustrates the trading partner relationship between wholesalers, manufacturers, and hospitals.

Historically, as far back as 1972, Bergen Brunswig, one of the largest drug wholesalers, began using the remote computing services of Management Horizons Data Systems (MHDS) to develop purchase orders in print format. Bergen would then print and mail them to the manufacturers. In 1972 they began a pilot with Eli Lilly in which the

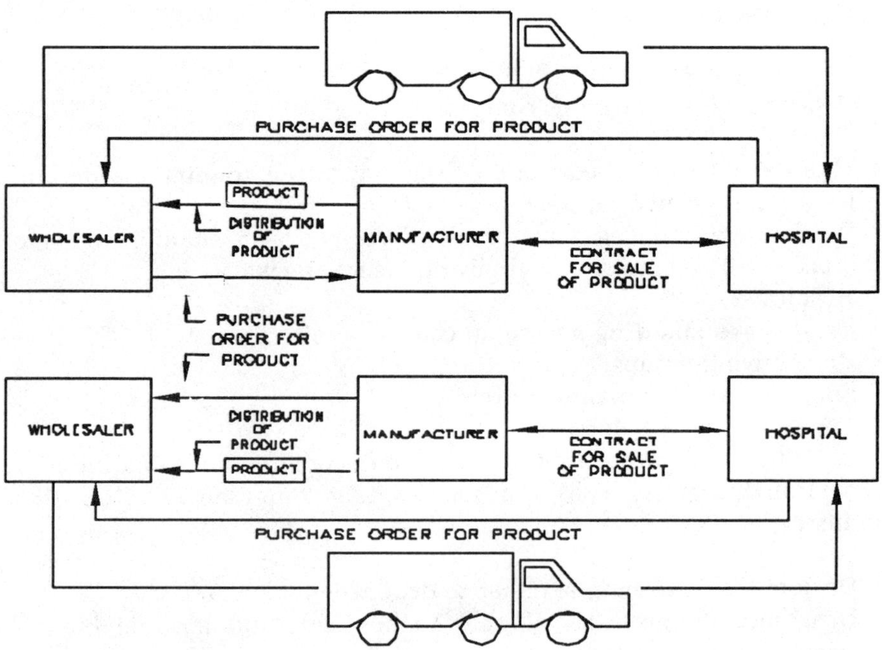

Figure 6-1 Trading partner relationship between wholesalers, manufacturers, and hospitals.

purchase orders, in data format, were transmitted directly from the MHDS data center to Lilly. In line with the technology of the day, the data format they developed was comprised of 80 character records and contained all of the data necessary to conduct business, in fixed length data fields.

At about the same time, the Business Systems Committee of the National Wholesale Druggists Association (NWDA) met to discuss this same possibility: ways of transmitting ethical orders directly to manufacturers. As this organization represented wholesale druggists, they were under some pressure to help their membership to alleviate pressing business problems. The wholesaler was searching for expense cutting measures to reduce internal costs to counteract the unacceptably low level of return on net worth (RONW) of under 10% and net profit after taxes of under 1% that they were realizing and to maintain high levels of customer service.

Implementing this new technology, electronic transmission of purchase orders, promised to reduce order lead time, which in turn would decrease inventory and safety stock requirements. In fact, implementing EDI was one of the prime factors in raising RONW to over 15% through 1984 and net profit margin to 1.25% over the same period. More recently, those figures dropped due to operating expenses decreasing at a slower rate than gross margin. 1987 has shown a turnaround of those figures again.

By 1974, MHDS had developed the system to which it attracted 16 drug wholesalers in 32 locations. The system transmitted "suggested order quantity" information to the drug wholesaler for review by its buyers. The first manufacturer to receive information from this system was Eli Lilly, followed by Mead Johnson, Burroughs Welcome, and others over the next two years.

In 1975, Informatics General Corporation, which had purchased MHDS, approached NWDA with the idea of the industry clearing house for electronic purchase orders. The Business Systems Committee was enthusiastic. After receiving responses to a Request for Proposal sent to several potential third party providers, they selected Informatics. In 1978, NWDA endorsed the Informatics "Ordernet" clearing house system, which prompted Informatics General to name its new Division, the ORDERNET Services Division. Except for Eli Lilly, which continued to receive orders directly, all other manufacturers from the MHDS system became clearing house customers.

With the endorsement from the NWDA the following occurred:

- ORDERNET Services agreed to enhance the Ordernet purchase order formats.
- ORDERNET took on the responsibility of sales and marketing of the system
- ORDERNET started selling on a one by one basis, with the strong active support of the NWDA. Richard C. Cook, then director of operations and research was a strong believer in the system, and strongly supported the program.
- NWDA gave ORDERNET the opportunity to present the program to wholesalers and manufacturers at trade shows and meetings.
- ORDERNET agreed to refrain from marketing to any entity competitive to wholesalers, namely hospitals and chain drug stores, for a period of two years, which gave the wholesalers a differential advantage in the marketplace.

On the strength of this existing system, the American Surgical Trade Association (ASTA), whose membership is made up of distributors of medical/surgical products, approached ORDERNET Services about a year later to develop a similar system. Not only were they interested in transmitting purchase orders electronically, but also transactions for sales tracing and rebate reporting. A similar data format, called COMM-NET, also fixed length, was developed for this industry.

It is interesting to note that even with a large degree of commonality between the drug/pharmaceutical companies and the med/surg companies, the sales tracing and rebate reporting transactions have never been used for the drug sector. That is because a similar service, provided by Drug Distribution Data (Division of IMS America), already existed. EDI has been evolutionary, not revolutionary in this industry, based soley on business need.

There are three main areas of EDI usage in this segment of the health care industry:

- Purchase order transactions sent from the wholesalers to the manufacturers.
- Chargeback family of transactions transmitted between wholesalers and manufacturers.
- Invoice sent from the manufacturers to the wholesalers.

By 1986, 99% of drug wholesalers were using EDI and specifically the Ordernet, industry specific purchase order transactions. Ninety percent of pharmaceutical manufacturers were doing the same, representing the largest penetration of EDI usage into an industry.

Electronic Purchase Orders

Let's examine the benefits each of the trading partners receives from sending/receiving the purchase order electronically. The wholesalers are able to reduce order lead time, thereby reducing safety stock and inventory requirements. In addition they have eliminated time-consuming manual tasks related to handling of paper transactions. By sending complete and correct electronic transactions to the manufacturer, they improve their chances of receiving timely deliveries of the required items.

The manufacturers have also eliminated manual procedures, including interpretation and completion of incoming purchase order information. In so doing, they have eliminated transcription and interpretation errors which, in turn, have all but eliminated shipments of incorrect product and returns based on incorrect shipment. In addition, they are able to rapidly process the incoming electronic orders which allows them to send the product sooner than was possible prior to EDI. This, in turn, improves the customer service that they can provide. Finally, by receiving machine readable, accurate and complete purchase order data, they have set the stage to disseminate this information to various computer applications throughout the company, e.g., invoice generation, and to strategic personnel, e.g., auditors, functional business managers, and top level strategic planners.

Chargeback Family of Transactions

The development of three electronic transactions in the industry specific Ordernet standard – the bid award notification, the chargeback debit memo, and the chargeback reconciliation – needed to process chargeback claims from the wholesaler to the manufacturer, represents a departure from the traditional view of EDI, that of substituting an electronic transaction for a standard business paper transaction. As there were no standard paper transactions in place, claiming and reconciling chargebacks had been a long and arduous procedure in the paper, telephone environment. This procedure has been streamlined and shortened substantially in the electronic environment.

The chargeback process is based on a specific business need of the health care industry. Because large hospitals often negotiate for price of product directly with a manufacturer, while having distribution and billing handled through a wholesaler, there is an agreement that the manufacturer will reimburse the wholesaler for the price differential between the normal selling price to the wholesaler and the lower selling price to the hospital.

The first of the electronic transactions to be used in large volumes is the chargeback debit memo, which the wholesaler generates with details of a hospital's purchases in order to initiate a return credit from the manufacturer. In order to maintain a positive cash flow position, the wholesaler needs credit in time to make future purchases from the same manufacturer. Over 80% of chargebacks are transacted electronically in this industry.

Unfortunately, in most cases, the wholesaler learns that the hospital has negotiated a special price with a manufacturer after its first invoice has been rejected. In order to eliminate this problem, the wholesaler requests that the manufacturer send them an electronic bid award notification transaction as soon as they establish a special contract with a hospital. In that way, they are aware of special pricing ahead of time and can invoice correctly the first time, improving their chances of being paid in a timely manner. Manufacturers are beginning to develop applications to generate the bid award transaction, both to comply with the wholesalers request, and to eliminate the manual procedures of logging contracts and tracking chargeback debit claims and a good part of the staff required to carry out these procedures.

Finally, there is a third transaction to complete the set, the chargeback reconciliation, that debits or credits the wholesaler based on the original chargeback debit memo and the hospital contract terms. This transaction is also gaining in popularity at this time.

The Electronic Invoice

The third area of EDI activity in this segment of the health care industry is of the invoice transaction. With the generation of the electronic purchase order, the wholesaler has complete and timely information against which to reconcile incoming invoices. If these invoices are received in paper form, the information must be interpreted and key entered, a process which is fraught with errors. However, with electronic transmission of machine readable data, an invoice reconciliation application can be developed which would allow the wholesaler to reconcile manufacturer invoices at the line item level. By automating this procedure, the wholesaler has a good deal to gain: he would be in a position to authorize payment sooner, based on complete reconciliation, and he would, therefore, be able to decrease his cost for product by taking advantage of discount terms. Since the net profit margin is so low in this industry, there is a great deal of appeal to lowering costs in this way. In addition, the wholesaler could greatly reduce its accounts payable staff. However, it is the manufacturer that must generate the invoice. Because the typical manufacturer is a high profit company, realizing about 25% net profit, it has not initiated generation of this transaction until pressure has been applied by the wholesaler. Therefore, usage of the electronic invoice has not, as yet, reached nearly the volume of either the purchase order or the chargeback transaction.

Figure 6-2 illustrates the flow of information that would exist in the electronic environment with use of the invoice transaction:

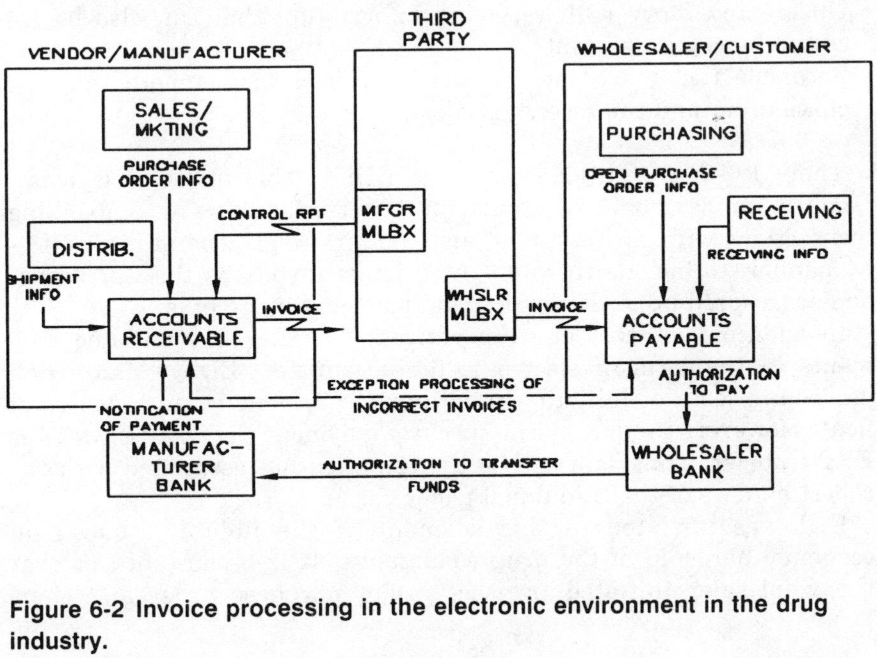

Figure 6-2 Invoice processing in the electronic environment in the drug industry.

- The invoice generated out of a vendor's computer system using both purchase order and shipment information.
- The invoice transmitted electronically to the wholesaler in standard data format, and with accurate and complete data.
- Third party control reports verifying that the invoice was sent through the system and was retrieved successfully by the trading partner.
- Machine readable invoices are automatically reconciled against the wholesaler's open purchase order and receiving information to determine whether they are correct.
- Automatic authorization of payment, then either check processing or electronic funds transfer through a financial institution in time to take advantage of discount terms.
- Incorrect invoices handled as exceptions, utilizing accounts payable staff.

Of course, in order to effect this flow with automatic processing the wholesaler must have developed the necessary applications to:

- Preserve a file of open purchase orders to which accounts payable has access.
- Update inventory with receiving information that can also be accessed by accounts payable.
- Reconcile the invoice at the line item level against both the purchase order and the receiving information.

There is some additional usage of EDI in this industry segment. Some manufacturers are exchanging electronic shipping and billing transactions with carriers in order to obtain freight charges in a timely manner, to include them on the original invoice to the wholesaler, and/or to speed up authorization and payment of the bills.

In addition, at least one innovative wholesaler has initiated payments in the form of electronic funds transfer (EDT). Many companies are leery of initiating this form of payment because of loss of float. However, the payer can specify a payment date along with his EFT transfer. That data can be the same as that associated with the collection date of the traditional paper check.

EDI was initiated in this segment of the industry, based on economic hardship of the drug wholesalers. It is because of this that the wholesaler initiated transactions of purchase order and chargeback debit memo have become the *de facto* mode of doing business. However, the addition of new transactions generated by the manufacturer, the bid award and chargeback reconciliation transactions and more recently the invoice, has been exceedingly slow to gain acceptance. There are still substantial benefits to be derived from EDI in this industry. NWDA has continued to be an active participant, encouraging its wholesaler members and manufacturer associate members to increase their participation in EDI by transacting business in any and all business areas in which they can realize benefits of decreased costs, staff reductions, and savings of time.

Manufacturers as Supplier to Hospitals and Hospital Buying Groups

In the previous section we discussed hospital pharmacy purchases that are agreed to by contract directly with the manufacturer, but are distributed through the wholesaler. For pharmaceuticals, 80% of purchases are done through a wholesaler, with only 20% direct. There is another segment of the hospital/manufacturer relationship in which the hospital purchases and receives shipment directly from the manufacturer. This arrangement is most prevalent, with 80% of purchasing done direct and only 20% done through a wholesaler, for the solutions required in high volumes and with short lead times by the medical/surgical department of the hospital.

Here, the leading manufacturers of parental solutions have attempted to tie-in customers with proprietary, PC-based ordering systems. One such system, ASAP Express, developed by Baxter Pharmaceutical, also has the ability to send orders to other manufacturers. The system initially sends all orders to Baxter, which picks off its own and routes the remainder through the GEIS network to the mailboxes of the other recipients. Most other manufacturers are not anxious to receive orders in this way, so selling manufacturer mailboxes has not been an easy task. The QuickLink system developed by Abbott can also accept orders for other manufacturers. In addition, a few other ordering systems have been developed that can access a variety of manufacturers.

However, no one all-vendor system seems to have captured the market. Meanwhile, hospitals are forced to support a variety of PC systems in order to send all of their orders. Most important in this scenario is the fact that all of the systems mentioned thus far handle the ordering transaction only, but offer little to help the hospital control its inventory or automatically initiate orders.

In addition, most hospitals do not have centralized procurement departments; pharmaceuticals are ordered separately from medical/surgical supplies as are general purchases of office products, etc. With so many internal departments ordering autonomously, no one department has automated the procedure with a sophisticated piece of material management/ ordering software.

Today, some of the forward looking hospitals have begun to restructure their departments and centralize the purchasing function. They have installed mainframe software products put out by such companies as MSA or McCormick Dodge, which keep track of inventory and initiate orders. Potentially, these order can be translated to the X12 standard and transmitted to the manufacturers. Only with this approach will the traditional EDI scenario of store and forward take hold in this portion of the industry.

Manufacturers as Customers to Their Suppliers

There is a tremendous amount of potential for EDI as business transactions pass between the drug manufacturer and its vendors. However, at this time there is little concerted effort to develop the trading community. Manufacturers buy from various industry groups, among them chemical, paper, and plastics. While the paper and chemical industries have already endorsed the X12 standard and have begun to trade electronically, activity is still very limited, with chemical focusing not toward customers, but rather back to their own suppliers. So, EDI in this direction would entail work in new corporate departments to develop new systems. As the major drug manufacturing firms become interested in implementing EDI through their purchasing/accounts payable functions, pressure will be brought to bear upon their suppliers. As there is a good deal of commonality of suppliers between the manufacturers, a trading community of suppliers will, in time, become EDI-active. It seems certain that the drug manufacturers will support the ANSI X12 standard transaction sets.

Wholesalers as Suppliers to Hospitals, Chain Stores, and Retail Stores

While 99% of wholesalers order from their suppliers via EDI, what is the potential of receiving orders from their customers in this same medium? Currently, very little. The reason is that the wholesalers' position in the industry is one of customer service. In the early years, high levels of customer service were synonymous with frequent deliveries. Stores would call in orders and the wholesaler would send them out. Today, customer service is still of prime concern, but ordering patterns and methods have changed.

The vast majority of hospital and store customers are ordering via direct order entry to the wholesaler, using a mechanized way of passing either inventory or ordering information. Many have adopted the use of hand-held source data entry devices such as that produced by Telxon, to place orders with wholesalers. These units are also used for current inventory information; the numbers of packages of each brand, product, and size on the shelves is entered and transmitted to the wholesaler. To the extent that product is barcoded, which is the case for all health and beauty aids, the counting process is facilitated.

Many stores have barcoded labels that automatically identify the brand, product, and size, with counting left to the ordering clerk. The wholesaler, then, develops an internal order to replenish the agreed upon stock level of this customer. Other stores control their own inventory levels and send order information.

The direct ordering system provided by each wholesaler to its customers serves the same purpose as the proprietary ordering system supplied by the drug manufacturer to its hospital customers; it serves to tie them to that wholesaler. There is little chance that the traditional store and forward brand of EDI will take hold here either. The level of service available today is too high for there to be pressure to change.

Summary

EDI in the drug industry between drug manufacturers and wholesalers started more than 15 years ago. Its use was prompted by the need to bolster net profits by decreasing internal costs and cutting back on safety stock inventory levels. Penetration has been almost

100% from its inception to the current time, in great part due to the efforts of a strong and active industry trade group, the National Wholesale Druggists Association (NWDA), which was instrumental in analyzing the needs of the industry, developing the industry specific formats, and endorsing a third party to provide the communication link, the EDI services, and the marketing arm for the industry. No other industry has even come close to this penetration of EDI as the accepted mode of doing business.

Until just a few years ago, the ORDERNET, fixed length industry specific standard was the *de facto* standard of the industry. However, with the growth and widespread acceptance of the ANSI X12 variable length public standard, the NWDA sought to have its member and associated member wholesalers and manufacturers respectively consider adopting X12 for new implementations. The jury is still out on this issue. While X12 offers the mainstream approach being taken by other industries, it is a more complex format that is more difficult to handle, and requires more sophisticated software to process.

The drug industry has taken the evolutionary, not revolutionary, approach to EDI. It has implemented only those transactions that could offer genuine benefits and has integrated these few into the way they transact business. Therefore, in spite of the prevalence of electronic trade in the purchase order and more recently chargeback transactions, movement into new transactions and business areas has been slow.

Likewise, EDI implementation from the manufacturer back to its supplier and from the hospital to the manufacturer has not yet started to take off and will not move quickly until economic indicators within the industry make it more painful to continue business as usual than it would be to change. Finally, EDI potential from the wholesaler to the hospital or retail customer doesn't seem to exist at the present time. Service levels are already high using automated procedures and hand held devices. There seems to be a good deal of room for improvement in the functionality and memory available in these devices. Improvements here would probably find a more receptive audience than introduction of EDI into this segment of the industry.

Chapter

7

EDI in the Automotive Industry

The automotive industry is comprised of several different parties including:

- New and used automobile and truck customers.
- Automobile manufacturers.
- Truck manufacturers.
- First tier suppliers.
- Second and ensuing levels of suppliers.
- Auto and truck after-market suppliers.

We will be discussing the automotive industry primarily as being comprised of the major automobile manufacturers and their first tier suppliers of auto components, tools and machinery used in the assembly process, and various and sundry office needs. That is because these companies have acted as a unit in developing EDI capabilities. While data requirements are fairly homogeneous for the truck manufacturers and their suppliers, and they have opted to support the same Automotive Industry Action Group, AIAG/ANSI X12 transactions, they have chosen to form a separate truck advisory group to study how to implement these transactions for their industry.

The automotive/automobile industry, then, is made up of a handful of large, sophisticated automakers (OEMs) and several thousand suppliers, ranging in size from major corporations to small companies resident in garages, with no computer capability. A large percentage of these suppliers are located in the Midwest, within one day's travel from Detroit, the capital of the U.S. auto industry.

As far back as the early 1970s the major automakers had developed internal, proprietary data formats to replace the traditional paper transactions of material releases, some engineering specifications and warranty data. They encouraged their suppliers to pull this data and to format and send notification of shipment. Data was available on the automakers' private network or could be sent to the same network at prescheduled times. However, any one supplier might have been required to support a handful of different proprietary standards, one for each auto manufacturer customer. This meant that the supplier would have to develop front and back end software links between the applications it was using to process releases and to develop notification of shipment for each of the proprietary standards it was supporting. While certainly not ideal, the suppliers were loath to refuse as this became a condition of doing business in the industry.

In the mid-'70s, the auto industry started a pilot with the truckers of parts. General Motors, for example, began to receive electronic freight bills to replace the paper bills it had been receiving.

Over the last decade, the industry has faced the problem of a downward trend in the purchase of American made automobiles, with foreign made cars, particularly those imported from Japan, gaining in popularity and taking over market share. There were several reasons for the change in buying preference from domestic to foreign cars, not the least of which was that products introduced in the American marketplace by the Japanese were known for fuel economy, were small, fairly priced, and of high quality, while many American-made cars at that time were large, expensive, fuel guzzlers, and of dubious quality. Even when the industry acknowledged that the public wanted smaller and more economical cars, we missed the boat by building small, economical, and low-quality cars. "Small" and "cheap" became partners in crime, and the customer base quickly started escaping from the sinking ship of American manufactured vehicles.

In order to improve quality in our cars without pricing ourselves out of the marketplace, some drastic measures were necessary. There was the need to become more efficient (leaner and meaner) by cutting internal costs and streamlining processing. In order to do this, there was the additional need to improve the relationships with supplier trading partners.

By the late '70s, automakers were looking for more efficient means of handling and processing data, and in 1981 the Automobile Industry

Action Group, AIAG, was formed and staffed by executives on loan from the major automakers. Their mandate was to:

- Look into ways of increasing productivity of North American automakers and suppliers.
- Seek out common solutions in data formats and communications.
- Evaulate how just-in-time manufacturing schedules would impact the industry.
- examine how barcoding would affect ordering, receiving, and other inter- and intra-company processes.

By the following year, the AIAG had developed a fixed length standard data format. While it was adopted by AMC which had not previously developed a proprietary standard, it was studied and rejected by other automakers who suggested that the variable length ANSI X12 standard be examined for a fit of functionality to the needs of the industry.

While EDI prospects for the automakers seemed good, as they were sophisticated companies with massive computer capability and data processing and communications staff, the same was not true for many of their trading partners. The emergence of microcomputers in 1983-1984 gave a tremendous impetus to the implementation of EDI in these smaller companies.

As prospects of high sales in the auto industry grew, the automakers also informed their suppliers that they expected them to start doing EDI on a regular basis. General Motors sent a letter to their first tier suppliers saying that EDI would be a requirement of doing business. As it turns out, this first letter was not really enforced because GM had not, as yet, developed a corporate plan to implement EDI itself.

In order to facilitate the implementation of EDI in the supplier companies, the automakers helped to develop an EDI specification for software requirements and communications interface that they then gave to potential software vendors. They used the previous experience of the grocery industry and adopted the identical communication standard of 2400 baud line with bisynchronous 2780/3780 communication protocol. The data standard called for in the new software for suppliers was still the proprietary standard of each of the major automakers. While the ANSI X12 standard was in the process of being endorsed by the industry, no one was actually supporting it. The new software, which would run on a microcomputer at the supplier location, needed to recognize which automaker had generated a material release and map from that proprietary standard to the print format.

By 1985, products started coming to the market which fulfilled the requirements of the industry and which were fairly inexpensive.

However, in the mid-80s, when GM bought EDS (the company that has since developed their EDI gateway software), several savvy EDI staff members moved to the new organization and new EDI implementations were temporarily put on the back burner. The next year, when Chrysler bought AMC, it devoted all of its resourses to integrating the new company into the corporation, and also slowed its implementation of EDI.

However, by 1987, the story was reversed. The automakers were devoting large amounts of energy into developing short and long range plans for EDI. Ford developed its corporate strategy for implementing EDI and, just this year, announced extensive specifications of what its suppliers must do in EDI and in barcoding. They distributed a massive document and set deadlines, which they intend to enforce.

Just to show how serious they are about EDI, Ford has said that they consider timely information on a par with quality of parts and level of service. The other automakers have expressed similar thoughts, ranking quality information as a top priority.

Cutting Internal Costs

Just-In-Time Manufacturing Schedules

Traditionally, auto manufacturers maintained very large inventories of parts and partially assembled components of automobiles in order to support the manufacturing and assembly schedules. However, the maintenance of a large inventory also causes a tremendous drain on cash flow. The first step necessary to reduce large inventories was to change the existing philosophy of assembling and stockpiling components, to one of assembling a complete automobile. Next, the manufacturing schedules needed to be developed to support this new philosophy. These new manufacturing schedules are aptly named "just-in-time." As their name implies, supplies are expected to be delivered just in time to be used in the manufacturing process. It became obvious fairly quickly that just in time deliveries would not be possible without just in time information. Enter EDI!

Automating Internal Systems

With the vast number of auto parts suppliers and the proportionately large numbers of releases against annually negotiated purchase orders, the auto manufacturers were being buried in paperwork that was time-consuming, people-intensive, error-producing, and overall, much too expensive for the rote work that it was. Automated procedures had to be put into place to replace the existing manual procedures. Internal application programs were developed to:

- Accept data pertaining to car orders from dealers.
- Turn those specifications into releases for component parts.
- Develop manufacturing schedules to assemble the ordered cars.
- Receive information on shipping schedules.
- Update inventory with received parts.
- Track the progress of each automobile from beginning to end of assembly and then through delivery to the dealership.

Again the requirement was for information. Enter EDI!

Barcoding

Linked to the systems above was the requirement to maintain complete and timely information in-house. In order to assure delivery of the correct product, predefined product codes were included on the release. In order to accurately track receipts, suppliers were requested to include barcoding on packaging. This enabled the receiver to scan the packaging in order to automatically update inventory figures. Both product codes and barcoding have been tremendous boons to efficiency within companies.

Automating Data Handling

However, even if the data sent to or received from a trading partner is absolutely correct and complete, errors can be insinuated into the data at the receiving location during a manual process. These errors can cause the wrong product to be shipped, the wrong quantity to be shipped, or the wrong delivery schedule. Any of the above can be very costly to the customer as it will stop the manufacturing process and cause downtime. It is equally costly for the supplier who may have to ship and pick up the product at its own cost, and who will surely fail to provide the kind of customer service required by its customers.

Ideally, data should be generated by a computer application, sent to the trading partner in machine readable form, and fed directly into a computer application by the receiving party to ensure that what is received is what is used. Again, enter EDI!

Evaluated Receipts Settlement

Traditionally, the decision to pay for product received is made by a customer after it receives the invoice and conducts a reconciliation of the invoice charges against the open purchase order and the receiving information. Often, the reconciliation process is manual and, at best, complicated, requiring matching data from three different internal departments – purchasing, distribution, and accounts payable. Because of this it turns out to be a lengthy process, which effectively delays paying the invoice and losing discount terms. Ideally, product could be paid for as soon as it is received in good condition, as long as price has been agreed upon advance.

It is in line with this theory that evaluated receipts settlement was developed by the major automakers in the automotive industry. The requirement is, of course, for timely and accurate data, first in the release the customer generates, which is based on prices pre-negotiated in the purchase order, then in the advance shipping notice the supplier generates from which the customer internally develops anticipated receiving information, and finally in the automatic counting and entering of product received by scanning the barcoded labels on the packaging.

Since payment will then be based on the actual receiving information, the customer generates and returns to the supplier a receiving advice which the supplier then uses to reconcile against its shipping information.

With material release, advance shipping notice and receiving advice passing between trading partners, it would only be reasonable to standardize these transactions so that they could be interpreted and processed automatically by an internal computer application. Electronic data interchange may be the answer.

Electronic Funds Transfer

Once payment amount has been determined and payment has been authorized, the only step left is to effect the transfer of funds. In most instances, this is currently done with a paper check which is mailed to the supplier and which he then deposits in his bank account for collection. While not a very efficient method because of the handling required mail time delays, it is fairly well thought of because of the float time generated from the date the check is actually generated until the date the cash is collected. Buyers in general are reluctant to give up float, the automakers being no exception. However, through electronic funds transfer (EFT), they have found a fast, efficient method of transferring the funds on a predetermined schedule.

Float has been eliminated, but as authorization to pay is dated, funds are not available for collection sooner. Both parties benefit from EFT – the buyer by eliminating handling and processing of checks and by paying in a timely manner to take advantage of discount terms and adhere to the terms of the purchase order agreement, the seller by being assured of payment on a specified date and thereby, improving its cash management.

Accompanying the electronic transfer, the buyer can take the opportunity to provide payment information and the seller can use this information to reconcile against its open invoices.

Trading Partner Relationships

In order for the auto manufacturers to adopt just-in-time manufacturing schedules, they would have to be assured of just-in-time deliveries of top quality product by their suppliers. Seeing that it would be difficult to encourage the suppliers to provide such responsive service in the traditional, adversarial customer/supplier relationship, it became obvious that the relationship would have to change.

While any customer, especially one as large as the typical auto manufacturer, has the clout to impose requirements on a supplier, it is generally more productive to offer inducements and support. At the same time that the manufacturer was asking for just-in-time deliveries, it was also volunteering to provide long and short term forecasts of product needed. This would allow the supplier to plan for increased need for product and would give him the opportunity to strike a better deal with his suppliers for component parts or raw materials.

Also, while requiring that the supplier maintain high levels of product quality, monitoring its output with customer defined quality specifications, the auto manufacturers were promising their chosen vendors the purchase of larger quantities and single sourcing. Additionally, there has been a move to develop longer term relationships by negotiating purchase orders for longer periods of time. Traditionally, the purchase orders would cover purchases for one model or calendar year. However, recently that has been increased to, in some cases, the expected lifetime of the model.

In order to support the entire relationship, the auto manufacturers required electronic exchange of data, first in a proprietary format, and more recently in the ANSI X12 format. Many of the suppliers were not prepared to support any data format; indeed they may not even have owned a computer.

By developing the current cooperative relationship between OEMs and suppliers, both parties have benefited. One manufacturer estimated that it would save $200 per car by using electronic exchange of data for the normal business transactions between themselves and their suppliers, so even the end customer, the auto buyer, may benefit.

It appeared that many of the problems being experienced in the auto industry could be alleviated by using electronic exchange of data. As we saw, as far back as 20 years ago, companies were supporting proprietary standards for a limited number of standard business transactions. At that time, most, if not all systems were interactive; most required key data entry. The automakers are still supporting those proprietary standards today. However, the plan is to phase out the old and bring in the new (AIAG/ANSI X12) over a period of time. This will mean a great deal of work on the parts of the companies involved, but the feeling is that it will be well worth it in the quality of data transmitted as well as the variety of transactions able to be supported.

EDI Activity in the Auto Industry

Figure 7-1 lists all of the ANSI X12 transaction sets currently in use by the auto industry or anticipated to be in use in the near future. A complete list of ANSI X12 transaction sets can be found in Appendix

EDI TRANSACTION SETS IN USE BY AUTOMATIVE INVOICE

TRANSACTION SET	ANSI X12 TRANSACTION SET #
REQUEST FOR QUOTE	840
QUOTE	843
MATERIAL RELEASE	830 *
PURCHASE ORDER	850
PLANNING SHEDULE	830 *
SHIPPING SCHEDULE	862
ADVANCE SHIPPING NOTICE	856
RECEIVING ADVICE	861
APPLICATION ADVICE	824
PAYMENT REMITTANCE ADVICE	820
TEST RESULTS	863

Figure 7-1 EDI transaction sets in use by automotive invoice.

H. Let's take a look at this EDI activity today and then at the future applications we can expect to see implemented in the next five to 10 years.

EDI In Purchasing

Purchasing encompasses both the pre-ordering and ordering transactions. In pre-ordering, the automaker may request a quote for pricing and delivery schedules on a new automobile component, expecting a quote returned from the supplier. In ordering, the automakers are huge purchasers of both productive (used in the production of an automobile; sold to consumer) and non-productive products (used in the manufacture/assembly of a car).

Request for Quote (RFQ) – ANSI X12 #840

The electronic request for quote is transmitted to a potential supplier of product with product specifications and quantity and delivery schedule requirements. It may or may not be a standalone document, as complete specifications may require drawings and other textual data and it rarely can be responded to in a totally automated manner.

Response to Request for Quote (QUOTE) – ANSI X12 # 843

The quote is returned to the automaker in response to the request for quote and can be used as support document to the purchase order.

Material Release - ANSI X12 # 830[1]

Normal business procedure for the procurement of productive material in this industry is for the auto manufacturer and its supplier to negotiate price and estimated gross quantity for each product that will be supplied in an annual purchase order agreement. Because the purchase order is generated only once per year, it was not in the first group of transactions planned for conversion to electronic form. However each automaker orders many tens of thousands of different products, so the intention is to convert it in the future, at which time purchase order terms and conditions will automatically be placed into a database of product information as soon as the agreement is reached. Orders for product during the course of the year are effected by use of a material release.

Releases are usually generated automatically, out of a computer application that tracks product requirements, inventory on hand, and manufacturing schedules. With just-in-time schedules, releases specify not only what and how much is required, but also when and where it is to be delivered. Often there is little lead time, so the supplier must be prepared to receive and act on the releases in a timely manner. In order to do that, the supplier must have software in place that front-ends a computer order/entry application and translates the release from the ANSI X12 data format to the internal format required by the application program. Alternatively, the data can be read, interpreted, and responded to in a more manual procedure.

The automakers are making a concerted effort to encourage their suppliers of productive material to receive the data format material release and to generate the electronic response of the advance shipping notice.

---

1 Same ANSI X12 transaction used for dual purpose. See Planning Schedule following.

Purchase Order – ANSI X12 # 850

For non-productive material, purchasing is conducted by sending the traditional purchase order. Ford relates that it has about 250 of its major suppliers of non-productive material up on EDI, while GM has about 60.

Let's look for a minute at the purchasing function in the various automakers and how their configuration helps/hinders their EDI implementations. Ford has centralized processing in its purchasing area. That means that all purchasing is conducted through one central gateway. With EDI capability at this gateway, they can trade with any and all suppliers that are "EDI ready" with no additional marginal work for each partner.

GM, on the other hand is completely decentralized. That would normally be a detriment as each location would have to develop software. In order to facilitate purchasing, however, they have instituted purchasing through regional centers, which utilize a common software application with EDI capability. Conversion from proprietary to ANSI X12 standard is being handled by these regional centers.

EDI for Forecasting/Planning

Planning Schedule – ANSI X12 # 830[2]

The planning schedule containing forecasts for productive auto parts are usually cut on a weekly basis by the automaker. It reflects anticipated needs at least 12 through 14 weeks out, and may contain data for several months. The planning schedule is used by the supplier to plan his own procurement of products and raw materials and to pre-schedule manufacturing tasks to fulfill the anticipated need.

---

2 Same ANSI X12 transaction used for dual purpose, see Material Release above.

EDI in Shipping/Receiving

Shipping Schedule – ANSI X12 # 862

The automaker generates a daily shipping schedule which describes its product needs for that day, sometimes calling for several deliveries during the day. This transaction contains data reflecting the day's just-in-time manufacturing schedules. It is examined by the supplier as soon as it is received and responded to in an advanced shipping notice transaction.

Sometimes, the shipping schedule is also used to effect in-sequence shipping. An in-sequence shipping schedule specifies not only what is to be shipped and when, but also how the product is to be loaded onto the vehicle. For this process, product is loaded in reverse order of its anticipated need, according to the day's manufacturing schedule, so it can be unloaded from the rear of the vehicle in the exact order in which it will be used. Particularly bulky parts such as car seats or high dollar parts such as engines are candidates for in-sequence delivery.

Advanced Shipping Notice – ANSI X12 #856

The advanced shipping notice is returned to the customer in response to the shipping schedule. The supplier scans the barcoded shipping label of the products being staged for shipment in order to produce the advanced shipping notice. It then notifies the customer that the shipment is ready to be shipped. The notice reiterates the composition of the shipment and requested receiving location from the shipping schedule and gives the estimated time of delivery. The auto manufacturer then uses this notice to expedite unloading of the vehicle and set up receiving records. When the product is received, its barcoding potentially can be scanned as it is unloaded, which will automatically generate a received status in the receiving record.

Receiving Advice – ANSI X12 # 861

Once product is received, the automaker generates a receiving advice which it returns to the supplier. Some automakers respond with information on all of the product that has been received. Others reconcile the actual receipts against the anticipated receipts from the advanced shipping notice and respond only with discrepancies in the Receiving

Advice. Both methods inform the supplier as to what the receiver intends to pay for, the former as the complete advice of what has been received and the latter in conjunction with the advanced shipping notice.

Application Advice – ANSI X12 #824

This transaction is currently being developed and will be pilot tested by Chrysler. The reason for it is to notify the sender immediately upon receipt of data whether or not errors were found by the application program during its edit for content. It will be especially important when delivery is scheduled shortly after receipt of the release. In this instance, the supplier will respond to a customer's material release with an advance shipping notice as usual. Then, the customer will immediately edit the data and return an application advice while the supplier is still on line. This process, known as fast batch, will be somewhat of a cross between normal store and forward EDI and an interactive process.

EDI and Payments

Payment Remittance Advice – ANSI X12 #820

The payment remittance transaction was developed to accompany and support the payment. It is generated by the customer and can contain a complete payment history tying back to the original purchase order, material releases, receipt of product, previous payments, and related credits and debits. It should be used by the supplier to reconcile against its open invoice, previous payment history, and related debits and credits, to accurately and quickly apply payments.

Integrating Internal Applications

As is often the case, the whole is greater than the component parts. That is evident in the EDI plans of the automakers and their supplier trading partners. While we can discuss each transaction that has or will be developed in electronic data format, the real benefits come from developing applications to automatically handle these transactions, and even more importantly, from integrating these applications to make the timely and accurate data available throughout the corporation. When all of these transactions are implemented on a large scale in one company, the potential benefits will be realized. By tying together data

- From an auto dealer regarding an automobile ordered by a consumer.
- From the automaker regarding product requirements to fill the customer order.
- From the supplier regarding the anticipated shipment of product.
- From the automaker regarding actual receipt.
- From the automaker regarding payment through internal computer applications which:
  - Interpret, edit, and process dealer orders.
  - Evaluate material requirements to fulfill these orders.
  - Develop manufacturing schedules to support these orders.
  - Generate material releases to fill assembly requirements.
  - Accurately document product received.
  - Evaluate payment.
  - Authorize payment of funds.
  - Reconcile payments and apply funds

the automaker can poise itself to perform the highest level of customer service in the most timely and cost effective manner. Add to this automatic recognition and tracking of product with barcoding, quality assurance of product from suppliers, and just-in-time manufacturing philosophy to provide high-quality product and reduce internal costs. Finally, take into account the historical reporting and tracking possibilities through the internal departments of the business, and electronic transfer of funds. It all adds up to highest efficiency with lowest costs.

While not all of the above transactions are used by all of the automakers and their suppliers, all are being used in the industry, with increased activity happening at a rapid rate.

We cannot underestimate the importance of an active trade organization in the implementation of EDI throughout the automobile industry. The AIAG has provided the common ground from which to examine the data and processing needs of business transactions for all of the participating companies. They have been active from the start, staffed in part by executives on loan from the major companies throughout the industry and have dealt not only with EDI but with other related issues such as just-in-time manufacturing schedules, barcoding, and evaluated receipts settlement in order to streamline processing and integrate systems throughout the corporation.

Currently, the AIAG is working on developing documents which discuss how to run a business using EDI, and how to implement evaluated receipts settlement to eliminate the need for the invoice transaction. It plans on developing documents in the near future to cover cash management and discrepancy reporting. Additionally, this organization sponsors educational programs for its membership.

The successful roll-out of EDI to the auto industry has been attributable in good part to the support and guidance of this important organization representing the entire automotive industry.

Future Applications of EDI in the Automotive Industry

EDI In Engineering

With so many of the traditional transactions being converted to electronic data format, the automotive industry has begun to investigate other, more unorthodox applications of EDI. In doing that, they have broadened their definition to include interactive, computer assisted design (CAD) data, graphics, and textual data besides the current X12 data format.

Down the road, they are looking at more implementation in the engineering department, where requests for quote will be transmitted electronically and will include engineering specifications. While some free-form text may be necessary in this transaction, an X12 electronic format is currently being developed. These transactions would be accompanied by CAD data and other graphics to describe the product, possibly transmitted or sent via tape to the trading partner. There may even be an interactive portion of the transaction that can be examined by the trading partner or altered in an on- line session. The responding quote would then use a good deal of the data derived directly from the request for quote, eliminating the need to key enter data and the possibility of injecting errors into the already accurate data. Evaluation of the specifications and product design would still remain manual, as judgment and decisions are required. However, the rote portion of developing the responding transaction would be accomplished automatically. Needless to say, application is still the name of the game. Without internal computer applications to interpret and process the incoming data, no benefits would be realized from converting these transactions to electronic format.

EDI In Quality Control

Another area that may soon be using EDI transactions is quality control. Automotive components must adhere to stringent quality standards as well as pass specified endurance, strength, and heat tests. The automotive industry, along with other industry groups such as metals, represented by aluminum and steel, and paper are actively developing transactions which define and describe quality requirements and which relate quality test results. Currently there is a test results transaction (ANSI X12 #863) under development. Details of quality specifications will some day accompany the purchase order of a product and test results for the batch will be received along with the advance shipping notice. Application at the automaker site will evaluate the test results immediately upon receiving them and then develop its receiving record for the product.

EDI Between First And Second Tier Suppliers

First tier auto suppliers, that are major companies in their own rights will soon be requesting that their major suppliers be prepared to accept electronic purchase orders from them and return an advanced shipping notice. Sometimes, a company is not only a first tier supplier, but also a second tier supplier. It may feel the pressure to implement EDI both from OEM customers and other auto supplier companies. With the pressure on the first tier supplier to maintain rigid quality control and delivery schedules, they will want to pass the same burden on to their suppliers. Those companies, then, will have to make themselves EDI-ready in response to their customers' needs.

Summary of EDI In The Automotive Industry

The automotive industry has been used as a case study here because of the widespread conversion of business transactions into electronic format, the development of applications to process the EDI data received from trading partners, and the long range view the major automakers have taken in developing new applications for EDI in their companies.

The basis for interest in EDI, of course, was the need to cut internal costs and streamline the manufacturing environment. EDI application of material releases and advance shipping notices was developed as a response to just-in-time manufacturing schedules and was accompanied by widespread use of barcoding to improve the receiving process. Evaluated receipts settlement, eliminating the need for the invoice, was a natural outgrowth to eliminate the need for complex reconciliation and to insure payment on a specified date. EDI has benefitted both of the trading partners, the automaker and its supplier. Relationships have become closer, with longer purchase agreements, single sourcing, forecasting of future needs, and an environment of sharing more accurate data in a timely manner.

The Automobile Industry Action Group (AIAG) has been a consolidating force that has provided the forum for the major automakers to develop homogeneous data requirements for their business transactions. Without strong participation of the membership, this trade organization would not have had the strong influence that it has had. There is a good likelihood that each automaker would have gone its own way in developing future transactions as they had done initially with their proprietary formats, forcing the auto suppliers to develop and maintain several different front and back end links to their own applications to support the different formats.

Even with all of the plans in place to support the X12 standard, there are still many suppliers supporting the old proprietary standards. That is because the automakers have not totally converted their existing systems to the new standard or completed development of new systems. The widespread opinion is that the process of implementing EDI is long and arduous. However, the results are well worth the effort.

Chapter

8

EDI in the Retail Industry

In this chapter we will focus on three sectors of the retail industry: grocery, mass merchandise, and apparel. In particular, we will discuss each sector's economic environment, the impact it has had on the mode of conducting business, and the systems that have been developed. We have chosen grocery because of its choice of industry standard and depth of EDI usage in the variety of business areas involved and in the number of different transaction sets it supports; mass merchandise because of the influence exerted by the major customers/mass merchandisers on their suppliers; and apparel because of the innovative approach some manufacturers and retailers have taken to integrate their internal systems to support the use of several EDI transactions.

Grocery

Within the grocery industry, we'll discuss both the traditional delivery pattern from the manufacturer to the retailer and direct store delivery via delivery route to the retailer's back door. Within the former segment, companies have been doing EDI for some time, becoming interested in conducting business electronically in the late 1970s. Their initial effort was to hire the consulting firm of A. D. Little to evaluate the potential benefits of electronic trade for the industry.

The resulting study reported that the potential for benefits within the grocery industry (excluding the direct store delivery segment) was high. With only 50% of the normal paper transactions in the full procurement cycle converted to electronic form, direct savings of $84 million could be realized through the reduction of clerical costs and an additional $128 million through the use of systems and new procedures. These benefits would accrue to the supplier, the broker, and the customer in approximately 45%, 13%, 42% ratios respectively. Long term savings in the form of indirect benefits attainable through the development of computer software could be up to three times as large as direct benefits, depending on how the individual companies developed new systems and integrated them into their procedures to make effective use of the timely and accurate data available through EDI. The procurement cycle transactions referred to above are the purchase order, the shipping advice, the invoice, the payment advice, and purchase order changes and adjustments. Additional transactions which would facilitate complete electronic processing of the purchasing/deliver/pay process are price change announcements, price protection announcements, and promotions.

The study made specific findings, recommendations, and predictions. It found that in order to link the manufacturer and distributor electronically, each would require an EDI system. Such a system would not require large capital costs to get started. While EDI at that time was technically feasible, the major impediment was the lack of an industry endorsed message standard format. Communication standards were also needed; however, the study found that it was not nearly so critical. As there was no message standard format suitable for use, the study called for the development of one for the targeted transactions, and demonstration that business could be transacted electronically with it.

From this beginning, the key companies of the industry moved ahead, customer driven by such major retail chains as Super Valu, Giant, and Ralphs and with strong participation by major manufacturers and brokers.

Their first task was to develop the data standard. For this effort they enlisted the help of the Transportation Data Coordinating Committee (TDCC), which had developed the data standards for the transportation industry. The first version of the Uniform Communication Standard (UCS) was published in April of 1982, along with the final report of the pilot study. UCS was developed as a variable length standard with syntax rules and control envelopes as had already been developed for the transportation industry transactions. For communication, the bisynchronous 2780/3780 protocol at 2400 baud rate was the standard adopted because of its widespread use amongst companies. In addition, an 18 hour "operational window" time period per day during which each company was required to be active – i.e., listening for incoming transmissions – was also defined.

During the rest of 1982, the initial pilot companies, using the TDCC as a resource to assist in contacting other companies, tried to attract additional trading partners to this new mode of transacting business. At the beginning of 1984, the Uniform Code Council, formerly the Uniform Product Code Council, was given administrative control of the UCS standard just as they already controlled the UPC codes, being used extensively by the industry to identify grocery products.

Very early on it was obvious that the standard would not be static, but would require maintenance periodically. In order to support this effort, an advisory group set up the format of the maintenance committee. The resulting committee, the SMC (Standard Maintenance Committee), made up of volunteers from companies in all segments of the industry, has kept tight control over the standard, evaluating all requests on the basis of real business need. Because of this work, the standard has been quite stable over time, changing only when enhancements were necessary to facilitate a business requirement. In practice, the standard is updated every six months, with each company expected to enhance its system to process the changes within the next six months. In this way, everyone stays current in the standard and there is no need for any one company to support many versions of the standard.

In order to initiate transmission of EDI transactions, each company in the grocery industry must purchase a Communications ID (COMM ID) from the UCC. This ID is priced commensurate with company size, and is used, by convention, to identify all senders and receivers of electronic transmissions in this industry. The fees obtained are used to support the EDI project. Examining the Comm IDs already assigned provides a comprehensive list of all parties currently transacting business electronically, or planning to do so in the near future.

While many of the companies in the original grocery industry pilot decided to transmit directly with their trading partners, Super Valu opted to use McDonnell Douglas as a third party value added network immediately. It was established from the beginning that any third party that wished to provide services to the grocery industry would have to support an "open network." Specifically, this meant that the third party would support EDI transmissions even when only one half of a trading partner pair was its customer. In order to do this, it would need to accept data with no required logon sequence from a non-customer on behalf of a customer and/or need to transmit data via auto-dial facility to a non-customer on behalf of a customer as shown in Figure 8-1. Such a mandate existed in order to assure that every company wishing to do EDI would have the ability to do so without restrictions by their trading partners or third-party agents. If EDI was to become the de facto standard of the grocery industry, it would have to work for everyone, regardless of size and computer sophistication.

Today there is heavy use of microcomputers by both wholesalers and retailers. Almost all are using a third party and most have purchased, as opposed to developed, software to support the UCS standard. Many of the large manufacturers are using mainframe software. Those involved since the original pilot have developed their own, as no products existed at that time to act as the link between the existing application and the UCS standard. More recently, mainframe oriented companies have been purchasing translation software. EDI activity centers on the purchase order today with noticeably less being done with the invoice. In addition, large manufacturers have developed an electronic dialogue with the public warehouses in which

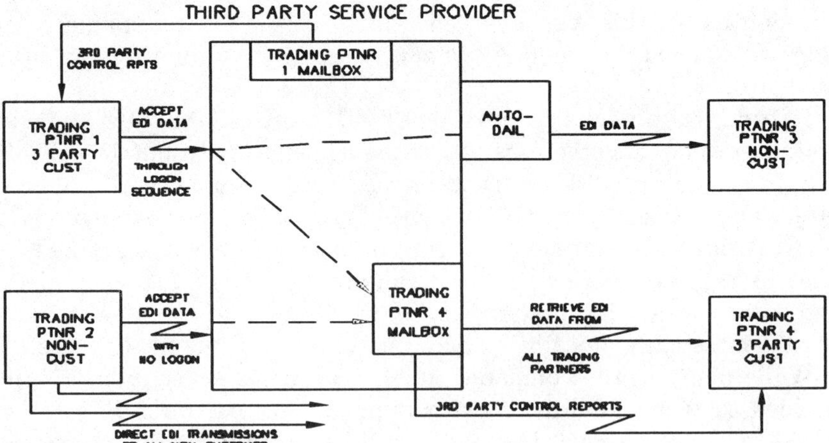

Figure 8-1 Third party support of "open network."

they store product. The standard used for these transactions is called WINS, Warehouse Industry Network Standard, which was developed in the same manner as UCS, utilizing the same data dictionary and with the same rules of syntax. Compatibility between the two standards provides the ability to pass information from a transaction in one standard to a transaction in the other.

The following EDI data flow shown in Figure 8-2 is possible with the targeted transactions, purchase order, shipping advice, invoice, payment advice, and purchase order changes and adjustments.

Typically, the purchase order is generated by the retailer, using data from its purchasing application. The data is generated in the predefined fixed length format required as input by a micro piece of EDI translation software, which then, translates the fixed length transaction into the variable length UCS standard, appends and prepends the appropriate control envelopes, and transmits the full file to the manufacturer trading partner or to a third party on its way to one or many trading partners. The manufacturer receives the UCS format, verifies it, and translates it into its own internal record format (through a piece of mini or mainframe translation software either purchased or homegrown). The order is then automatically evaluated by the order/entry application and verified for credit against internal customer files and for product availability against inventory files, and

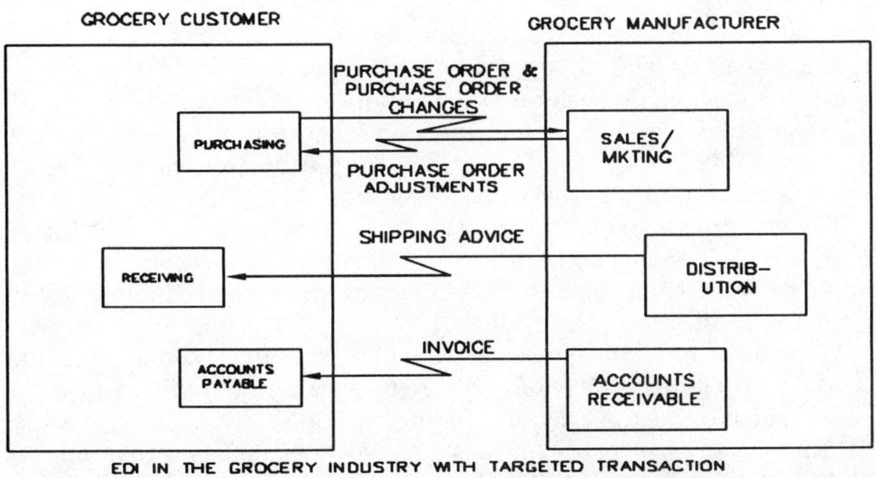

Figure 8-2 EDI in the grocery industry with targeted transaction.

is processed by the order processing application. An internal order to the appropriate company, distribution center, or public warehouse results. Using the same information as received in the purchase order, corrected for product quantities and delivery dates as required, the manufacturer can generate a shipping notice to be sent to its retailer trading partner to allow it to plan for the coming shipment, and can generate a bill of lading to be sent to its carrier to notify it of the impending shipment pickup. The carrier uses the bill of lading information in conjunction with standard freight rate tables to compute the freight bill. It generates an electronic freight bill transaction and returns it to the manufacturer.

In the event that the product is being stored in an outside warehouse, an EDI transaction is generated and sent to the warehouse, requesting it to stage the order for pickup by the carrier. In addition, various inquiries and responses travel regularly between the manufacturer and the warehouse.

The manufacturer notifies its public warehouse when it plans on shipping additional product. In turn, the warehouse returns notification of receipt and condition of the product. Not only do these transactions help both parties to control their inventories more accurately and in a more timely manner, but they also permit the manufacturer to fill incoming orders from the public warehouse stock days before it would have been available in the traditional paper/telephone environment.

Finally, the invoice is generated using the initial purchase order information along with changes due to stock unavailability. It is transmitted as soon as the order is picked up for shipment to the retailer.

The retailer uses it to reconcile against its open purchase order file and its product receipt information, and authorizes payment. Payment is made either by paper check or via Electronic Funds Transfer (EFT) accompanied by payment remittance notification.

In addition, changes and adjustments to purchase orders are transacted between trading partners as needed, and processed automatically by the application.

What does support of these transactions buy for the companies involved? An aggressive retailer can realize lead time and safety stock requirement reductions by shortening the order cycle. George Klima of Super Valu has predicted a saving of $600,000 per year for his chain. Manufacturers have not been vocal about savings; claims of getting more business when trading electronically have not been forthcoming. This is probably due to the limited extent, both in number of EDI trading partners and number of different transactions being transmitted electronically as well as to the consumers' demand for brand name products.

While both parties can realize productivity benefits, each is dependent on the use of intelligent, internal application programs to interpret and automatically act on the data received. Bottom line benefits for the manufacturer are difficult to measure. For example, the salesperson who used to travel to see individual customers just for the purpose of picking up their orders has become more productive, gaining many hours each week because electronic transmission has eliminated the need to travel. However, the company has probably not cut down on the number of salespeople it supports. With a higher percentage of business transacted electronically, benefits would undoubtedly be higher. The problem now is to attract new retailer trading partners to EDI without using valuable staff at each manufacturer company.

One solution is for the manufacturer to offer retailers special deals for electronic orders. As deals would normally be based on savings attributable to EDI, and as those have proved to be elusive and difficult to measure, this option is rarely offered. Another possibility is to start a second pilot for existing manufacturer and retailer trading partners, utilizing a broader set of electronic transactions. Even though several EDI transactions have been developed, most retailer/manufacturer partners have not progressed beyond the use of electronic purchase order and invoice, and only a limited number of manufacturers are using WINS transactions extensively with their public warehouses. If a group of EDI trading partners could be encouraged to move to the next level of EDI usage, incorporating electronic transmissions into new facets of their normal business environment, not only would they realize higher levels of benefits from trading electronically, but at the same time, those not yet participating at all would be at a competitive disadvantage and would begin to feel pressure to change their business environment from the traditional paper one to the electronic one. EDI, then, would not necessarily give the competitive advantage, but would provide the environment to keep a company from being at a marked competitive disadvantage.

Direct Store Delivery

The second segment of the grocery industry, direct store delivery, is just starting to use electronic data interchange in its everyday business. Direct store delivery covers all product delivered via delivery route directly to the retailer. In a grocery store, this can be up to 30-40% of the merchandise. Typically beer, soda, snack foods, bakery items, milk, and general merchandise such as pots, pans, makeup, vitamins, and household implements are delivered in this fashion. In convenience stores an even greater percentage of merchandise is delivered directly, often almost 100% of all products carried. Direct store delivery is a very labor intensive activity, with the vendor controlling the shelf space by counting existing inventory, delivering product to the store, and refilling the shelves with product.

As you remember, the A. D. Little study for the grocery industry as a whole had excluded this segment from consideration in their 1980 research as it had been decided to treat it as a separate issue at a later date. In April, 1987, a second study, DSD Store-Level Study, was published by A. D. Little. It dealt entirely with the business environment and potential benefits and costs of implementing EDI in the direct store delivery segment of the industry.

The study found that this is a prime area for achieving operational savings for both supplier and retailer. They estimated that with the 500 million deliveries made in this way per year, covering 10 billion line items, retailers could expect to realize $330 million and DSD suppliers, $175 million of direct benefits by implementing EDI. Indirect benefits could be even larger, up to three times as large for suppliers and potentially very valuable to the retailers who could automate their accounting operations and improve line item merchandise management.

This study used as its basis the excellent work begun in early 1985 with the formation of a UCS/DSD task force, whose mandate it was to extend UCS to cover business requirements of direct store delivery. The task force developed two groups of transactions, those to be transmitted between the office of the supplier and the retailer, comprised of contractual data, and those to be transferred from one party to the other at the back door of the retailer, containing information relevant to the specific store delivery. They realized that in order to process these two groups of transactions they would need internal applications to:

- Setup and maintain a trading partner relationship, with its products, prices, and contractual parameters.
- Transact day-to-day business.
- Perform billing and accounting reconciliations and authorizations for payment.

They labeled the full complement of direct store delivery transactions DSD/UCS; those dealing with data exchange between offices NEX/UCS (network exchange of UCS) and those between route driver and back door receiver DEX/UCS (direct exchange of UCS). All transactions are patterned after the traditional UCS standard and have been developed with the same architecture, syntax rules, and data dictionary. In addition, it was decided that the UPC code, being used so successfully in the rest of the industry to identify product to both supplier and retailer, would be employed in this segment in the same way.

Some important findings and predictions of the study are

- EDI in the direct store delivery segment of the industry can eliminate conflicts and improve productivity, thus eliminating the tension and adversarial relationship between supplier and retailer.
- Unique invoice formats and retailer turnaround documents are counterproductive and should be eliminated.
- DEX/UCS will become the predominant means of exchanging data at the store level in the next 10 years.
- DEX/UCS offers significant potential benefits to supermarkets, convenience stores, and DSD suppliers; an estimated 14%, 56%, and 18% of sales respectively.
- Indirect benefits will be realized through a reduction of retailer manual systems, and enhancement and development of new computer applications.
- A test program should be conducted by representative DSD suppliers and retailers to evaluate the standards and business procedures of office to office and direct exchange of EDI data.

In fact, seven retailers and nine suppliers established pilot trading partner pairs in 1987. They developed prototype systems and began operational tests in early 1988. As of June, six trading partner pairs were operational. Standard transaction sets are expected to be formalized in the fall and a report to the industry will be completed by A.D. Little in December 1988.

Let's look at the traditional business environment, systems, manual procedures, and staffing that exists in this segment of the industry. Today, a retailer buyer negotiates with and contracts to buy product from a DSD supplier. Information relating to that deal, such as authorized products, correct cost, and correct selling price, is key entered by a clerk at each location. That information must be maintained both at the headquarters and back door of the retailer. With each delivery, the supplier brings an invoice. The invoice is used by the retailer at the back door as a receiving document to check-in items. All items in the delivery are counted and prices checked prior to being loaded onto the shelves.

Receiving information collected from all deliveries during the day is sent to the main office at night, where it is key entered by clerks who must first interpret the product codes, quantities, and prices on each supplier's proprietary paper invoice forms, and then enter them correctly into the main office system. If discrepancies in products, quantities, or prices invoiced are discovered during the delivery check, corrections are handwritten onto the invoice, further complicating the data entry job. Worse yet, many invoices do not make it to the main office at all as they are misplaced or damaged during the day at the receiving location. In all, this is a terribly inefficient way of handling deliveries and presents an almost impossible task of collecting and maintaining accurate data.

By contrast, EDI would streamline the delivery process and provide timely and accurate data for both supplier and retailer. Figure 8-3 shows the office to office and store-level transactions that would flow between the supplier and retailer in the EDI environment.

After setting up the supplier/customer relationship for specified products and at agreed upon prices and delivery arrangements, the supplier generates a product information transaction that reflects the terms of the agreement. He transmits it to the buyer for his perusal and authorization. The transaction describes the product, its cost, retail price, and other contract terms, and is transmitted to the retailer buyer who evaluates the information and returns an item authorization transaction as response. Once this initial information is set up by both parties, all orders, deliveries, and adjustments are verified against it. Orders received on the headquarters level are responded to by shipping advices and periodical invoices and statements. The retailer returns payment advices. Both parties transmit discrepancy and adjustment data as needed. On a day to day basis, delivery invoices, adjustments, and acknowledgments of receipt are

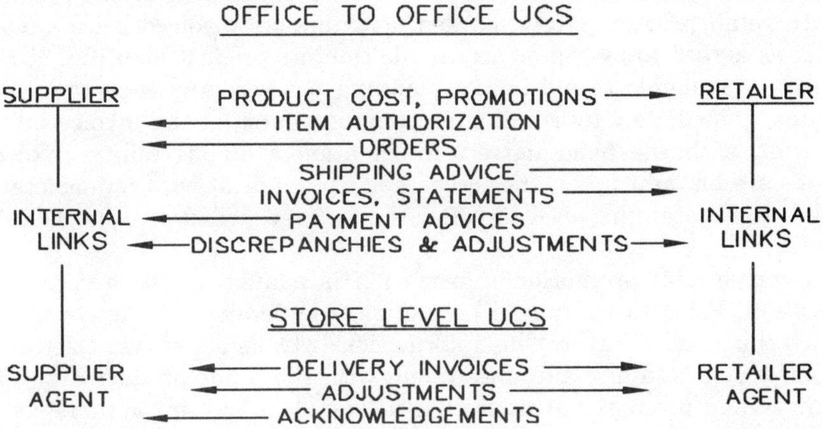

Figure 8-3 Office and store level EDI in direct store delivery environment.

transferred between the selling agent (route driver) and the buying agent (back door receiver).

There are two ways of effecting this transfer,

1. The route driver arrives at the retailer site with a handheld device on which he has the invoice for today's delivery. That device is then attached to the retailer's system, which displays the product identification (UPC code), retail price, and quantity, along with general information about the selling party. Once product has been counted, the invoice can either be adjusted to reflect the actual quantities, or can be authorized by electronic signature as is. Either way, final invoice information is available to be carried back in the handheld device by the driver and to be transferred to headquarters by the retailer.

2. The route driver arrives with a "smart card," a floppy computer disk, which again has the invoice on it. This is then slipped into a reader box attached to the retailer's computer and is displayed in the same way as above. After making necessary adjustments, the corrected and authorized invoice is again available to both parties.

By having all of this information available at the receiving site, the retailer is assured that the vendor is delivering an authorized product with retail price correctly marked, and that its invoiced price is correct as agreed to by the buyer. In addition, its product identifier (UPC code) is available to aid in the scanning process. Any exceptions are found immediately by running a computer match of the invoice information with the headquarters information available online. Exceptions are brought up on the screen and can be dealt with immediately. This eliminates the need for after-the-fact reconciliations and adjustments.

Even special promotion information is available at the receiving location. Prior to running a promotion, the vendor sets up its terms with the retailer buyer. This information is transmitted, via electronic transaction, and is maintained along with the other product information. When promotional product is delivered, prices are automatically verified by the retailer's system. Some retailers are shortcutting the receiving process even more. On their receiving menu they have options as follows:

1. Invoice total – this allows them to just count total cartons, verify it against the vendor's invoice, authorize on the basis of that count, or adjust the invoice as necessary dependent on actual count.

2. Item review – this requires them to check item by item as discussed above, which is the most time consuming method. It is used initially with most trading partners and is replaced with No. 1 or 3 if deliveries are usually accurate as reflected in the invoice.

3. Blind entry – with this option, items are scanned and automatically counted. Information flows directly into the computer system. In this way, the retailer still gets the integrity check and count without spending the time to visually check and count delivered product. This is the most time and cost effective as it eliminates all data entry and physical counting tasks.

On the vendor side, an automated route generating system would not only aid the distribution by staging the individual deliveries correctly and on time, it would also make available all invoices associated with the daily route to the route driver. After making all of his daily deliveries, his handheld device or smart card would contain the adjusted and corrected copies of all those invoices. Upon return, these would be read into the vendor's computer system. Periodic invoices would then be computed from daily corrected invoices, eliminating the need for monthly adjustments and reconciliations.

With user-friendly handheld devices or smart cards and user-friendly menus, this is a system that is easy to use by both the route driver and receiver who have traditionally been unfamiliar with computers. Other functions could be made available at the receiving site if a microcomputer replaced the terminal there. This would make more information accessible, would support the use of other menu options, and would enable a print copy of the invoice if necessary.

The main benefits the DSD supplier and retailer expect to gain from transacting main office transactions and from automating the receiving process are:

1. To assure product integrity by:

   - Allowing the receiver to verify that the product being delivered has been authorized.
   - Verifying that the invoice cost and retail price match the agreed upon prices in the retailer headquarters system.
   - Identifying the product's UPC code to enable the receiver to scan incoming product for identification and to count the quantity delivered.

2. To eliminate the need to key enter invoice data at the retailer location after the fact, which, in turn, eliminates transcription errors. Also to eliminate the same work at the supplier site. With all corrected invoice data resident in the handheld device or smart card that the route driver returns to the supplier at night, all that is necessary is to link the device to the supplier's system in order to make that information available to the application programs.

3. To enhance accounting accuracy by identifying differences between the supplier invoice and the delivery at the time of receipt and by resolving those authorization and quantity differences at the back door. In addition, this new method of transacting business eliminates the need to retain and handle paper.

> As long as each party has access to the data it needs to conduct business, there is no need to retain backup copies of paper.

In order to assure that all parties will be able to trade electronically with all of its trading partners, this group has adopted a similar attitude to standardization of communications capabilities. Not only does each party need a Comm ID, which it must purchase from the UCC in order to identify itself in electronic transmission, but each must also provide a standard plug connection on its handheld device, microcomputer, and headquarters mainframe computers.

In addition to the above benefits, new business opportunities are anticipated by using the electronic method of transmitting data. One possible opportunity is to provide the same level of receiving service in an unattended mode. The route driver would be able to plug his handheld device into an available connection in order to transfer data to the receiver's computer at the same time that he is able to leave the product in a locked receptacle. When the receiver arrives, validation can be accomplished. Another possibility is to send a smart card along with the product or through the network to support deliveries by a third party such as UPS. All in all, new logistics methods would be possible in the electronic environment, which offer timely and accurate data in support of direct store deliveries.

It is anticipated that EDI will become the accepted mode of doing business in the direct store delivery segment of the grocery industry within the next 10 years. The reason for this optimistic opinion is that there are such great benefits to be derived. Those participating in the current pilot will begin to realize those benefits; those not yet active will begin to realize the competitive disadvantage. With the competition that grocery chains and convenience stores find in the marketplace, they must take advantage of the cost savings and efficiencies offered by transacting business electronically using NEX/UCS and DEX/UCS data formats.

Super Valu

SuperValu is an example of a major grocery retailer implementing EDI throughout the company. The main reason, according to George Klima, of SuperValu, is to eliminate information float. With EDI, accurate and timely data is received. With enhanced internal applications, that data becomes available for use by all functional areas of the company. Because of this, fewer different electronic transactions are needed with EDI than were previously sent and received in the traditional paper environment. Also, functional business areas start to become integrated.

SuperValu was one of the leaders in support of the UCS standard in the grocery industry. With top management support, they have embarked on an aggressive program to incorporate EDI into all areas of the company and to eliminate paper transactions for both inter- and intra-company messaging. In order to do this, they have conscientiously evaluated the data requirements for transacting business as a prelude to redesigning internal applications to support business needs. They have developed a data flow where human intervention is required only for exception processing. All in all, they believe that the implementation of EDI did not really cost them anything because its cost was balanced by the savings they realized when they eliminated several applications they had planned on developing.

Let's take a look at the cost savings that Super Valu is realizing and/or predicting by trading electronically in various transaction sets.

- With the 6500 purchase orders they generate per week, they are saving $1.20–$1.30 per purchase order.
- By ordering from EDI-capable vendors, they can reduce order lead time by one day.
- They predict a 15 person reduction of buyers by March 1989.
- They expect to save $6000 per day in purchase order/receiving/invoice reconciliation costs by the same date.

In order to achieve these goals, they have developed and continue to develop new applications to use data more efficiently in the electronic environment. In addition, they move aggressively to increase both their number of EDI trading partners and the number of different electronic transaction sets that they transmit and receive. By March 1989, they hope to be processing and paying 80% of their invoices electronically.

Following are some of the new applications that they have already developed and some that are currently in the development phase.

New Applications

- Request for inventory count – used to get an accurate count of product on hand, and as input to the invoice reconciliation process.
- Receiving against invoice – reconciliation of the invoice count, the open purchase order, and the quantity being invoiced.
- Computer generation of chargeback – developing a debit transaction to reflect reconciliation errors.

Under Development

- Promotional announcement processing – in this system, the vendor or broker maintains SuperValu files with the buyer's approval. It is being developed to ensure that manufacturer promotions are taken advantage of by SuperValu. The computer program recognizes a promotion opportunity, places the order, and then calculates and passes on allowances to the individual stores. Currently, SuperValu is handling 200 promotional announcements per week. This application will represent savings for SuperValu in the million dollar range, as many promotions are missed today.
- Price changes – SuperValu gets about 20 price changes per week. With the new system, which will receive notification of price changes electronically and then process them automatically, benefits will be:

  – Receipt of accurate and timely price change data.
  – Improved customer service.
  – Improved buyer/seller relationship.
  – Maintenance of accurate SuperValu files by price bracket.

- Item maintenance – a new system, in pilot today, in which the vendor maintains the item UPC code plus other alias codes in its computer for the customer. Benefits of this system are timeliness and accuracy, as above.

SuperValu realizes that they will receive maximum benefits from EDI only by increasing their volumes and the variety of electronic messages that they support. Because of this, they maintain very aggressive goals. Their integration of EDI data into daily processing routines has been a strong example to others in the grocery industry.

Mass Merchandisers

For purposes of this discussion, a mass merchandiser is defined as a low-level retailer carrying a large variety of merchandise. Such a store competes for consumers mainly on the basis of price and customer service, as its products are comprised of the same standard lines that all of its competitors carry. Demand for product in this type of store is inelastic, meaning that a small change in price brings about a large change in demand in the opposite direction; i.e., small price increase, large decrease in demand. This type of retailer must look for ways of decreasing internal costs in order to raise net profit margin.

As mass merchandisers are notoriously large purchasers, it is natural for them to attempt to increase efficiency in the purchasing area. The first step in that direction is to centralize their purchasing areas. With all purchasing done through one department, they are already able to realize substantial benefits over a distributed environment, no matter the medium; paper, telephone, or electronic. By centralizing purchasing they:

- Devote only one staff of buyers to the purchasing function.
- Order from their suppliers as one major customer for all locations.
- Control inventory for all locations out of a single system.
- Get substantially lower costs and better delivery schedules for the large quantity purchases.

Of course, in order to purchase from a central system, the mass merchandiser must have appropriate systems in place in its various locations to collect sales, receiving, and return data; transfer that data to the central location; make all of the necessary decisions at the central locations, and send updated information back to the store locations.

Service Merchandise, one of the pioneers in EDI, which supports the ANSI X12 standard, does all of their purchasing out of a central location, which is on-line to its various stores daily. For each sale, sales information is entered at the store location via a point-of-sale system. Likewise, product receipts and returns are entered at the store site. Each night the store transactions are pulled down and are used to develop purchase orders from the entire chain to the various vendors. Then, files with new prices and new inventory figures are generated and downloaded to the individual stores along with the purchase orders for that store. These are then accessed at the store location the following morning. As goods are received, the open purchase order is used to create a receiving report.

If Service were not transacting business via electronic purchase orders, they would not be able to realize the benefits of all of the central and store level systems that they have developed. By centralizing the purchasing function and developing all of the intra-company communication links, they poised themselves to handle the purchasing function in the most cost effective manner. However, the benefits that Service realizes from implementing sophisticated point of sale systems at the store location and intra-company links to the central ordering application would not have been realized in the traditional paper environment because they still would have been experiencing three days mail delay and manual data entry tasks at the vendor site. So, EDI became the vehicle to eliminate mail float, and enhanced vendor order/entry and order processing applications became the vehicle to eliminate manual errors and processing float.

The standard data format that Service chose to support for inter-company communications is ANSI X12. Intra-company files are stored in the company's fixed length internal data format.

As a result of being large purchasers, mass merchandisers are also major payers of invoices. In order to support this effort, they must have large departments of accounts payable clerks whose job is to match the incoming invoice to the open purchase order and to the receiving information and to verify that the product was ordered and was received in good condition. Not only is this procedure time consuming, and expensive, it is also fraught with errors. Again, Service Merchandise developed an automatic matching system to perform what had traditionally been a manual reconciliation process. However, in order to eliminate the time, staff, and internal error rate, the invoice must be received electronically and in a machine readable standard format.

Service was one of the first mass merchandisers to develop a full-fledged program to bring up trading partners. In 1985, directives came from their chairman of the board down to the MIS department, to design and develop the systems necessary to support the electronic purchase order and invoice. The user community became active after the fact.

Service has a tremendous amount of clout with their vendors since they are such a large customer. The initial letter to the vendor community, sent by the vice president of merchandising was fairly mild, telling the vendors of Service's desire to use EDI. The letter following gave dates by which the vendor was expected to be live. The top 200 vendors were given the choice of transmitting directly with Service or through a third party. One hundred fifty of those 200 chose to transmit directly, causing Service to develop its own network to handle the communications with them. They chose to support 2780/3780 Bisynchronous protocol for communication access, since most companies could support it.

Smaller vendors were told to transmit through McDonnell Douglas, the third party EDI service provider that Service had chosen to endorse.

McDonnell, in turn, developed a trading partner marketing program to get Service's trading partners on line. They sponsored marketing meetings, which were attended by Service, and invited trading partner prospects. With the pressure that Service exerted and the efforts of McDonnell many of the trading partners implemented EDI.

However, over time the trading partner program fell into disuse and the pace slackened considerably. Even though close to 300 trading partners, including 240 of the top 600 are trading with Service via EDI today, they were disappointed with the ongoing trading partner program as run by McDonnell and have recently chosen to endorse an additional third party in order to encourage marketing to their potential trading partners.

One of the things that became apparent as the Service MIS staff got ready for electronic trading was that a good deal of change was necessary to make their computer applications EDI-worthy. For one thing, they had to include all necessary edits so that any error would cause the transaction to kick out as an exception that would then be reported on and handled by a person. For another, they had to find a way to codify all fields. In the past incoming narrative data was read and interpreted and outgoing was printed on the purchase order form to be read and interpreted by the receiver. In the EDI environment, all data must be understood by a computer program and must be acted upon automatically. Especially troublesome are terms and deals. Even though it is not legally necessary to include terms on a purchase order, traditionally they have been included. However, terms are often fairly complex, depending on the deal that has been worked out by the buyer with the vendor. It was necessary to simplify and standardize the terms so they could be included in electronic format. Most retailers include terms on the purchase order for informational purposes only. It gives the vendor the opportunity to match incoming terms to their own records and report exceptions/disagreements back to the customer. However, they are often ignored by the vendor in favor of its own files.

Most importantly, the "gateway" computer application, the application receiving EDI data, needed to be integrated with ensuing internal applications in order to pass along the accurate and timely information. In addition, certain information had to be retained in order to be used for matching and reconciliation at a later time in the processing stream, for example, the purchase order to match against the stock received, and the receiving information to reconcile against the invoice from the vendor.

As systems were developed for the EDI environment, the underlying philosophy was to allow correct transactions to flow automatically through the system with no intervention and to kick out error conditions in exception reporting to be handled by staff.

Has EDI been successful for Service Merchandise? They have reported reducing their accounts payable staff and effort by 80% using the electronic invoice with their automatic matching system. Of course, not all of these saving can be attributed to EDI. The systems they put into place provided the means to take advantage of the EDI data, but EDI provided the timely and accurate data.

Service Merchandise

Because Service Merchandise anticipated integrating EDI into several facets of their business and because they had very optimistic plans for bringing up a large percentage of their trading partners, they took a very organized approach to the project. Figures 8-4, 8-5, and 8-6 contain lists of the tasks they accomplished in the planning, organizing, and implementation stages they went through to bring EDI to fruition within their company.

Following are discussions of each task.

Planning for EDI

1. Identify and prioritize your objectives.

   In the case of Service, the objectives were to:

   - Reduce lead time.

1. IDENTIFY AND PRIORITIZE OBJECTIVES.
2. DEFINE SCOPE OF THE PROJECT
3. SELECT TRADING PARTNERS
4. CHOOSE A STANDARD TO SUPPORT
5. DEVELOP A PLAN FOR COMMUNICATING WITH TRADING PARTNERS
6. DEVELOP A PLAN FOR HANDLING TRANSLATIONS TO/FROM YOUR INTERNAL APPLICATION
7. DEVELOP A REALISTIC BUDGET FOR THE EDI PROJECT
8. SECURE MANAGEMENT SUPPORT

Figure 8-4 Service merchandise planning tasks.

1. DEDICATE RESOURCES TO THE PROJECT
2. PUT PROGRAM IN PLACE TO APPROACH TRADING PARTNERS
3. SELECT 2–3 PILOT PARTNERS
4. EVALUATE CURRENT PAPER TRANSACTIONS
5. ESTABLISH PROTOTYPE PILOT PROCEDURES
6. DEVELOP CLEAR & EASY TO UNDERSTAND DOCUMENTATION

Figure 8-5 Service merchandise organizing tasks.

- Reduce internal costs.
- Reduce error rate in ordering and receiving.
- Eliminate manual key entry errors.

Realize that objectives will be realized over time and that integration of applications within the company make indirect benefits possible.

1. DEVELOP SALES PROGRAM TO PROMOTE EDI TO TRADING PARTNERS
2. HELP TARGETED TRADING PARTNERS TO DEVELOP COST EFFECTIVE EDI PROGRAM
3. ENCOURAGE TRADING PARTNERS TO COMMIT TO A TIME FRAME
4. OFFER SERVICE MERCHANDISE STAFF AS CONSULTANTS
5. INVITE TRADING PARTNERS TO MARKETING SEMINARS
6. GET TOP MANAGEMENT TO PARTICIPATE IN EDI PROJECT
7. OFFER INCENTIVES TO TRADING PARTNERS
8. FOLLOW UP! FOLLOW UP! FOLLOW UP!

Figure 8-6 Service merchandise implementation tasks.

2. Define the scope of the project.

Service decided to handle EDI as a central capability, buffering the standard from their application systems. They chose this as the path of least resistance in the long term, realizing that as new transactions were added to their EDI environment, they would constantly need to upgrade their existing application programs. This path also turns out to be the least expensive. Development or purchase of translation software that can translate all transactions and all versions of a standard can be utilized by all internal departments and divisions of the company.

Service also included evaluation of current business procedures and change for the EDI environment in the scope of their EDI project. As EDI is a reciprocal arrangement between trading partners, they planned on developing a teamwork approach with their targeted partners.

3. Selecting trading partners.

The advice here was to select pilot partners early, choosing a small number with which you do a high volume of business. This will not only serve to keep the project visible throughout the company but will help to uncover all possible system bugs by offering the widest range of transaction data usage.

After initial pilot, Service wanted to move right into multiple implementations with other targeted trading partners. Because of this, they had already selected their targeted vendors by targeting their top 600.

4. Choose a standard to support. Investigate standard support within your industry and especially those supported by your trading partners. Join an industry group and take an active part in that group and in the standards committee in order to assure that your data and business functional needs will be met. Service chose to support the ANSI X12 standard.

5. Develop a plan for communicating with trading partners.

   Service offered their top 200 vendors the choice of communication either directly or through a third party. All others were expected to communicate through a third party. This, they thought, would eliminate the communication support they would have to offer to smaller, usually less sophisticated vendors. Other options would have been to sign with one or more service providers, giving their trading partners a choice or to support direct communications with all partners.

6. Develop a plan for handling translations to/from your internal application.

   Service is totally committed to the ANSI X12 public data standard, being unwilling to support any company proprietary standards. In evaluating their options, they discovered that purchasing translation software was less expensive than developing a similar capability in-house. Not only is initial development expensive and a drain on corporate MIS resources, but incorporating standard maintenance procedures into such a piece of software requires in-depth expertise of the standard and dedicated data processing staff.

7. Develop a realistic budget for the EDI project.

   In order to effect a successful implementation of EDI, Service realized that they would have to spend time and money on:

   - Educating user and data processing staff.
   - Traveling to standard committee, industry trade group, and trading partner meetings.
   - Designing, programming, and testing of internal systems to support their EDI implementation.

- Developing documentation for internal use as well as for trading partners.

Without budgeting these expenditures in advance, the project would have floundered from lack of resources.

8. Secure management support.

   In the case of Service, the CEO led the bandwagon for EDI; they were never lacking in top management support. However, they were aware that they had to get the support of management at all levels, especially the direct involvement of the account representative of each EDI targeted trading partner. Without user involvement, developing new business procedures for the electronic environment would not have been possible; rather than getting the support and advice of the user community, they would have antagonized just those staff members whose support was necessary to insure a successful implementation.

With this plan in place, let's look at the Service plan of attack for organizing the program.

1. They dedicated resources to the project by choosing a person to attend committee meetings, and assigned technical people to evaluate the business requirements of the user community, design system enhancements, program, and then install them.

2. They put into place a program to approach trading partners, running seminars, visiting trading partner locations, and sending out mailings. They also enlisted the aid of the third party service provider that they had contracted with to co-sponsor the trading partner marketing seminars.

3. They selected two to three pilot partners, using high volume, current interest, and current EDI activity as criteria for their choices.

4. They evaluated their current paper transactions in terms of the data requirements for transacting business. They found that a good deal of data traditionally transmitted on paper is redun-

dant or extraneous. In developing data requirements for their EDI transactions, they eliminated these redundancies and pared the purchase order to the 300-350 characters absolutely necessary for the supplier to process the order. In this way they built in a cost savings in transmission charges.

5. They established the procedures in the pilot that they would use to test each trading partner's communications and data transmissions, run parallel EDI and paper systems, and cut over to production. By developing the prototype procedures up front, they were able to set up trading partners in a timely manner to fulfill their goal of bringing up several hundred vendors.

6. They developed clear and easy to understand documentation explaining the data requirements, communication requirements, and procedures to support EDI. This was made available to prospective trading partners to facilitate their own EDI implementations.

Finally, they developed an implementation program to encourage trading partners to trade electronically with them. While Service certainly can influence vendors to comply with their requirements, they were also asking their trading partners to develop new business practices on their behalf. Therefore, they realized that success in this venture would be possible in direct relation to the support that they offered.

Toward this implementation goal they:

1. Developed a sales program to sell trading partners on the EDI concept. They worked on a presentation that would visually explain how EDI would work, what the hardware and software requirements would be, and what benefits they could expect to realize from electronic trade with Service.

2. They helped their targeted trading partners to put together a cost-effective system for communication and translation that would use their current hardware.

3. They encouraged their trading partners to commit to a time frame of implementation so they could schedule trading partner implementations.

4. They offered their own staff to provide assistance to trading partners, as needed.

5. They sent invitation letters to selected trading partners to attend marketing seminars. Realizing that the Service account representative has the leverage with the trading partner, the letters were directed from them to the sales/marketing representative of the supplier. Letters showed Service commitment by being signed by the vice president of purchasing.

6. They got top levels of management to take part in the project. Their CEO was very vocal on the matter of EDI, both within the company to staff and outside to trading partners, again showing the strongest possible commitment to the goal of trading electronically with suppliers.

7. They offered incentives to targeted trading partners to induce them to sign up. Even though the supplier would realize benefits by implementing EDI, Service offered a favorable vendor status to those who did sign up to trade electronically.

8. Finally, follow-up. After the initial letter, after invitations, and after meetings, only 10% of its targeted suppliers signed up without follow-up. All others got follow up material and sometimes on site visits before they decided to implement EDI. Service realized that if they did not give the extra effort, they would fall short of their goals.

Summary

Using this organized approach, Service targeted their top 600 suppliers for EDI implementation. They targeted purchase order as the first electronic transaction with invoice following closely on its heels. Service's objective was to encourage its trading partners to adhere to a short time frame in implementing both transactions.

They initiated their program in 1985. Since then, they have brought up close to 300 vendors, with 240 of their top 600. Of those, 150 of their top 200 opted to transact business directly with Service. All others have chosen to use a third party provider as communications intermediary. The Service program had a very strong commitment from top management, which provided the environment in which MIS could design and develop the systems necessary to support electronic transmission of business transactions.

While Service has realized substantial benefits in efficiencies by sending the electronic purchase order to its vendors, the greatest benefits have been realized in accounts payable. In that area, they have reduced their costs by 80% through use of an automatic matching system for purchase order, receiving, and invoice information, which automatically reconciles the invoice on the store and line item level.

Apparel Sector

In looking at the apparel sector of the retail industry, we see a continuum of establishments which include:

- The mass merchandiser, which competes almost entirely on price as discussed above.
- The value-oriented department store, predominantly competing on price with some sensitivity to fashion.
- The mainline department store, a blend of price and fashion sensitivity.
- The department store, competing almost entirely on fashion, with little sensitivity to price.
- The specialty store, focusing on a particular market niche. This type of establishment may be anywhere on the price sensitivity scale, depending on the amount of competition in the market niche and the quality of merchandise that it carries.

As we might expect, there is a direct relationship between an establishment's price sensitivity and its use of new technology to streamline procedures and cut internal costs. Examples of new technology being employed by this industry group are barcoding, point-of-sale systems, and electronic data interchange (EDI).

Let's look at the general economic conditions that exist in the retail industry today. The consumer has an increased amount of disposable dollars; however, the value of the dollar has decreased, even with low inflation rates in recent years. Cost of goods is increasing, especially for those firms employing American labor. In addition, we are over-stored. With population shifts out of the major cities, shopping centers have sprouted up ad infinitum in suburban areas all over the country. Each retail location is expected to carry a full line of inventory to cater to its local population. Because of the proliferation of store locations, coupled with inventory requirements, earnings are depressed. Add to this the number of mergers and acquisitions that have been occurring in recent years, and you get a very uneasy business picture, comprised of companies desperately looking for the means to increase efficiencies and decrease costs.

While mergers and acquisitions may ultimately provide the environment in which companies can realize benefits of scale, in the shorter term this same situation can delay the use of new technology by providing a distributed and varied computer, system, and procedural environment. Even though EDI is most efficient and cost effective when implemented as a central corporate function, that may not be possible in the recently merged corporation.

One of the main business problems facing retailers is a lack of control over their inventory. They see inventory management as one way to improve their business situation. In the past, buying decisions were not based on actual sales activity, as sales were rarely tracked as they occurred. In order to manage inventory, one must be able to identify it down to the lowest level (in this industry, size and color); track it in several categories such as sold, available for sale, and in transit; and make buying decisions based on criteria such as selling record, seasonal demand, promotion, etc.

A positive force in the effort to identify inventory within the industry has been the adoption of the UPC code (long used in the grocery industry) to identify items down to the style, color, and size level. Both vendors and retailers have accepted this code, eliminating the need for each partner to maintain product aliases and to cross-reference to its own product numbering scheme. It has also provided the vehicle by which a point of sale system can track items down to the color and size level. Use of the barcoded representation of the UPC code has also been adopted by many companies, allowing them to scan the barcoded labels attached by the manufacturer to the item upon receiving, which automatically enters the items in the on-hand, available-for-sale inventory. They scan the label again at time of sale into their point-of-sale (POS) system, which then reduces the on-hand inventory figure and tracks the sale with no additional key entry. The accumulation of sales information provides the basis to develop trending or tracking reports, which assist buyers in making smart buys by pointing out slow and fast moving items. As the use of UPC codes grows, companies can gain better control of their inventory; however, in order to do this, they need smarter internal systems and more sophisticated point-of-sale systems. For this very reason, point-of-sale software developers are being driven to enhance their products with scanning capabilities, more memory, price look-up capability, and maintenance of historical data for development of sales trends and tracking reports.

In order to track inventory quantities, the retailer needs a way to accurately receive product. Here, manufacturers can assist the process by marking the shipping cartons with an industry standard barcode that uniquely identifies each container, and attaching the correct UPC label directly to each item. The retailer then reads the barcode on the shipping container, references an electronic packing list, and compares the electronic list of carton contents to the items that it has received and counts the items within each carton. Quantities received are then entered into its inventory file.

In some cases, the manufacturer pre-notifies the retailer of an impending shipment by sending an advance shipping notice that describes the load in terms of the sequentially numbered carton identifiers comprising the shipment and in terms of the products and quantities contained in each. When product is received, the retailer need only identify the sequentially numbered cartons in the shipment in order to identify the whole load. This eliminates the need to scan or count each individual item in the load, reducing the time lag between receipt of goods and placing them on the selling floor.

In order to improve the buying decision, the retailer is not only installing point-of-sale systems to assist him in tracking each sale, but also inventory management systems to make the buying decisions. Whereas in the past the retailer was willing to receive a size and color mix of items for a particular style, today he is ordering according to demand. By doing that, the retailer should realize a reduction in over and understock conditions and elimination of the need to drastically mark down unwanted product in order to unload it.

VICS, the Voluntary Inter-Industry Communication Standards Committee, can be credited with accelerating the EDI process for the retail and supplier to retail industry. It was formed because many large companies felt that the existing industry associations were not addressing the needs of the industry, and were not effectively supporting implementations of these new technologies. Member companies of VICS are manufacturers, textile mills, and retailers. This organization has used the already existing Uniform Code Council for the grocery industry, which has a strong implemented base, as its organizational example. While they chose to support the ANSI X12 standard for EDI instead of the UCS standard, they did decide to use Uniform Product Code Version A (UPC-A) managed by the UCC as the methodology for identifying items in this industry. Initially, the leaders in the industry worked through VICS to set up prototype guidelines of data usage for the industry. The full membership evaluated them and tailored them for use by all. VICS published an implementation guide in April 1981 that contains guidelines for use of the ANSI X12 standards for the retail industry and continues to update the guidelines on a semi-annual basis.

Let's take a look at how two innovative apparel manufacturers and a specialty store chain have integrated EDI in their businesses.

Levi Strauss & Company

Prior to its support of the ANSI X12 standard data format, Levi had implemented proprietary formats for electronic communication with a number of customers and suppliers. For the last several years, Levi has been a strong advocate of the X12 standard. They have held leadership roles of various X12 subcommittees and task groups, and of the VICS committee.

About 25% of the purchase orders Levi receives come in electronically, some in the customer's proprietary format. Within the next 24 months they expect to migrate those trading partners supporting proprietary formats to the X12 standard. Today, they support only a public data standard for all business transactions and all trading partners. Levi is also using the UPC code to identify its manufactured items as do many manufacturers and retailers today. Some still support their own internal numbering schemes.

Levi is a team player, realizing that the buyer/seller relationship in their industry must be strong in order for each to derive maximum benefits from the new technology that they are employing. The relationship is based on the supplier being extremely responsive to its customers' needs. Levi believes that the entire cycle from capturing point-of- sale information to replenishment of inventory should be supported by automated or semi-automated systems and electronically attained information. They are not only a strong proponent of EDI within their own company, but also very supportive of implementing automated systems by and for the retailer in order to assist them to track sales, receive more efficiently, manage inventory, and order correctly.

In order to test the waters for EDI interest, Levi surveyed its customers. They report that response was even higher than expected in favor of automated systems and electronic transmissions. Because customers, in general, did not have systems in place to assist them to order new stock, Levi used the favorable response they received to justify developing a model stock management system that they offer to their customers. In order to use the system, the customer sends Levi either its point-of-sale information relating sales within a time period or inventory-on-hand counts. Levi runs these figures against replenishment models established by the customer and can either provide a suggested purchase order to the buyer or actually place an order and report back to the customer via EDI. By using such a system, the customer knows that it will always have the appropriate levels of inventory for the entire Levi line of apparel.

In the receiving area, Levi has implemented a system to assist the customer to shorten its receiving process and free up staff at the same time. When an order is staged for delivery, Levi sends the customer an advanced shipping notice that provides the detail of the impending shipment and its delivery schedule. Included in the information in this transaction are the serially generated numbers that uniquely identify each of the shipping cartons and the detailed information of what items are included in each. The serial numbers are represented on the outside of each shipping container by the industry standard 128 barcode. Normally, a receiver would have to open each carton, and identify and count each item in a shipment. However, in this case the customer can use the advanced shipping notice it has received as its receiving record for the product. With this advance information, he need only scan the number on a shipping carton to know everything that is included in that carton. Not only does this speed up the receiving process, it provides information prior to arrival of the shipment to help plan storage or floor placement of the goods. Levi also premarks each item with its barcoded UPC code by placing a tag on it. This frees the retailer from having to mark each item and sets the stage for either scanning these barcoded tags or entering the code into a point-of-sale system when the product is sold.

Using the advanced shipping notice as a receiving document can also eliminate the need for a separate invoice to the retailer. Since all of the invoice information, except price, has already been transmitted in the advanced shipping notice, and since prices were already agreed to, the invoice becomes unnecessary to the payment decision. Since the retailer would have had to invest funds into development of a new invoice reconciliation application in order to handle the electronic invoice, use of the advanced shipping notice can also eliminate the need for this new development. Currently, most retailer reconciliations are based on tolerances, but that picture should change within the next few years as the use of electronic data becomes more widespread.

As for electronic funds transfer, Levi relates that there is little activity in this area. Companies will need to understand the gains they can realize before implementing EFT. The main concern is loss of float. There may be value to both parties in generating float neutralizing terms for the electronic environment.

The main focus today for Levi are those EDI transactions that flow between its customers and itself and value added services that it can provide for the retailers in the area of inventory management.

KG Mens Stores

KG Mens Stores, a chain of 115 specialty stores carrying mens' clothing, is a showcase customer of Levi, having implemented EDI and taken advantage of the value-added services that Levi provides.

About five years ago, they took a close look at the industry and at their economic situation, and realized that they needed to reduce their safety stock and inventory, and cut internal costs because they earn a low margin of profit and a low turnover of inventory. Prior to double digit inflation, inventory level had not been perceived as a major problem. They also saw that competition was growing, not as much from other specialty chains as from the traditional department stores that were beefing up their specialty departments. So, KG was not only interested in reducing inventory levels, but needed to be sure of carrying the right inventory. Buying traditionally had been done by lot, containing a mix of size and color within a style. They were sometimes unable to fill customers' demand using this buying technique. At the same time they had to offer large markdowns on merchandise they were unable to sell.

Another reason to try to improve buying was that shipping costs were getting higher. KG wanted to buy right for each store in order to minimize shipping costs and product transfers between stores.

Fortunately, purchasing at KG was a completely centralized function. They regularly purchase merchandise from about 500 vendors. Their main philosophy has been to incorporate new technology to provide bottom line benefits. Because they perceived that benefits would be highest in the purchasing area, they started there and contacted their vendors over a year ago to inquire about their interest in trading electronically. They considered developing their own standard data format, but decided instead to support the ANSI X12 standard. They are an active member of VICS. Internally, they developed application for their mainframe computer that utilized VICS/ANSI X12 guidelines.

Today, their purchasing application is almost completely automated. Sales information is accumulated at the store level, tracking by UPC code on style, size, and color. Nightly, that information is pulled by the central computer. 90% of orders are then generated automatically through an automated replenishment system that uses trends of similar items for new products, seasonal adjustments, and other parameters, in addition to the actual sales figures to determine order levels. Store level responsibilities at KG include customer service, morale of employees, unload of shipments, and display. While ordering decisions are made centrally, 100% of the product is drop-shipped to the individual store locations. KG has no warehouses, so they require quick response from their vendors. With timely shipments, they order smaller amounts and more often. Today, they order every two weeks to refill stock levels and count on receiving shipments in a timely manner.

In order to facilitate receipt, two of their major vendors, Levi Strauss & Company and Haggar Apparel Company, generate and transmit to them an advanced shipping notice (ASN) based on their original electronic purchase order. The ASN contains shipment details and delivery schedules as well as the identifying code on each carton in the shipment and the contents of each. Upon receipt of the shipping notice at the central location, the store manager is notified of the items that he will receive and when they will arrive. He can then schedule staff and plan store space requirements for receipt and display of the merchandise in the shipment. Products from these vendors are premarked and arrive with a barcoded tag on each item. Cartons are identified by identifying code, carried out to the floor, and items are hung directly on the racks. Quantities received are counted and entered into the store inventory or scanned and automatically entered upon receipt.

KG has commitments from all vendors to support UPC code premarking in the future. KG plans on using the advanced shipping notice and receiving information to generate payment authorization in the future. Today they already have an automated system of matching and reconciling paper invoices, so there is no pressing need for a new system. They do not expect to support receipt of a separate electronic invoice. So far, they have no plans to support electronic funds transfer or payment remittance. As they are concerned with bottom line benefits, they are putting effort into developing the applications from which they expect to realize the greatest benefits.

KG credits VICS with accelerating the EDI process for the apparel industry.

Haggar Apparel Company

Haggar is looking at EDI as a tool to implement its quick response program. Because they manufacture most garments domestically, they feel competition based on price from offshore manufacturers. They are looking for tools, other than price, with which to fight this competition. Their strategy is to give good service and quick replenishment to attract retailers to their product line.

About three and a half years ago they were first asked to accept a customer's purchase order in its own proprietary standard. They agreed, and had to develop a front end for their order entry system in order to accept them. Today, they are strongly in favor of supporting the ANSI X12 standard. As an active member of VICS, they support the VICS guidelines for usage in the general merchandise sector of the retail industry.

Traditionally, the sales representative at Haggar actually visited his accounts, took a physical inventory, and generated an order based on seasonal adjustments and the physical count of items remaining on the racks. Merchandise was sold by the lot of assorted sizes and colors within a style. The buyer at the retail location would approve the order and the sales rep would bring the completed order in-house. Because of the logistics of travel to multiple customers, it would take from seven to 10 days before the order was received and key entered into the Haggar order entry system. Typically, this process would be carried out monthly, which meant that the retailer was required to carry a full month's inventory of items. If a particular size or color sold out, he was stuck until the next order arrived. Since most retailers kept no detailed sales information on the size and color level, they were not in a position to make "smart" buying decisions.

More recently, retailers are capturing point-of-sale information at the size and color level for each SKU (stock keeping unit) and are ordering to more closely meet customer demand. This puts some pressure on the manufacturer to have the required colors and sizes of each style on hand to meet retailer demand.

In order to support its retailer customers, Haggar began to premark items by tagging them with the UPC code. This gave the retailer the opportunity to use the ticket information as entry to their point-of-sale system, either through scanning of the barcoded representation of the code or by entering the code itself. The challenge for the retailer was to put systems in place to take advantage of electronic transmission of the purchase order and capture of UPC information.

Haggar, similar to Levi, wrote a replenishment system to assist the retailer in ordering correct quantities. When the retailer furnishes sales information or residual inventory to the Haggar replenishment application, the system would develop a reorder based on a model stock configuration agreed to by the buyer. The system can handle not only a basic stock configuration, but also three promotional levels based on dates. Success was easily measured; the system tracked initial stock configuration by style or model number as well as ongoing sales for Haggar. Significant results were noted, both in increased sales to Haggar and decreased inventory requirements for the retailer.

Haggar today is receiving electronic purchase orders from about 15% of its retailers. Sales reps still go out to the others to generate orders. Haggar credits VICS with a great deal of the success of EDI in this industry. The organization has made EDI visible, pointing out the benefits to participating companies. Having VICS active in supporting the standard has provided a buffer between ANSI X12 and the manufacturer or retailer, who need only consider data requirements for their own business situation.

In bringing up EDI trading partners, Haggar found that those already doing EDI with other suppliers were the easiest to bring up. They found that most of their customers who have implemented EDI have bought mainframe software to accomplish the translation from internal format out of their purchasing system into the VICS/ANSI X12 format. Similarly, Haggar bought mainframe translation software. Most of their effort in implementing EDI has been to make orders flow faster and more efficiently. EDI is just a tool to facilitate the flow of information between trading partners. All benefits accrue from efficient and innovative use of the timely and accurate data received.

Haggar has noticed that on the retailer side, because of the large effort, staff commitment, and capital outlay for installing a point-of-sale system, EDI implementation is sometimes slowed to a halt. Haggar believes that there are enough benefits from EDI to justify EDI implementation prior to installing a point-of-sale system. They currently have two or three store groups sending and receiving EDI data with no point-of-sale system. While these groups must still do manual inventory counts, they do realize the benefits of eliminating printing, mailing, and handling of documents, keypunching data entry, and manual errors, such as transposing numbers.

Haggar offers quick response service to their EDI customers by giving them priority within their system. Because of the fast turnaround, customers need to order smaller quantities at shorter time intervals. Most order weekly or biweekly; one sends sale information daily.

For the majority of its department store customers, Haggar packages for the store level. It scans contents of the store carton and generates a packing slip that it places on the carton. The retailer takes the packing slip and compares it to the actual physical count of the shipment.

Today, three customers, representing about 300 stores, are receiving advanced shipping notices from Haggar. While two others are receiving electronic invoices, Haggar reports that there has been little interest in the invoice. They anticipate instead, increasing use of the advanced shipping notice.

Additional EDI activity includes transmitting price/sales catalogs in standard data format to some trading partners. These will contain updated prices of the SKU's that the trading partner orders. As with Levi, they have not initiated any EDI/EFT or payment remittance activity. Likewise, there has been no EDI activity with carriers.

On the vendor side, Haggar receives advanced shipping notices from its major fabric suppliers. Potentially, this can save them a good deal of time when goods are received. Traditionally, when fabric was received, the width was measured, it was tagged with a barcode, and a corner of the fabric was cut off to be sent to the lab and analyzed for color before it could be stored. This process took several days to accomplish, so inventory received was not freed up for use in new product until a week after receipt.

Today, when a supplier sends an advanced shipping notice, they include length, width, and color information. In addition, the fabric is tagged prior to shipment. Upon receipt, the barcoded tag is scanned and the fabric is immediately ready for storage and use in new product. Haggar saves both time and money by getting timely and accurate information from its supplier and reduces its inventory requirements at the same time. Currently, they are doing no electronic ordering, but hope to start later in 1988.

Haggar transacts its EDI business through a third party and encourages its trading partners to do the same. In the apparel sector of the industry, Haggar reports that the major manufacturers such as themselves and Levi made the first move toward EDI. However, today, retailers are calling to initiate electronic trade. Each side has their own economic reasons to do EDI; however, this is a win-win situation, with both sides benefitting.

Chapter

9

EDI Futures

Predictions exist of rapid growth in EDI activity and in the amount of products and services purchased in support of that activity. Today, we are observing new industries becoming interested in trading electronically. Even small, non-computer oriented companies are being impacted by the EDI revolution because their larger and more sophisticated trading partners are requesting that they begin to transmit or receive transactions electronically. Currently, it is estimated that 3500 companies use EDI in at least one business area. Predictions are that 10,000 companies will be using EDI in the next two years.

In addition, companies that are already active in EDI are making plans to increase their participation by increasing the depth of their activity (bringing up more trading partners in the business areas in which they already have implemented EDI) and breadth of their activity (beginning to transmit and receive new transactions in the business areas in which they already are active and implementing EDI in new business areas within the company). Both activities will tend to cause an outward spiral of increased participation related to volume of data transmitted electronically and number of companies implementing EDI.

In what new directions can we anticipate EDI activity? In this chapter we'll look at potential use of EDI for:

- Financial applications.

- International trade.
- Government applications.
- Multi-media.

EDI In Financial Applications

Within corporations, financial applications that use or generate the electronic invoice or its equivalent are being developed actively. However, financial applications that effect payment have been slower to take hold. For one thing, corporate trade payments were not widely embraced by the corporate community for many reasons, not the least of which was desire not to lose float. Electronic funds transfer, a variation on the same theme is slowly gaining acceptance. Either method of transferring funds is based on a buyer organization authorizing its bank to transfer funds to a seller's account or financial institution. Both utilize the banking community as a clearing house of the payment transaction.

At a recent EDI Seminar, Bank of America presented its view of the current and potential data flows in the electronic environment. Figures 9-1 and 9-2 show the current paper transaction flow and several possible EDI flows that were presented that day.

CTX, corporate trade exchange, is based on use of the NACHA (National Clearing House Association) format transaction, which can either be used alone to authorize payment and relate limited information or as an envelope to the ANSI X12 payment remittance transaction to authorize payment only. In addition, the payment remittance can effect the entire transaction, acting as both authorization and remittance history. In all of the above cases, not only is authorization to pay passing through the banking community but also payment remittance information. It would be the responsibility of the bank to strip the information it needed to effect the money transfer, and forward the rest along to the trading partner.

Figure 9-1 illustrates the current flow of dollars and information inter-corporation and through the banking system. The paper check representing dollars and the stub representing information are sent from payer company to payee. The payee retains the information and deposits the check in its bank. Dollars are transferred from payee to payer/banks and the check is returned to the payer company.

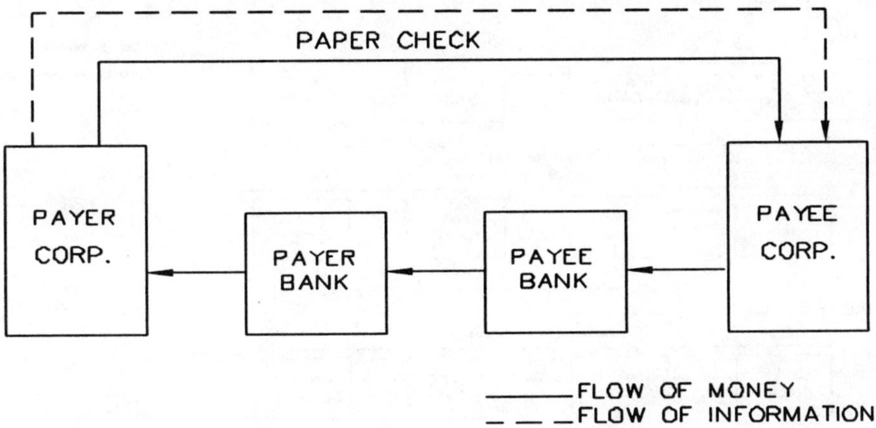

Figure 9-1 Current flow of data and money in banking system.

There are several alternative flows possible in the electronic environment. Figure 9-2 illustrates four of them. In all four, dollars continue to flow through the banking system. The "Navistar" model, so named because Navistar is using this method, shows information flowing from payer to its bank and, at the same time, from payer to payee. The bank reconciliation model shows information flowing through the banking system and being reconciled to data already retained prior to being passed to the payee bank and on to the payee. The payment advising model shows information passed from payer to its bank and then routed directly to the payee, bypassing the payee's bank. Finally, the third party model shows transmission of data through a third party provider to both the payee and its bank. Information to the bank is used to effect money transfer from payer's to payee's accounts.

Even though payments must travel through a bank, the payment remittance information could, alternatively, take a separate route, flowing directly from the customer to its vendor. The banking community is anxious to effect the former, for good reason. With growth of electronic funds transfer as a method of payment, the bank would stand to lose a good deal of business attributable to paper checks and a good deal of lockbox activity. They are anxious to make up this deficit with added EDI activity. However, banks do not currently have

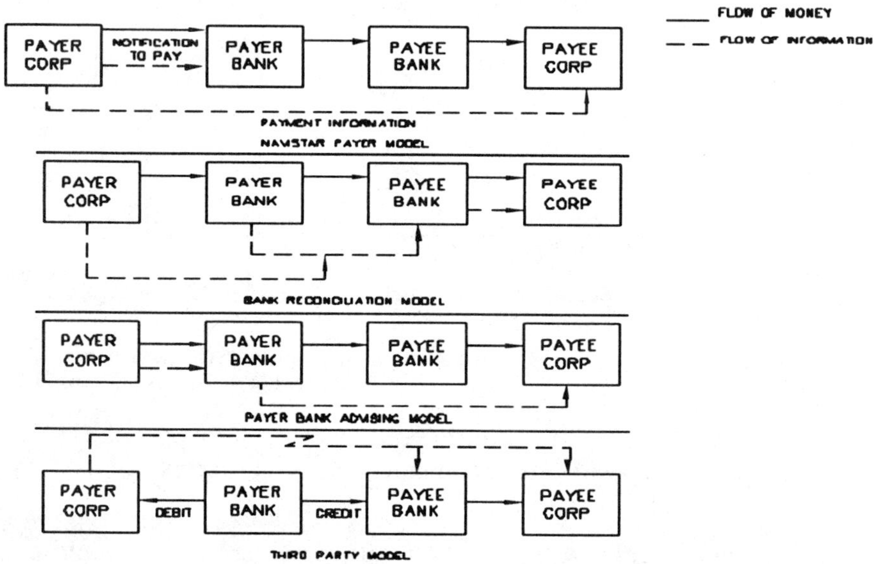

Figure 9-2 Various possible flows of data and money in EDI environment.

the systems in place to handle payment remittances, effect communications to a widespread group of trading partners, or handle the vast amounts of data that can be anticipated. In addition, the banking community realizes that if it provides no value added services to the handling of the remittance, it can charge only commodity type prices for passing the data through its system and may not even get the data at all. Therefore, the banking community is, today, an industry in search of an application. It is unclear just what value added services the banks will offer and whether the business community will concur that they are true value added services for which it wants to pay. It is clear that corporate treasuries are anxious to obtain detailed payment information in a timely manner, with which they can update their accounts and develop historical tracking reports.

For those banks that work aggressively to develop value added EDI services, they stand to profit from increased electronic activity by charging for those services and by taking a share of customers from non EDI-capable banks. Banks that offer undifferentiated accommodation EDI services will not realize profits from EDI. In developing new systems, banks must realize that payment systems that can accommodate only financial data will be at a disadvantage in the long term. They must be prepared to handle business data to the advantage of their customers.

EDI and International Trade

Following is a list of some of the important events in the evolution of international EDI.

As far back as 1961, the UN/ECE committee on Development of Trade established a working party on the Simplification and Standardization of External Trade Documents, which became the first instance of a development effort for standardization of international trade procedures and documentation.

In 1968 the Transportation Data Coordinating Committee, (TDCC), formed with the support of the U.S. Department of Defense to develop messaging standards for inter-organizational communication of business transactions, became the first instance of inter-company EDI in the United States. The standards resulting from this effort were and still are used by the rail, motor, ocean, and air carriers and shippers.

In 1979, the American National Standards Institute (ANSI) chartered the Accredited Standards Committee (ASC) X12 to develop a standard for the inter-industry electronic interchange of business transactions. The syntax and structure of the resulting standards were based on those developed by TDCC but contained the functionality and data content to allow them to be used by all industries and organizations.

In 1983, major auto manufacturers from the U.K., Italy, France, Belgium, Sweden, the Netherlands, and Germany formed a committee to develop electronic data interchange standards for the automotive industry in their respective countries. That committee became the ODETTE EDI Standards Committee the following year. The automotive industry still represents the largest group of EDI users in Europe.

In 1984, ANSI X12 and TDCC formed a joint electronic data interchange (JEDI) committee to consolidate the data element dictionaries and data segment directories of the two standards. At the completion of this task, TDCC became the official "gatekeeper" to assign new data element ID's, new data element code values, new data segment ID'S, and new transaction set ID's for both standards.

In 1985, after a year and a half of work, ODETTE, with assistance of the Automobile Industry Action Group (AIAG), its U.S. counterpart, developed standard message formats for the European auto industry.

Then, in November of 1985, North American and European EDI interests (from more than 20 countries) assembled to discuss the feasibility of establishing a joint syntax for an international standard format to be used in international trade. They met again in March of 1986 and then at least monthly for the next 18 months under the cochairmanship of Dennis McGinnis of North American Philips and R.J. Walkers, Chief Executive of SITPRO, Simplification of International Trade Procedures Board. The result is an international EDI syntax called EDIFACT, EDI For Administration, Commerce, and Transport.

The EDIFACT syntax became a draft international standard in April 1987. In September 1987 it became a full international standard by unanimous vote. The EDIFACT data element dictionary will be identical to the UN Trade Data Element Dictionary, and standardized code lists will coincide with ISO code lists where they exist.

EDIFACT messages are under development on several fronts. The invoice was the first to be approved as a Universal Standard Message (UNSM) in December of 1987. EDIFACT is destined to gain strong backing from the North American, Western European, and Eastern European business interests because it is in the unique position of being developed prior to specific business practices becoming so entrenched that they could not be changed. The thing that makes EDIFACT different is its focus on business function instead of replacement of a specific paper document. With the focus on function, transaction sets are developed as a series of predefined segments containing the information strings required to transact a particular business application. Each party to the transaction will find, in the segments, all of the information it needs to transact business.

A tremendous boon to international support of EDIFACT came when the U.S. Customs Commissioner, William Von Raab, announced early in 1988 that the U.S. Customs Service would support the EDIFACT standards developed by international business interests. Customs had previously been talking of developing a proprietary autobroker interface which was being met with criticism as an inappropriate direction to take at this time. Following his lead, the U.K. and Australia announced their support of EDIFACT. With this kind of government support, companies considering implementing EDI to support international trade can now be certain that there is a standard for message formats that is universally accepted, that that standard is EDIFACT, and that the business community will now begin to move rapidly toward an electronic environment.

EDIFACT has been described by Alice Rigdon, Customs Representative to the European Community in Brussels, as "a snowball coming down the top of the hill that got a big push from Customs Commissioner Von Raab." It is agreed that EDIFACT will be a fact of life for international trade communications.

How will generation and interpretation of EDIFACT transaction sets fit into the domestic EDI systems that corporations have established? While the EDIFACT syntax is very similar to the ANSI X12 syntax, some differences do exist. Most mainframe translation software products on the market today can handle international standards as well as domestic. Homegrown software would have to be enhanced to cover new syntax situations. In addition, data requirements for international trade are more extensive than those for domestic transactions. The sender of an EDIFACT transaction would need to have available all data elements required for this message standard in order to generate a complete transaction; the receiver would need systems to interpret and act on the expanded set of data fields he will receive. While some additional programming would be needed to handle EDIFACT standard messages, neither the syntax nor the data differences are extensive enough to cause major problems to an already existing EDI application.

Certainly the potential benefits of eliminating paper in international trade would far outweigh the extra development costs required to support the EDIFACT standard.

Government Support of EDI

Aside from U.S. Customs support of the EDIFACT standard for international trade, there are several other areas of the government, using or in the processing of implementing EDI domestically.

Active for about five years are the commissaries of the military. A large percentage of purchasing of food products is done electronically, with commissaries generating the UCS standard purchase order and transmitting it to food manufacturers via an EDI third-party service provider.

The Department of Defense recently announced that it will support only ANSI X12 standard transactions in its new development of systems to support electronic transmission of business transactions. In practice they actually mean that they will support X12 for the purchasing function, and TDCC for transportation transactions in the logistics area. EDI in logistics has been been getting a lot of attention recently, with plans for development in two separate areas: one, transactions within the military (intra-government messaging) and two, transactions between the military and commercial interests outside of the government.

The general feeling in the Department of Defense is that paper transactions represent old technology, and electronic transactions will shortly be the de facto way of doing business.

In a report written by Tom Heard and Mike Bridges of the Logistics Management Institute, they presented six areas requiring development in order to assure payoff from EDI implementation at the Department of Defense. They were:

- Establish an EDI program office to coordinate the entry of DOD into the electronic environment.
- Upgrade electronic processing capabilities to take advantage of the timely and accurate data that they will receive.
- Install EDI in 145 of their largest shipping locations. This would represent over 80% of all movements of product.
- Configure a telecommunications network to make communications between the DOD and its trading partners possible and cost-effective.
- Modify federal regulations and DOD directives that explicitly prohibit DOD from conducting business electronically.

The treasury has announced that it will support Vendor Express, a payables system which will pass CCD+ corporate trade payment formats through the banking community. It will also support use of the ANSI X12 payment remittance transaction. However, it has put some limitations on the transaction's functionality (one payment per invoice) because of limitations which exist in its own software. This may, in turn, act to limit its usefulness to the corporate community.

Plans for implementing EDI are in the formulative stage in several other areas of both the civilian and military areas within the government. Just these few instances show how widespread interest in electronic trade is. Luckily, the ANSI X12 standard has developed enough support in a wide variety of industries to convince government departments to investigate support of the same standard prior to choosing the path of developing its own proprietary standard formats.

Because of the desire by government representatives to make the ANSI X12 standard work for the needs of the government, they have been taking an active part in the standards organizations in both development and maintenance roles. The recently formed Government Task Group of the ANSI X12 Committee has been busily defining requirements for transactions that will be transmitted between government agencies and corporations. This effort shows signs of growing as the government plans on integrating more of its internal applications to electronic transmission of business transactions.

Multi-Media EDI

The most prevalent form of EDI today is of batched transactions in a standard data format that are either transmitted in a data stream directly to a receiving trading partner or to a third party on its way to the eventual recipient trading partner. Applications have been identified that do not lend themselves entirely to the batched, store and forward EDI scenario. Some even require on-line activity. For example, an EDI advanced shipping notice (ASN) is received by an auto manufacturer. It may reflect changes from the original material release on which it is based. The auto manufacturer wants the opportunity to examine the ASN, develop a response in the form of a follow up material release and send it back immediately to the vendor. The on-line segment of the procedure ensures immediate action, which in this case is vital to maintain the just-in-time manufacturing schedules. While this is not technically EDI because it requires human intervention, it belongs in this discussion because it utilizes EDI data and generated EDI data. As companies use EDI data more extensively throughout their organizations, there are likely to be a multitude of new applications, such as this, based on the availability of timely and accurate EDI data.

Another application of multi-media EDI arises from the need to include graphics along with data to form a full business transaction. For example, the data fields in a request for quote often cannot adequately describe the product being requested. One picture being worth a thousand words, this transaction calls for graphics to accompany the data. At this time, such a combination does not comprise an EDI data stream even though both are transmitted over the same medium. At some time in the future, EDI data transactions may act as envelopes to graphics representations.

A third example of multi-media EDI is already being employed in some measure, but has tremendous growth potential directly related to the aggressive corporate EDI goals we are beginning to see. When a company launches a campaign to not only implement EDI with a few major partners, but to convert an entire business area's output to the electronic environment, it soon realizes that many of its trading partners are not at all EDI-ready; in fact, they may not even own computers.

In order to accomplish its own goals of generating only EDI transactions, it may be necessary to find methods of passing transactions to those trading partners that cannot handle EDI data in human readable print format. Usually, the company is not interested in supporting this effort. Therefore, it plans on sending all transactions through a third party service provider who will pass along the transactions in standard data format to those trading partners that can accept it and convert the transactions destined for trading partners that cannot accept it into human readable, print format.

Once converted, this data dan be printed and mailed, transmitted via facsimile machine to the trading partner's receiving location, or sent as an electronic mail message to the receiving trading partners electronic mail mailbox.

This solution is about as far from state-of-the-art as you can get. However, as a practical solution, it serves the purposes of allowing the sending company to convert its entire application to EDI output, while allowing small, unsophisticated companies to receive data from that output without impacting its own procedures.

Summary

As is always the case, new technologies inspire new application. So it is difficult to predict the direction that EDI will take in the future. It seems certain, though, that the number of applications using EDI data will grow as more and more uses for the data are identified. Finally, EDI will become the accepted mode of doing business. It will not be too far into the future, that EDI will no longer provide the competitive edge, just as typewriters and computers no longer do, but lack of EDI will surely mean a competitive disadvantage.

Appendices

Appendix A

EDI Publications

Automotive Industry Action Group
AIAG Industry Actionline
Kathleen Vokes
313-569-6262

Automotive Industry Action Group
EDI Implementation Guide
Date Conley
313-569-6262

EDI Council Of Canada
Interchange
Marshall Spence
416-621-7160

EDI Executive Publications
EDI Executive
Debbie Shaw
404-973-4683

EDI in Business
Paul Daisy
201-972-2970

Eurotech Forum
Trade-Flash
Alfredo Sarich
32.27369715

International Thomson Transport Press
Electronic Shipping News
Patricia Braxo
212-714-3100

Metals Industry Implementation Guideline
Kathleen Almand
202-452-7196

National Council International Trade Document
NCITD Newsletter
Eugene A. Hemley
212-925-1400

ORDERNET Services Div. Sterling Software
ORDERNET Services EDI News
Thomas E. James
614-459-7500

Phillips Publishing, Inc.
EDI News
Susan J. Aluise
301-340-2100

SITPRO
Interchange
Ken Cottrill
01-930-0532

Uniform Code Council, Inc.
UCS Bulletin
Chris Frapwell
513-435-3870

Appendix B

EDI Software

Mainframe

ALCO Standard Corporation
Lawrence A. Hall
215-296-8400

American Business Computer
ABC Sales Department
313-855-4520

Control Data
Clint Hileman
216-529-5420

Crowntek EDI Services
Christopher Smith
313-553-7667

Data Design Associates
Betty Fulton
800-556-5511

EDI Solutions
Darcy Running
612-831-9059

EDI, Inc.
Robert C. Marien
301-670-0811

Intec Systems
Rick Parks
417-739-4214

Lek Product Marketing Company, Inc.
Larry E. Kramer
612-688-8010

MSA
Frank Buchheit
404-239-3411

Metro*Marl Integrated Systems, Inc.
Bob Lyttle
516-484-0949

ORDERNET Services
David Schenk
614-459-7500

Superior IS
D. Carl Garrison
713-654-1716

TranSettlements, Inc
Bob Canis
404-996-8109

Union Pacific Technologies, Inc.
Phil Seifert
314-622-3097

Micro

APL Group, Inc.
Bill Fairbairn
203-762-3933

Advanced Communications Systems
Bob Stone
800-223-5424

American Business Computer
ABC Sales
313-855-4520

American Custom Software, Inc.
Robert Sparkman
615-537-6516

B & L Information Systems
Mike Fabis
616-465-6207

Baggerly & Associates
Steve Stallings
714-625-7917

Birmingham Computer Group, Inc.
Dennis Burgio
313-540-0640

Brenner, Inc.
David Laxton
513-251-6655

Can/Am Tech, Inc.
U.S. 412-261-2889
Canada 416-528-4323

Central Data Systems
Ken Reisman
313-478-7000

Chase Manhattan Corp.
Linda McLaughlin
212-552-5762

Columbus Computer Business Systems
Scott Staples
416-498-6778

Computer Alternatives
Tim Sujek
313-528-9189

Computer Dimensions, Inc.
Dan MacDonald
313-465-9794

Computer Methods
Miles Leggo
313-522-2120

Computer Strategies
Diane Goense
616-957-4444

Control Data
Clint Hileman
216-529-5420

DISC
John Snyder
301-486-0410

DNS Associates, Inc.
Hugh W. Stewart
617-862-8569

Data Systems Services, Inc.
Paul Koncz
313-478-8485

Document Interchange Systems Corp.
Jim Houser
212-438-4397

EDI, Inc.
Robert C. Marien
301-670-0811

Electronic Data Xchange, Inc.
Steve Flink
215-277-8383

EmTech Corporation
Mark Daugherty
617-281-1721

Genzlinger Associates, Inc.
Vance Genzlinger
313-879-7070

INFO Data, Inc.
Peter Delong
313-352-6755

Independent Business Software
Gary Carpenter
616-243-0900

Intec Systems
Rick Parks
417-739-4214

JETICS
Hank Unruh
703-893-4404

LEK Product Marketing Company, Inc.
Larry E. Kramer
612-688-8010

Louis A. Wright & Associates, Inc.
Roy Gutknecht
313-459-7760

Martin Marietta Data Systems
Gerry Van Dagna
800-654-3935

Metro*Mark Integrated Systems, Inc.
Bob Lyttle
516-484-0949

National Electronic Mail Associates
Tom Hoppenjans
606-341-3524

ORDERNET Services
Thomas E. James
614-459-7500

RAILINC Corporation
Phillip Hennessee
202-639-5566

Release Management Systems
John Bennett
313-553-7667

St. Paul Software
Gary Anderson
612-641-0963

Superior IS
D. Carl Garrison
713-655-1435

Supply Tech, Inc.
Wendell Holladay
313-357-3430

Trax Systems
Scott Nelson
714-661-7661

Valenite GTE
Jess Alderson
313-589-2235

Wagner Data Systems
Lester T. Povlich
800-558-5596

White Ware Inc.
David Whitehouse
313-769-2505

Mini

ACS Network Systems
Jim Bert
800-426-3836

American Business Computer
ABC Sales
313-855-4520

American Custom Software, Inc.
Robert Sparkman
615-537-6515

Assets Data Corp.
Christine M. Trahey
516-737-2400

Birmingham Computer Group, Inc.
Dennis Burgio
313-540-0640

Comsen, Inc.
Fred R. Nichols
717-691-8123

Control Data
Clint Hileman
216-529-5420

Digital Equipment Corporation
William M. Carlisle
603-884-3322

EDI Solutions
Darcy Running
612-831-9059

EDI, Inc.
Robert C. Marien
301-670-0811

Intec Systems
Rick Parks
417-739-4214

Louis A. Wright & Associates, Inc.
Greg Lanthier
313-459-7760

M3 Software Corporation
Tom Schulte
313-433-3803

Metro*Mark Integrated Systems, Inc.
Bob Lyttle
516-484-0949

National Systems Corporation
Michael Gibbons
212-947-1230

ORDERNET Services Div. Sterling Software
Thomas E. James
614-459-7500

Pittsburgh Software Company Inc.
P. Bryan Heidorn
412-683-8010

Radley Business Computers
Don Draheim
313-855-6181

Appendix C

EDI Third Party Service Providers

American Custom Software, Inc.
Robert Sparkman
615-537-6516

Control Data
Clint Hileman
216-529-5420

Dakom HB
Swedish Data Communication Systems
Mr. Bjorn Passad
46-8635280

Electronic Data Systems (EDS)
Joe Klimaski
313-696-2296

GE – Canadian GE Information Services
Jack Brooks
416-858-5215

Harbinger Computer Services
James B. Langford
404-320-1636

IBM Canada Ltd.
Patricia V. Ransom
416-941-6607

IBM Information Network
Gerry D. Mead
813-878-3942

Industrial Network Systems, Inc.
Frank R. Paterson
419-893-8789

MEMA – TRANSNET
Don McGrath
201-569-8500

Martin Marietta Data Systems
Gerry Van Dagna
800-654-3935

McDonnell Douglas – EDI*Net
800-435-8880

ORDERNET Services Div. Sterling Software
Thomas E. James
614-459-7500

Pubnet/Assn of American Publishers
Richard E. Bates
212-689-8920

RAILING Corporation
Phillip Hennessee
202-639-5566

SP*EDI Net
Bob McCord
817-924-7759

Telecom Canada
Jim Farris
613-567-0731

TranSettlements, Inc.
Margaret E. Carlock
404-996-8109

Western Union Corp.
Joanne Rinkus
201-825-5001

Appendix D

Cost Analysis Document

Analysis of the Current Business Environment

Business Documents

	P.O.'s	Invoices	Other
# sent/recvd per week	____/____	____/____	____/____
# sent/recvd per month	____/____	____/____	____/____
# sent/recvd per year	____/____	____/____	____/____
# of line items (avg)	____/____	____/____	____/____

Processing and Handling

Cost to send a purchase order (include key entry time, order development time, approval time, etc) __________

Cost to receive a purchase order (include handling time, key entry time, interpretation of data time, etc.) __________

Cost to make a payment (include receipt of invoice, verification against open purchase orders, approval of payment, key entry, etc.) __________

Cost to send or receive other transactions __________

Other __________

Paper and Mailing

Cost of paper, envelope, and time to get a transaction into the mail.

____

Error Handling

Cost to handle incorrect purchase order sent (include telephone time to make correction, receipt of wrong product, handling return, etc.) __________

Cost to handle incorrect purchase order received (include telephone time, shipment of wrong product, material return, payment for return shipment, damage to returned goods, etc.) __________

Cost to handle incorrect payment made (include loss of available funds, telephone time, etc.) __________

Other error condition – Describe __________

NOTE: Eliminating an error condition offers the greatest opportunity to benefit in time and cost savings.

One Time Costs to Develop/Buy Software and Hardware

Cost estimate of in-house application link software development ____________

Cost estimate of in-house translation software development ____________

Cost estimate of translation software product ____________

Cost estimate of alternate translation product ____________

Cost estimate of communications software product ____________

Cost estimate of hardware ____________

Ongoing Costs

Transaction Analysis

Transaction Type: ________________________________

Estimate Per (day, week, month, or year)

Transaction Header Area

		Segments	Characters
A.	Basic header information	5	150
B.	Number of names & addresses in header _______ (multiply by 4 for segs., by 40 for chars.)		

		Segments	Characters
C.	Free form message lines in header? If yes, (1 seg. and 60 chars for each line)		
D.	Shipping schedule in header? If yes, (1 seg. and 40 chars. for each ship date)		
E.	Carrier information in header? If yes, (4 segs. and 120 chars.)		
F.	HEADER TOTAL		

Each Line Item

		Segments	Characters
G.	Basic line item information	1	60
H.	Does product require free form description? If yes, (1 seg. and 60 chars. for each description line)		
I.	Is shipping schedule in line? If yes, (1 seg. and 40 chars. for each ship date)		
J.	Must product be shipped to multiple shipping points? If yes, (4 segs. and 160 chars. for each ship location)		
K.	Are manufacturing specs. included in line? If yes, (3–8 segs. and 90–200 chars.)		
L.	Is carrier information included in line? If yes, (4 segs. and 120 chars.)		

M. Are free form message lines included in line item? If yes, (1 seg. and 60 chars. for each message line) ______________

N. LINE ITEM TOTAL ______________

Total of All Line Items

	Segments	Characters
O. Number of lines in average business document		
P. Line item total (multiply N by O)		

Summary Area

	Segments	Characters
Q. Summary segment	1	30
R. Transaction header and trailer	2	50
S. Total transaction set segs. and chars. (add F + P + Q + R)		

Total segs. and chars. transmitted per ______________

T. Interchange & Group headers and trailers each transmission (for each group in transmission add 2 segs. and 50 chars. and then add 2 segs. and 60 chars. for interchange) ______________

U. Number of transmission per ________ ______________

V. Control segments per ________ (T β U) ______________

W. Number of business documents per ________ ______________

X. Number of document segs./chars. per ________ (S β W) ________________________

Y. Total segs/chars. per ________ (X + V) ________________________

Third Party Costs

One Time Costs

	Party Name	Party Name	Party Name
	________		________
Training	________		________
Startup charges	________		________
Initiation fees	________		________
Hookup charges	________		________
Consulting	________		________
Mailbox	________		________
Interconnect Charges	________		________
Other	________		________

Ongoing Third Party Charges Per Month

Monthly base fee	________		________
Numer of transactions sent	________		________
Number of segments sent	________		________

Number of characters sent ________ ________

Number of transactions received ________ ________

	Party Name	Party Name	Party Name
Number of segments received	________		________
Number of characters received	________		________
Connect time @. per minute	________		________

Note: at 2400 baud, estimate 15,000 characters per connect minute

Ongoing Third Party Charges Per Month (continued)

Mailbox charge ________ ________

Report charges ________ ________

Other ________ ________

Other ________ ________

Other ________ ________

Other ________ ________

Appendix E

Feasibility Study Instructions

1. Identify functional business area study is being done for. List names of functional business area managers conducting study and MIS and Communications support managers.

2. Develop the list of transactions you currently send from/receive into this business area. Write estimated number of transactions in current environment and with EDI. If you are not thinking of converting all transactions into EDI, note that as a "0" or "phase 2" as the case may be.

3. Perform an analysis of your current "gateway" application, the one that would need to generate or receive EDI data (e.g., order entry application, purchasing application).

   Develop a data flow diagram showing

   - How data is currently input into system, e.g., key entry, tape from trading partner.
   - What manual procedures are required from the time the paper transaction is received in-house or generated by the application, e.g., opening or stuffing envelopes, interpreting paper transactions, answering or making telephone calls.
   - What data is required for gateway application and how they flow into subsequent applications.

Make note of the number of staff you currently need to perform the manual tasks above, and the time it takes.

Also get figures on the error rate you are experiencing because of such problems as:

- Incorrect interpretation of transactions received,
- Program malfunctions or inappropriate actions due to incorrect data entry,
- Incorrect or late shipments sent/received, and
- Amount of returned goods sent/received.

4. Develop a revised data flow for the application as it would work with EDI.

    - Show automated data entry in format acceptable to application if you are the receiver, otherwise, show generation of machine readable data file to replace paper transaction print format.
    - Show application link that maps standard format to application format if you are the receiver, otherwise, show link that generates standard format from application output.
    - Include a control mechanism in the new application to

        – Keep track of your EDI activity,
        – Generate or accept and reconcile standard functional acknowledgments to your in-house EDI activity figures,
        – Read and interpret third party reports and reconcile them to your EDI transmission activity figures.

    Consider additional functionality to give functional business managers, auditors, corporate administrators access to selected data in order to improve planning, auditing, and tracking.

5. Develop a list of potential trading partners with names and telephone numbers of functional business manager and MIS and communication support contacts.

6. Compute "EDI potential" by doing a cost/benefit analysis. Use the following parameters to evaluate benefits and costs.

"EDI potential" = EDI benefits – EDI costs

EDI benefits = Market factors + Short and long range benefits

EDI costs = Setup costs + Ongoing costs

Ask yourself the following questions for MARKET FACTORS.

- Are you getting pressure from major trading partners to do EDI?
- Do you need to show that you are state-of-the-art because your entire industry is starting to implement EDI?
- Do you need to cut internal costs to remain competitive?
- Do you need to improve your image by providing better and more responsive customer service?

A "yes" denotes a positive market factor, several "yeses" denote strong positive pressure. Sometimes, strong market factors can mean that you will implement EDI in spite of high costs.

SHORT TERM BENEFITS are derived from reducing or eliminating costs associated with manual handling and processing of transactions and with labor and material.

Investigate the following costs and develop a matrix comparing current vs. EDI costs. Look for substantial cost savings in key entry and error handling.

LONG RANGE BENEFITS are, as their name implies, futures. In order to realize a benefit in this category you will often require additional software, new arrangements with trading partners, or the like. However, make this an important part of the analysis, as the savings derived here will overshadow those realized in the short term.

For each category, note the current environment:

- Do you have systems in this area?
- How much manual effort is involved?
- How does the current system works?

- What problems and bottlenecks exist?

Then note how you might improve conditions by using EDI data:

- What new systems could be developed?
- How could those that already exist be improved?
- How could information be disseminated to staff within your company?
- How could EDI data position your company for more favorable vendor status?

Try to quantify potential benefits.

Develop an estimate for SETUP COSTS for EDI. Your internal MIS department can estimate time and effort to enhance your current application programs.

Ballpark figures for purchase of EDI products are as follows:

- Basis communication software $100-500
- Translation software – Micro $1000-5000.

  – Mini $9000-11000.
  – Mainframe $18,000-25,000.

Estimate ONGOING COSTS. You can use the Cost Analysis document for this purpose.

7. Develop a business area recommendation showing a positive or negative trend for "EDI potential" over time.

*** Remember to amortize setup costs over several years and to distribute them over the functional areas that will utilize the same software and hardware. ***

Appendix F

Feasibility Study Worksheet

1. Functional Business Area ____________________

 Managers ____________________

 ____

 ____

 ____

 MIS Support Contact ____________________

 Communication Support Contact ____________________

2. TRANSACTION SENT/RECEIVED ANALYSIS

 Transaction 1. ____________________

	CURRENT	PROJECTION
FOR EDI		
SEND		
RECEIVE		

Transaction 2. ______________________________

	CURRENT	PROJECTION
FOR EDI		
SEND		
RECEIVE		

Transaction 3. ______________________________

	CURRENT	PROJECTION
FOR EDI		
SEND		
RECEIVE		

Transaction 4. ______________________________

	CURRENT	PROJECTION
FOR EDI		
SEND		
RECEIVE		

Transaction 5. ______________________________

	CURRENT	PROJECTION

FOR EDI

SEND

RECEIVE

3. CURRENT GATEWAY APPLICATION

For each application that will be impacted by electronic trade of the transactions above, develop a current system analysis with data flow diagram showing:

a. Manual procedures – handling
key entry
interpretation
telephone

b. Input procedures – key entry

c. Staffing requirements – data entry clerk
salesperson

d. Data requirements

e. Data flow to subsequent applications

4. REVISED EDI GATEWAY APPLICATION

For each gateway application analyzed above, develop business specifications for the following:

a. Changes to gateway application to support file input

b. Control requirements to keep track of EDI activity

c. Data access to replace paper copies

d. Acknowledgment reconciliation to trace EDI activities

e. Mapping specifications between EDI standard format and internal application format

5. LIST OF POTENTIAL TRADING PARTNERS. CONTACT NAMES OF EDI COORDINATOR, BUSINESS AREA USERS, COMMUNICATIONS SUPPORT STAFF FOR EACH PARTNER

   1.

   2.

   3.

   4.

   5.

6. COST/BENEFIT ANALYSIS

Market Factors

- Are you getting pressure from major trading partners to do EDI? ______________________
- Do you need to show that you are state-of-the-art because your entire industry is starting to implement EDI? ______________________
- Do you need to cut internal costs to remain competitive? ______________________

- Do you need to improve your image by providing better and more responsive customer service? ______________________

Short Term Benefits

Evaluate CURRENT vs. EDI costs for the following:

	CURRENT	EDI
Transaction handling		
Error correcting		
Key entry		
Telephone time		
Material costs		

Long Range Benefits

Identify current position and note possible improvements, cost savings in the EDI environment.

	CURRENT	EDI
Inventory level		
Cash flow		
Customer service		
Business efficiency		
Administrative control		
Audit trail		

Favorable vendor status ________________

Favorable delivery schedules ________________

Favorable prices ________________

Setup Costs

Estimate setup costs for EDI for each of the following:

Computer hardware and software purchase ________________

Communication hardware and protocol software purchase ________________

Software development ________________

Coordination with trading partners ________________

Third party initial charges ________________

EDI consulting ________________

Participation at trade shows and standards committees ________________

In-house meetings ________________

Ongoing Costs

Estimate ongoing costs for EDI for each of the following:

Note: You can use the sample cost analysis document for this procedure

Maintenance of software ________________

Transaction costs ________________

Communication ________________

Set-up trading partners ________________

Processing ______________________________

Parrallel current system ______________________________

7. BUSINESS AREA RECOMMENDATION

"EDI POTENTIAL" – parameters over time and with varying degrees of EDI activity.

Discuss phased approach to implementation, if appropriate.

9. DEVELOP BUSINESS AREA RECOMMENDATION FOR HOW TO PROCEED WITH EDI IMPLEMENTATION

Appendix G

EDI Network Services Request for Information

Attach additional sheets whenever necessary.

I. DESCRIPTION

1. Vendor Name ______________________
2. Address ______________________
3. City, State, Zip ______________________
4. Telephone Number ______________________
5. Sales Rep Name ______________________
6. Technical Rep Name ______________________
7. List name and addresses of 3 local references:

____

____

____

8. List name and address of a user group:

____

____

____

9. What is the size of your company in terms of gross sales?

____

____

____

10. What is the size of your company in terms of EDI gross sales? ______________________________

11. What is your company organization?

Unincorporated? ____________________
Partnership of private corporation? ____________________
Public corporation? ____________________

12. How long has your company been in the EDI business?

Network Based Services

13. Do you provide network based translation? YES NO

14. When a translation error occurs, at what level do you reject?

Transmission	YES	NO
Group	YES	NO
Transaction Set	YES	NO

15. Is the reciver responsible for the cost in correcting a sender's translation error? YES NO

16. Please desribe your procedures for assigning cost under different error conditions. ______________________

____

17. Given the following three parites, sender, translator/netowrk, receiver, who is responsible for initiating recovery from a translation failure at the following levels?

Transmission (Envelope) ______________________
Group ______________________
Transaction Set ______________________

18. Do you provide error reporting at the following levels?

Transmission	YES	NO
Group	YES	NO
Transaction Set	YES	NO
Individual Transactions	YES	NO

19. Please describe the method of notification whenever an error is detected, especially when the error involves an interconnect.

____

____

____

____

20. Please describe the type of error reports (including statistics) that are currently in production. ______________________

____

____

____

21. Do you provide identification of specific problem causing error (i.e., mandatory field missing, numeric field not numeric)? YES NO

22. After translation, can we selectively pull transaction sets (i.e., pick up invoices weekly, purchase orders daily)? YES NO

23. How long will copies of a transmission be retained in a mailbox for recovery purposes?

____

24. How are back-up copies distinguished from new transmissions in a mailbox?

____

25. Provide the number and location of access points to the network.

____

26. Detail all network expansion plans. List specific locations to be added to the network and time frames.

____

____

____

27. Provide detailed description of network redundancy.

____

____

28. Are there disaster recovery plans in place? YES NO

29. Provide details of plans in case of a disaster to your service.

____

____

____

30. How would our company activate a disaster plan if we lost a major location?

____

____

31. What type of network support is available?

____

32. Where is the network support located?

____

____

33. Is there a separate cost associted with this network sup port? YES NO

34. How is the network support cost assessed?

____

____

____

____

35. What are the hours of network operation?______________

36. Explain the security features on the network.

____

____

____

37. What protocols are supported?

____

____

38. What line speeds are supported at the access point?

____

____

39. What line speeds are supported at the host?

____

40. Is asynchronous error checking software supported? YES NO

41. Do you currently have in production outdial capability with time-based store and forward? YES NO

42. What are the standard framing bits on the network transmission?

____

____

____

____

43. Describe any special restrictions that we should be aware of.

44. Does the network support interactive transmission or is it only bulk file transfer?

45. Describe how you will provide interconnects to other EDI networks.

46. List the names of the interconnects currently in production and the dates initiated.

47. List the names of the interconnects currently in test and the dates initiated.

____

____

____

____

48. List the interconnect references.

____

____

____

49. Do you support "open communication standards?" YES NO

50. How long have you supported "open communication standards?" ____________________

51. How many clients are currently using "open communication standards?" ____________________

52. What is the telephone number of "listening process" for the "open communication standards?"

____

____

____

53. How many years have you provided a generic message transfer system for delivering TDCC, UCS, and/or ANSI messages? ____________________

54. How many of your clients currently use each of the following:

________ TDCC ________
________ UCS ________
________ ANSI ________

(List the inductry subsets that are in use.)

55. How many clients are trading with one trading partner?

____

56. How many clients are trading with multiple trading partners?

____

57. What is the average length of time required to add trading partners to the network?

____

58. What are the procedures for changing or terminating existing or active trading partner relationships?

____

____

____

59. How long does it take to establish a trading relationship?

____

60. How much of that time is usually required for administrative agreements between trading partners?

____

61. Do you have a formal checklist for adding trading partners to a network YES NO

62. Could we use the same checklist for approaching our trading partners? YES NO

63. Please attach a copy of that checklist.

64. Do you offer mailbox and broadcast services? YES NO
Please describe.

65. Please provide detail on all available options and associated costs for accessing network from host.

66. Please provide costs of character segment transmission.

67. Please provide volume discount schedule.

68. Please detail the storage charges.

69. Please detail the administrative fees.

70. Please provide billing options and formats.

71. Please identify fees associated with customized reporting.

72. Please attach copies of standard reports.

73. Please provide an explanation of and charges for any additional features that you may offer (e.g., range for parameter edits performed on data content).

Security/Recovery

74. Can the service be used at a recovery site, if necessary? YES NO

75. a. Is there a security built into the system? YES NO

b. If yes, describe briefly:

____

76. a. Does the system have balancing procedures? YES NO

    b. If yes, are they automated or manual?

____

____

____

____

77. a. Does the system provide audit trails? YES NO

    b. If yes, describe briefly:

____

____

____

____

78. Error handling:
    JCL Abend Messages YES NO
    Program Abend Messages YES NO
    Messages Keyed to Documentation YES NO
    Can User Elect Abend Options YES NO

Documentation

79. Attach a copy of the service documentation.

80. a. Does the service allow flexibility in naming standards? YES NO
    b. If not, is this negotiable? YES NO

81. Does the documentation include:
    a. System Flowchart and Narrative YES NO
    b. Program Listings YES NO
    c. Input/Output File Layouts YES NO
    d. Tape Control Instructions YES NO
    e. Distribution Instructions YES NO
    f. Control Instructions YES NO
    g. Step Operating Instructions YES NO
    h. Step Narratives YES NO
    i. User Manual YES NO
    j. JCL Deck and List YES NO
    k. Estimated Step Run Times YES NO
    l. Report Examples YES NO
    m. Restart Procedures YES NO
    n. Error Description for Condition Codes/Abends YES NO
    o. Other ______________________________
    o. Other ______________________________

82. Is the documentation available oneline? YES NO

Training Factors

83. Will you provide in-house training for:
    a. Technical Staff YES NO
    b. Operations Staff YES NO
    c. User Staff YES NO

84. Will you provide a management overview in-house? YES NO

85. a. Will you provide training materials? YES NO
    b. If so, describe:

____

____

____

____

Contractual Factors

86. a. Do you use a standard contract? YES NO
    b. Attach a copy?

87. Are you willing to negotiate the contract contents? YES NO

88. Does the contract provide for a free, no obligation trial period? YES NO

89. Can a final version of this questionnaire be used as an addendum to the contract? YES NO

Signature ____

____

Today's date Name of person completing this questionnaire

Appendix H

ANSI X12 Transaction Sets

AMERICAN NATIONAL STANDARD – HAS PASSED FULL PUBLIC REVIEW

ASC/ANSI Document Number	Transaction Set ID	Document Title	Current Version Number
X12.1-1986	850	Purchase Order	002001
X12.2-1986	810	Invoice	002001
X12.3-1986	–	Data Element Dictionary	002001
X12.5-1987		Interchange Control Structure	002001
X12.6-1986		Application Control Structure	
X12.7-1986	840	Request for Quotation	002001
X12.8-1986	843	Response to Request for Quote	002001
X12.9-1986	855	Purchase Order Acknowledgment	002001
X12.10-1987	856	Ship/Notice Manifest	002001
X12.12-1986	861	Receiving Advice	002001
X12.13-1986	832	Price/Sales Catalog	002001
X12.14-1986	830	Planning Schedule	002001
X12.15-1986	860	Purchase Order Change Request	002001

ASC/ANSI Document Number	Transaction Set ID	Document Title	Current Version Number
X12.16-1986	865	Purchase Order Change Request Acknowledgment	002001
X12.20-1986	997	Functional Acknowledgment	
X12.22-1986	–	Data Segment Directory	002001

DRAFT STANDARD FOR TRIAL USE – HAS PASSED FULL X12 REVIEW, BUT NOT YET PUBLIC REVIEW

ASC/ANSI Document Number	Transaction Set ID	Document Title	Current Version Number
X12.11-198x	869	Order Status Inquiry	
X12.23-198x	870	Order Status Report	
X12.28-198x	846	Inventory Advice	
X12.33-198x	867	Product Transfer & Resale	
X12.37-198x	862	Shipping Schedule	
X12.38-198x	823	Lock Box Transaction	

IN VARIOUS STAGES OF DEVELOPMENT - NOT YET DRAFT STANDARD

ASC/ANSI Document Number	Transaction Set ID	Document Title	Current Version Number
X12.17-198x	857	Notification of Readiness To Ship	
X12.18-198x	858	Shipment Information	
X12.24-198x	821	Financial Transaction Report	
X12.25-198x	822	Customer Account Analysis	
X12.26-198x	844	Product Transfer Account Adjustment	

ASC/ANSI Document Number	Transaction Set ID	Document Title	Current Version Number
X12.27-198x	845	Price Authorization Acknowledgment/Status	
X12.30-198x	868	Electronic Form Structure	
X12.31-198x	847	Quality Information	
X12.32-198x	866	Waiver Request	
X12.34-198x	864	Text Transaction	
X12.35-198x	854	Purchase Order Change (Seller Initiated)	
X12.36-198x	848	Material Safety Data Sheet	
X12.39-198x	835	Product Availability Inquiry	
X12.41-198x	863	Report of Test Results	
X12.42-198x	815	EBDI Security Structure	
X12.43-198x	819	Operating Expense Statement	
X12.44-198x	824	Application Acknowledgment	
X12.45-198x	828	Payment Status Inquiry	
X12.46-198x	825	Payment Status Report	
X12.47-198x	827	Payment Return Information	
X12.48-198x	829	Payment Cancellation Request	
X12.49-198x	831	Control Totals	
X12.50-198x	849	Response To Product Transfer Account Adjustment	

Bibliography

Robert A. Payne and A. L. Payne

Comprehensive Articles & Books

Akerman, G. C. and Cafiero, W. G., *Introduction to Electronic Data Interchange: A Primer*, General Electric Information Services Company, 1985.

Anderson, Dr. David, *Logistics Data Interchange: An Emerging Competitive Weapon for Shippers*, Temple, Barker & Sloane, Lexington, MA, 1986.

Blissmer, Robert H. and Hoffman, Susan S., "EDI Inspires Visions of a Paperless Society," *InformationWEEK*, May 18, 1987, pp. 48-52.

Borsellino, Matt, "The New National Dream?" *Materials Management and Distribution*, May 1987, pp. 36, 38 f.

"Buyer Distrib Link Simplified," *Purchasing*, February 13, 1986.

Buys, Clifford R., *Motor Carrier/Shipper Electronic Data Interchange*, American Trucking Association, Alexandria, VA, 1986. [Second edition published 1987]

Buzzell, Robert A., ed., *Marketing in an Electronic Age*, Harvard Business School Press, 1985.

Calderwood, Lynne, "Distribution Group Learns Data Exchange Well on Way," *Materials Management and Distribution*, June 1987, pp. 16 f.

Campbell, Randy, "Are You Ready for EDI?" *Business Software Review*, October 1987.

Canright, Collin, "EDI: The Acronym That Means Business," *Systems/3X World*, January 1987, pp. 40-46.

-------. "Seizing the Electronic Information Advantage," *Business Marketing*, January 1988, pp. 81-82, 84, 86.

Carroll, Paul B., "Computers Bringing Changes to Basic Business Documents," *The Wall Street Journal*, March 6, 1987. [Also reported in *The Asian Wall Street Journal*, March 10, 1987.]

"A Case for Electronic Document Interchange," *Infosystems*, January 1987, p. 58.

Chester, Jeffrey, "EDI: Not Just a Giant's Game," *Infosystems*, January 1988.

------. "Electronic Data Interchange," *Infosystems*, June 1986, pp. 48-50.

Chilton, David, "EDI Still Revving Up for Takeoff," *Computing Canada*, October 1, 1987.

Clauson, Keith S.; Zelinski, Thomas; Monczka, Robert M., "Implementing EDI: The Great Chase," *Purchasing and Technology – 1986 & Beyond*, National Association of Purchasing Management, 1986.

Coffman, Cathy, "Paying the Bills Could Save Money," *Distribution* March 1986.

Communications – COMPAT 88, Euromatica S.A., Brussels, Belgium, February 29, 1988.

The Competitive Edge, Electronic Data Interchange Council of Canada, 1987.

"Computer-Based Sales Orders Catch On Fast," *Sales & Marketing Management*, March 1987.

"Concept of EDI Catches on After More Than a Decade of Unrecognized Value," *Computer Daily*, September 12, 1986.

"EDI And QR: A Lot More Than Alphabet Soup," *Chain Store Age Executive*, January 1988, pp. 89-90.

"The EDI Concept Is Simple; The Problems Are Many," *Computerworld*, July 9, 1986, p. 16.

"EDI: Data On the Fast Track," *Distribution*, June 1987, pp. 38-41.

"EDI Gains Maturity," *Computerworld Australia*, December 11, 1987.

"EDI: Let Computers Do Your Talking," *Textile World*, December 1986, pp. 50, 55-56.

"EDI Systems Are Spreading Rapidly Across Industries," *Computer Daily*, August 22, 1986. [Also reported in *Computer Age EDP Weekly*.]

EDI: The Mission Possible, EDI Strategies, Marietta, GA, 1987. [Videotape]

The EDI Yellow Pages Directory, July 1987. [Edition II March 1988]

"Electronic Data Interchange - An Accomplishment in Acceleration," *Tymshare Today*, Autumn 1983, pp. 10-12.

Electronic Data Interchange and Paperless Trade: The Implementation Guide, Euromatica S.A., Second Edition 1988.

"Electronic Data Interchange," *ThruPut: Significant Trends in New Communications Services*, LINK, December 1985.

"Electronic Document Delivery: the Choices – and What It All Means," *Purchasing*, August 21, 1986.

Emmelhainz, Margaret A., "Electronic Data Interchange in Purchasing," *Guide to Purchasing*, National Association of Purchasing Management, Oradell, NJ, 1986.

------. *The Impact of EDI on the Purchasing Process*, Ohio State University, Columbus, OH, 1986.

------. *1.17 Electronic Data Interchange in Purchasing*, National Association of Purchasing Management, Inc., University of Dayton, Ohio, 1986.

Feldman, J., "The Bytes That Bind: Electronic Data Interchange," *Handling & Shipping Management*, May 1984.

"Getting There With EDI," *PurchasingWorld*, November 1985, pp. 58-60.

Glatzer, Hal, "When Delivering EDI Mail, Postman Rings Instantly," *Software News*, May 1987, pp. 70-75.

Guilbert, Edward A., "Transacting Business In the World of Electronic Data Interchange," *That's Transportation 1983*, Myasthenia Gravis Foundation, February 13, 1984.

Guilbert, Edward and Steiner, Richard H., *The World of Electronic Data Interchange*, Visual Aids Electronics, Washington, D. C., December 9, 1986. [Cassette]

Guinipero, Dr. Larry C., "Paperless Buying Nets Multiple Benefits," *Electronic Buyers News*, April 6, 1987.

Harrington, Lisa H., "Edward A. Guilbert: The Maven of EDI," *Traffic Management*, November 1986, p. 14.

Harris, Catherine L.; Foust, Dean; Rothman, Matt, "An Electronic Pipeline That's Changing the Way America Does Business," *Business Week*, August 3, 1987, pp. 80, 82.

Herman, James G., "Strategic Offense Initiative," *Network World*, April 13, 1987.

Hill, Thomas, "Saving Time and Labor with Electronic Data Interchange," *PC Week*, August 4, 1987, p. C/15.

Hoffman, Susan S., "Do Small and Midsized Firms Have a Choice?," *InformationWEEK*, May 18, 1987.

------. "IBM's Lucente: EDI Will Be As Vital As the Telephone," *InformationWEEK*, December 7, 1987, p.12.

Horwitt, Elisabeth, "Move to EDI Gathers Steam as Standards Clear, Benefits Grow," *Computerworld*, December 15, 1986.

Huguet, J. H., Jr., "Computer-to-Computer Ordering; The Sales/Marketing Implications," *Marketing News*, September 14, 1984.

Humphreys, Doug, "An Overview of EDI: What Is It?" *Computing Canada*, March 19, 1987.

Hurst, Randolph, "Electronic Data Interchange: Is This the Way to Go?" *CEDA Current Annual*, May 1985, pp. 55-56. *An Introduction to Electronic Business Data Interchange*, American National Standards Institute Accredited Standards Committee X12, 1985, 1987. [July 1987]

Johnson, Mark L., "Electronic Reordering," *Home Center*, February 1987, pp. 59-63.

Jones, Russell, "An Esperanto for Data Processors," *Computing*, London, England, May 15, 1986.

Kastiel, Diane Lynn, "Companies Increase Reliance on 'Paperless' Transactions," *Crain's Detroit Business*, July 21, 1986.

------. "'Paperless' Transactions in Hot Demand," *Business Marketing, July 1986.*

Kemezis, Paul, "EDI Being Translated Into Money by More Corporations," *Data Communications*, October 1987, pp. 64, 66, 68.

Kerrigan, Douglas, CFC, "A Paperless Office By the 1990s?" *Business Forms & Systems*, August 1987, pp. 40 f.

Lallande, Ann, "Electronic Networks Raze the Paper Mountain, May Even Save the Firm," *International Management*, March 1986, pp. 51-57.

La Londe, Bernard J., and Emmelhainz, Margaret A., "Electronic Purchase Order Interchange," *Journal of Purchasing and Materials Management*, Fall 1985.

LaPrairie, Paul, "Do You Know What You Are Missing?" *Materials Management and Distribution*, February 1987, pp. 17-18.

Luber, Alan, "Paperwork? No, Communication," *PurchasingWorld*, November 1987, p. 88.

Maclure, Clare, "EDI Shows Need for Law Reform," *Computer Weekly*, London. England, October 29, 1987.

Metz, Peter J., and Norris, Richard C., "Treading A New Logistics Path," *Handling & Shipping Management Presidential Issue*, 1986-1987, pp. 56-64.

Milbrandt, Ben, *Electronic Data Interchange (EDI): Making Business More Efficient*, EDI in Business, Willowbrook, IL, 1987.

Mitchell, Mary, "Strategic Tool," *Communication Solutions*, Compuserve, Columbus, Ohio, Fall 1987.

Mitchell, Russell and Heywood, Peter J., "Detroit Tries to Level a Mountain of Paperwork," *Business Week*, August 26, 1985,

Monczka, Robert M., and Carter, Joseph R., *EDI: Managing Implementation in Purchasing*, National Association of Purchasing Management, 1987.

Norris, Richard C., *Business Data Interchange*, Auerbach Publishers Inc., 1984.

------. *Electronic Data Interchange for the Grocery Industry: Feasibility Report*, Arthur D. Little, April 1980.

"Plugged-in Purchasing [Electronic Data Exchange]," *Canadian Business Journal*, August 1987.

Pollack, Andrew, "Technology: Doing Business by Computer," *New York Times*, July 10, 1986. [Also reported in *Miami News*, July 12, 1986, and *Tuscaloosa News*, August 3, 1986.]

Powell, Gil, "Electronic Ordering Has Arrived," *Office Products Dealer*, May 1985, pp. 64-68.

"Pursuing Closer Relations," *Business Computer Systems*, June 1986, p. 23.

A Review of Electronic Data Interchange (EDI) Developments in Europe, Euromatica S.A., Brussels, February 1988.

Roebuck, Bill, "EDI: What's Happening in Canada," *Materials Management and Distribution*, August 1985, pp. 30-31.

"Rubac's Universal Coding Explained," *Computerworld*, September 28, 1987.

"SA Needs to Look at Mail Box of EDI," *Computing S.A.*, October 26, 1987.

Safran, Gerson, "Electronic Data Interchange," *Jobber News*, Don Mills, Ontario, May 1987.

Sandberg-Diment, Erik, "The Invoice Is in the Ether," *The New York Times*, March 22, 1987.

Schatz, Willie, "On the Edge," *Datamation*, April 15, 1986, pp. 59-64.

Schindler, Paul E., "Easing Into the Electronic Invoice," *InformationWEEK*, June 2, 1986, p. 25.

------. "EDI Acceptance Snowballing," *InformationWEEK*, July 13, 1987, p. 18.

------. "Electronic Data Interchange: Its Time Has Come," *InformationWEEK*, May 18, 1987, p. 49.

Schindler, Paul E. Jr.; Hoffman, Susan S.; Layne, Richard; Maynard, Chris, "EDI Is Coming At You," *InformationWEEK*, October 5, 1987, pp. 20-21, 25-27.

Seideman, Tony, "Business Hears Warning to Automate," *The Journal of Commerce, December 4, 1987.*

------. "Electronic Data Interchange Alters the Way the World Does Business," *The Journal of Commerce*, December 2, 1987.

"Seizing the Initiative on Comms," *Computerworld Australia*, June 5, 1987.

Shaw, Jack, "Electric Business Data Interchange, A New Strategy for Transacting Business," *MSA Update*, March/April 1985, p. 16-17.

------. "EBDI: Cash Managers Forge Strategic Role in Electronic Era," *Cashflow*, October 1985.

------. "Electronic Business Data Interchange, Helps Improve Customer Service, Inventories, Cash Flow, and Working Capital," *MSA Update*, March/April 1985, p. 19.

Shwartz, Elizabeth, "Bridging Business's Abyss," *Office Management & Automation*, January 1987, pp. 17-19.

Silber, Sigmund, "A Case for Electronic Document Interchange," *Infosystems*, January 1987, p. 58.

Skiko, Edward J., "Skiko Delivers Profound Keynote Address at TDCC Forum," *Spectrum*, General Electric Information Services Company, Rockville, MD, February 1986.

Steinberg, Don, "Electronic Data Interchange Use Moves from the Few to the Many," *PC Week*, December 15, 1987.

Stix, Gary, "EDI: Not Just Do-It-Yourself," *Computer Decisions*, March 1987, pp. 20, 24.

------. "Ending the Supplier Paper Chase" (EDI), *Computer Decisions*, July 30, 1985, pp. 66-72.

Sutton, Howard, "Cost-Saving, Market-Building Alternatives to Expanding the Sales Staff," *Boardroom Reports*, April 1, 1987.

"Take A Byte Out of Order Delays," *Flooring*, December 1987, pp. 34-35.

Taylor, Patricia, "EDI Setting Standard for Future," *Computerworld*, December 14, 1987.

Thompson, Kevin D., "Hooking Up Electronically," *The Journal of Commerce, December 12, 1986.*

Vizachero, Rick, "ANSI Group Looks Into Electronic Data Interchange," *Government Computer News*, November 21, 1986, p. 12.

Wallace, Bob, "EDI Gives Competitive Edge," *Network World*, June 8, 1987, pp. 1 f. [3 part series]

What Is EDI?, Electronic Data Interchange Council of Canada, Etobicoke, Ontario, January 2, 1986.

Yee, Theresa, and Payne, Robert A., *The EDI Glossary*, EDI, spread the word! [Also published in *The Journal of Commerce*, December 2, 1987 and in *The EDI Yellow Pages Directory*, February 1988.]

Air

"Air Cargo EDI Task Force Updates Invoice Standard," *Traffic World*, May 4, 1987.

Airborne Express Wants to Stop Sending You Invoices, Airborne Express, Seattle, WA, 1986.

Ettorre, John J., "Customers Deemed Trophies of Hunt," *Handling & Shipping Management*, June 1987, pp. 20-22.

Moses, Jim, "EDI Making Inroads in Air Cargo Industry," *The Journal of Commerce*, December 2, 1987.

Seideman, Tony, "Data System Takes Wing In Air Cargo Industry," *The Journal of Commerce*, November 16, 1987.

------. "Federal Express Customers Use Courier's Own System," *The Journal of Commerce*, December 24, 1987.

"Slow-moving Documents Falling Behind Freight In Air Cargo Industry," *Traffic World*, June 22, 1987.

Apparel and Textiles Industries

Abend, Jules, "Tracking UPC Growth," *Stores*, September 1987, pp. 52 ff.

------. "UPC + QR = JIT Inventory Replenishment," *Stores*, May 1987.

"At A Moment's Notice," *Travelware*, November 1987.

Axelrad, Marge, "Retailers Enter Electronic Age," *Home Textiles Today*, March 16, 1987, pp. 1, 43. [VICS]

Baker, Rob, "Haggar Data Plan Streamlines Orders," *Women's Wear Daily*, January 13, 1987. [Similar articles appeared in *Dallas/Fort Worth Business Journal*, January 26, 1987; *Textile World*, February

1987; *Apparel Industry Magazine*, March 1987; *Bobbin Magazine*, April 1987.]

------. "The Jeans War Goes Electronic," *Women's Wear Daily*, November 1986, pp. 16 ff.

------. "UPC Wins Top Endorsement," *Women's Wear Daily*, June 26, 1986.

"A Balanced Corporate Strategy for Responding to the Direct Import Challenge," *Summerour & Associates Management Letter*, January 1986.

Blueweiss, Herbert, "QR...Bringing Order Out of Chaos," *Daily News Record*, September 22, 1987.

Bozman, Jean S., "Retailers Shop for EdI Norm at Conference," *Computerworld*, October 12, 1987.

Browne, John M., "Telecommunications Merge with Computer Technologies," *Bobbin Magazine*, November 1986, pp. 127, 128 ff.

"Chains Tighten Inventory with Quick Response Vendor Links," *Discount Stores News*, May 11, 1987.

Chavie, Rick, "Quick Response Helps Retailers Achieve Competitive Advantage," *Discount Store News*, January 4, 1988, p. 57.

Clune, Ray, "Much Work Seen Before EDI Systems Fully Link Mills to Apparel Makers," *Daily News Record*, March 23, 1987.

------. "NAHM Seminar Pushes Just-In-Time and Quick-Response Programs," *Daily News Record*, November 16, 1987.

Colgate, Anne Imperato, "Seminole On the Path of Quick Response," *Bobbin Magazine*, January 1988, p. 56.

"Computerized Information Exchange Aid to Retailers," *Mass Market Retailers*, November 16, 1987.

Crafted With Pride Update, Crafted With Pride In USA Council, New York, NY, September 1986. [Videotape]

Davis, Janice, "Stability Returns to I.S. At The Bay," *Computing Canada, April 3, 1986.*

"Defining Quick Response," *Earnshaw's*, September 1986, pp. M26-M31.

Doler, Kathleen, "Companies Oversee Apparel-Industry Adoption of EDI," *PC Week*, August 18, 1987.

------. "U.S. Apparel Firms Choose EDI To Gain A Competitive Edge," *PC Week*, August 18, 1987.

Duff, Mike, "Nonwoven Fabrics Industry to Study Electronic Coding," *H F D Retailing Home Furnishings*, October 26, 1987.

"DuPont – Man Made Fibers," *Southern Textile News*, December 8, 1986, pp. 11, 22.

"EDI and QR: A Lot More Than Alphabet Soup," *Chain Store Age Executive*, January 1988.

Engel, Leslie, "USA: The Lure of Domesticity," *Earnshaw's*, November 1987, pp. 52-54.

Frazier, Robert M., "New Technology for Quick Response: How U.S. Apparel Manufacturers Can Capitalize on Their Proximity to the U.S. Market," *The KSA Perspective*, Kurt Salmon Associates, March 1986.

Gillease, Paul G., "The Next Step for Quick Response," *Bobbin Magazine, January 1988, pp. 48, 50.*

------. "Quick Response: On the Fast Track," *Bobbin Magazine*, January 1988, pp. 44 ff.

Glatzer, Hal, "Who Minds the Store? Probably a Computer," *San Francisco Examiner*, November 12, 1987.

Haber, Holly, "Bar-Code Standards Set at SAFLINC Seminar," *Women's Wear Daily*, December 3, 1987.

Hoffman, Susan S., "The Personal Fit: Levi Uses EDI to Link Up Better With Its Retailers," *InformationWEEK*, May 18, 1987.

"How to Profit from QR Partnerships," *Textile World*, February 1987, pp. 43-44, 46.

"In What Way Is the Textile Industry Contributing to Quick Response and EDI?" *Women's Wear Daily*, June 1987, p. 31.

Kaoli, Miles, "Hinerfeld: 'Quick Response Determines Industry Success,'" *Apparel World*, February 1986.

Kasten, Matthew, "EDI Touted as Vital Link to Just-In-Time in Textiles, Apparel," *Daily News Record*, November 10, 1986.

------. "Mills, Apparel Mfrs. Adopting Voluntary 'Language' Standard," *Daily News Record*, May 23, 1986.

------. "Links With Stores Stressed at ATMI," *Women's Wear Daily*, April 10, 1987.

Kiley, David, "At Levi Strauss, Computers Take Blues Out of Marketing," *Adweek's Marketing Week*, November 9, 1987, pp. 52, 54.

"KSA's Cole: Unity Can Seal Revenue Leak of $25 Billion," *Home Textiles Today*, April 6, 1987, p. 10.

Laughlin, Lee, "Few Bugs Seen Barring Industry EDI," *Daily News Record*, March 12, 1987, pp. 1, 15.

"Levi Strauss and Co.," *Apparel Industry Magazine*, December 1987, pp. 48, 50. [Similar articles appeared in *Network World*, December 21, 1987; *Bobbin Magazine*, January 1987.]

"The Link Age," *Women's Wear Daily*, December 10, 1987.

Lloyd, Brenda, "Mervyn's Learns It Has to Keep Pace In a Changing Marketplace," *Daily News Record*, November 13, 1987.

Markman, Michelle, "Quick Response Gains Ground in Retail Sector," *California Apparel News*, September 25, 1986.

Maycumber, S. Gray, "From Fiber to Shelf, 20/20 Sport Manages Its QR Pipeline," *Daily News Record*, October 7, 1987.

McCarthy, Dan; Sarkissian, Richard; Blumberg, William, "Chains, Vendors Forge New Links in Communications Systems," *Discount Store News*, October 12, 1987, pp. 164, 168.

McEwan, Mary E., "Sock it to Them," *Women's Wear Daily*, September 1987, pp. 29, 32.

"Milliken: Retailers Are Getting Behind QR," *Textile World*, October 1987, p. 32.

"Now It's the Suppliers' Turn to Fit the QR Mix," *Textile World*, February 1987, pp. 46, 50.

"NRMA Endorses UPC for Vendors," *Home Textiles Today*, August 18, 1986.

"NRMA Predicts Closer Collaboration Between Stores Trading Partners," *Retailer & Marketing News*, September 1987.

Orgel, David, "Arrow Shoots for '87 Launch of Data Interchange Program," *Daily News Record*, December 10, 1986, p. 8.

O'Sullivan, Rick, "EDI Breaks the Communication Barrier," *Women's Wear Daily*, June 25, 1987.

Palmieri, Jean E., "19 Firms Agree to Adopt Universal Product Coding," *Daily News Record*, June 26, 1986.

Perkinson, Gary F., "EDI: Another Competitive Edge for Retailers," *Discount Merchandiser*, October 1987.

"QR = New Partnership Between Retailer, Vendor," *Stores*, May 1987, p. 44.

"QR Pilot Programs: The Results," *Chain Store Age Executive*, January 1988, p. 90.

"QR Working at Penney, Wal-Mart," *Stores*, May 1987, p. 52.

"QR Works for J. C. Penney," *Apparel Industry Magazine*, May 1987, p. 90.

"Quick Response: How Far? How Fast?" *Women's Wear Daily*, September 1987, pp. 9 ff.

"Quick Response Implemented at Hoechst Celanese," *Young Fashions*, September 1987.

"Quick Response: the Industry Responds," *Body Fashions/Intimate Apparel*, September 1986.

"Rallying to Meet Retailers' Demand," *H F D Retailing Home Furnishings*, July 18, 1987.

"Retailers Reach for New Ways to Cut Costs, Survey Shows," *Intimate Fashion News*, December 6, 1987.

Ruben, Howard G., "Levi Strauss Putting Big Bucks Behind Its 'Levilink' System," *Daily News Record*, December 10, 1986.

Santora, Joyce E., "Riegel Textile Maps Out Modernization," *Bobbin Magazine*, January 1987, p. 75.

Segal, Glen, "Information Processing Executes Quick Response," *Bobbin Magazine*, November 1986, pp. 72-76.

Seideman, Tony, "Automation Rouses Retailers," *The Journal of Commerce*, January 15, 1988.

------. "K Mart Suppliers Get Word: Automate," *The Journal of Commerce*, December 16, 1987.

------. "Retail Sector Use of EDI Seen Affecting Distribution Industry," *The Journal of Commerce*, October 9, 1987.

Sharp, Christopher, "Christmas Caution On Quick Response," *Women's Wear Daily*, November 2, 1987.

------. "Retailers Lead Way to Quick Response," *Women's Wear Daily, September 8, 1987.*

Smarr, Susan L., "Du Pont Forum Touts the Power of Partnerships," *Bobbin Magazine*, November 1987, p. 152.

Specht, Diane, "USA: Preparing for the Future," *Earnshaw's*, November 1987, pp. 62-65.

Spevack, Rachel, "Full Commitment Needed to Make UPC Systems Go," *Daily News Record*, January 12, 1988.

------. "Lee Taking Three-Pronged Approach to Speedier Response," *Daily News Record*, December 10, 1986, p. 8.

------. "Thigpen Outlines Three Key Areas for Apparel Makers," *Daily News Record*, December 11, 1986.

"Study Predicts EDI Linkage To Be Retail Requirement," *Daily News Record*, November 4, 1987.

Sullivan, Mark, "DuPont Program Proposes an Itinerary for Survival," *Sportstyle*, October 6, 1986.

Tahmincioglu, Eve, "Some Major Retailers Take EDI Express Route," *Footwear News*, August 24, 1987.

Taylor, Jena Knobler, "Pillowtex Unveils Quick Response, Plan to Counter Delivery Problems," *H F D Retailing Home Furnishings, December 7, 1987, p. 28.*

Troy, Colleen, "Industry Moves to Establish Standards for Bar Coding," *H F D Retailing Home Furnishings*, June 1, 1987.

Van Fossan, R. Craig, "How Quick Is Your Response?...Why Should You Care?" *Apparel Merchandising*, April 1986, p. 8.

"Wal-Mart Computers Talk to Vendors," *Chain Store Age Exec.*, January 1985.

Wallace, Bob, "Garment Firms to Adopt EDI Code," *Network World*, August 17, 1987, pp. 2, 5.

Walzer, Emily, "Quick Response in View," *Sportstyle*, October 19, 1987.

White, Robert, "Quick Response: What Is It?" *Apparel Industry Magazine*, December 1985.

------. "The Electronic Mailbox: Cracking the Code," *Bobbin Magazine*, July 1986.

Automotive Industry

Annis, Ted, "JIT Via EDI," *Manufacturing Systems*, November 1986, pp. 62 f.

Ashyk, Loretta, "Auto Firm Suppliers Like Group's Helping Hand," *Crain's Cleveland Business*, January 19, 1987, p. 19.

"Auto Industry Hits Stride in Standards Setting," *PurchasingWorld*, May 1986.

"Auto Industry Steers Toward Implementing EDI Standards," *Computerworld*, February 1986.

"Automakers Agree on Standards for EDI," *Handling & Shipping Management*, October 1986.

Blackham, John, "Just in Time: The Implications for Distributors," *New Zealand Interface*, August 1986.

Callahan, J. M., "AIAG Pushes Computerized Communications" (Automotive Industry Action Group), *Automotive Industries*, September 1984, p. 94.

------. "EDI to Save Billions of Dollars" (Automotive Industry Action Group), *Automotive Industries*, April 1986.

"Caterpillar Connects with EDI," *PurchasingWorld*, August 1986.

Cribbs, Gillian, "General Motors Vote Lifts Istel's Edict," *Computer Weekly*, London, England, August 27, 1987.

"Cummins, Suppliers Hook Up With EDI," *PurchasingWorld*, January 1988, pp. 84 f.

"Data Exchange Assumes Key Role," *Materials Management and Distribution*, November 1986, pp. 14-16.

Donovan, John, "Auto Industry Enforces Computer Communications Standards," *Plant Engineering*, May 8, 1986.

"An Electronic Net for Auto Parts," *Business Week*, July 11, 1977. [MEMA/TRANSNET]

"Far Better in the Far East?" *Automotive News*, July 27, 1987.

"Ford Says EDI Saves Millions," *Software News*, January 1987. Greenstein, Irwin, "Caterpillar Erects Paperless Network," *MIS Week*, January 20, 1986.

Hoffman, Susan S., "Do Small and Midsized Firms Have A Choice?" *InformationWEEK*, May 18, 1987.

McCullough, Patricia, "EDI Magic: First You Need A Plan," *Heavy Duty Trucking*, December 1987, p. 94.

Seideman, Tony, "Automakers Moving to Common Data Standard," *The Journal of Commerce*, December 29, 1987.

------. "Carmakers Take Gentle Route to Applying New Technology," *The Journal of Commerce*, December 28, 1987.

------. "Ford Adopts National Standards," *The Journal of Commerce, January 6, 1988.*

Slofstra, Martin, "Auto Parts Suppliers Urged to Go Electronic 'Just in Time,'" *Computing Canada*, May 30, 1985, p. 4.

"Still A Long Way Down the Road," *Computer Weekly*, September 3, 1987.

"TRANSNET Booms in Electronic Age," *Heavy Duty Trucking*, November 1986, p. 4B.

Watson, Terry, "EDI 'First Development in Paper War,'" *Computerworld Australia*, December 18, 1987.

"Without Standards, Telecommunications Means More Work For Us" (General Motors), *Infosystems*, Fall 1985, p. 12.

Banking (Corporate Trade Payments)

"ACH: Has Its Time Arrived?" *ABA Banking Journal*, May 1987, pp. 70 ff.

Akerman, G. E., *Electronic Data Interchange for Financial Institutions, GEISCO Ltd. 1986. [Draft]*

"Automakers Are On the Road to Paperless Payments," *Pensions & Investment Age*, August 1986.

"Bank Frees Its ACH Pkg.," *MIS Week*, April 6, 1987.

"Bank, GE Begins Accelerated International Trade Payment," *Daily Commercial News & Shipping Guide*, June 24, 1986.

"BankSpeeds Payments By Eliminating Paperwork," *The Journal of Commerce*, June 17, 1986.

"Bank Zaps Paperwork With Its EBDI Program," *PurchasingWorld*, July 1986. [First National Bank of Chicago]

Benmergui-Perez, Marlene, "Banks Eye Interchange System for Corporate Trade Payments," *Financial Post*, September 13, 1987.

Betts, Mitch, "Banks Cash In on EDI," *Computerworld*, December 7, 1987.

------. "Banks Moving Toward EDI Services," *Computerworld*, August 10, 1987.

Burr, Barry B., "EDS' Electronic Payment System Uses GM's Banks," *Pensions & Investment Age*, May 4, 1987, pp. 15 f.

------. "GM to Save Millions in Payments," *Pensions & Investment Age*, October 13, 1986.

------. "Navistar Joins Electronic Pay Age," *Pensions & Investment Age*, April 6, 1987.

Business Communications: A Long Way From Pony Express to Electronic Delivery, The First National Bank of Chicago, May 1986.

Cayer, Shirley, "Does Just-In-Time Have a Place In a Bank?" *Purchasing*, May 21, 1987, pp. 56-58.

------. "First Chicago Homes In On EDI's Potentials," *Purchasing*, August 17, 1987, pp. 94-95, 99.

Diamond, Sam, "Data Interchange Standard Picks Up Steam," *Computers In Banking*, September 1987.

"EDI: Coping With the Business World's Blizzard of Paper," *Banking World*, England, September 1987.

"Electronic Payment Service Debuts," *MIS Week*, October 27, 1986. [Mellon Bank]

Engstrom, Theresa, "The New Age of Payments Systems," *Institutional Investor*, October 1987.

Ferguson, Daniel M. and Hill, Ned C., "EDI and Payments Terms; Negotiating a Positive-Sum Game," *Journal of Cash Management*, September/October 1987.

------. "EDI/EFT Survey Results," *Credit & Financial Management,* December 1986, pp. 35-38.

Ferris, Tom, "GM Readies Electronic Bill Paying," *American Banker*, October 1986.

Gage, Theodore Justin, "EDI: High-tech Boat Treasury Managers Should Not Miss," *Cashflow*, October 1987, p. 25.

Giaquinto, Philip M., "Electronic Banking Changes the Industry," *The Bankers Magazine*, Jan.-Feb. 1987, pp. 38-41.

"GM's Ambitious EDI Program," *ABA Banking Journal*, February 1987, p. 56.

"GM to Save Millions by Electronic Bill-Paying," *Automotive News*, December 1, 1986, pp. 1, 51.

"A Good Idea, But Who Should Pay?" *ABA Banking Journal*, July 1987.

Gordon, J., "Electronic Transfer - C&FM Interviews Daniel M. Ferguson & Ned C. Hill," *Credit & Financial Management*, December 1986, pp. 28-30, 32.

Guenther, Robert, "U.S. Treasury Pays Suppliers Electronically," *The Wall Street Journal*, August 24, 1987.

Hoffman, Susan S., "Banks Must Prepare for EDI," *InformationWEEK*, September 14, 1987.

Hyatt, Charles S., "The Progress Decade: ACH in Ohio," *The Ohio Banker*, September 1986, pp. 22, 24. *Introduction to ACH Corporate Payments*, NACHA, 1987.

Kantrow, Yvette D., "Banks Want Role in Corporate-Data Exchanges," *American Banker*, June 22, 1987, pp. 1 f.

Level, Leon J., "Meeting the Needs of Multinational Corporations," *Journal of Bank Research*, 1986, pp. 254-257.

Liss,Ronald E.,"The ANSI X12 Committee: A Status Report on Standards for Cash Cycle Management," *Journal of Cash Management, August/September 1982, pp. 39-48.*

Lovell, Bernard, "Technology You Can Bank On," *Distribution*, October 1986, pp. 24-26, 30.

Hoffman, Susan S., "Big Banks Vs. EDI?" *InformationWEEK*, July 13, 1987.

Ludlum, David A., "GM Opens Electronic System," *Computerworld*, January 5, 1987, p. 83, 88.

Maier, S., and Marks, L., "Electronic Corporate Trade Payments," *Journal of Cash Management*, September/October 1987.

"Major Focus of Credit Research Foundation: Electronic Business Data Interchange," *Computer Age EDP Weekly*, February 2, 1987.

Mongelluzzo, Bill, "Bank Electronics Speeds Letters of Credit," *The Journal of Commerce*, November 17, 1987.

Monhollon, J., and Summers, B., "The Role of the Federal Reserve in the Electronic Payments Evolution," *Journal of Cash Management*, May/June 1987.

Morrison, John J., "EBDI: The Standards Are Coming," *Cashflow*, May 1987, pp. 40, 44-46.

O'Heney, Sheila, "Meeting Tackles Tough Issues Concerning EDP," *Computers In Banking*, November 1987.

------. "Steam Ahead," *Computers In Banking*, August 1987, pp. 53-60.

"The Paper-Free Future of Trade," *International Correspondent Banker*, February 1986.

Patrikis, Ernest T., "Global EFT Guidelines: What They Can Mean to U.S. Banks," *Bank Administration*.

Paustian, Chuck, "Electronics Aid Cash Flow," *Pensions & Investment Age*, April 20, 1987.

------. "Railroads On Track With Debit Program," *Pensions & Investment Age*, June 1, 1987, pp. 33, 35.

Poisson, A., "ACH Electronic Payments," *Business Credit*, December 1987, pp. 27-31.

"Railroads Roll With ACH Payments," *ABA Banking Journal*, August 1987.

Roberts, Julie, and Shaw, Jack, "Electronic Bridge: Making the Switch to Paperless Transactions," *Business Credit*, December 1987, pp. 22-26.

Sheppard, Donald A., "Standards for Banking Communication Systems," *Computer*, November 1987.

Steinberg, Don, "Banks' Fate May Hinge Upon Ability to Provide EFT Links," *PC Week*, October 13, 1987.

------. "Link to GM's EFT Net Speeds Payment Processing at PPG," *PC Week*, October 6, 1987.

"A Step Toward a Paperless World," *ABA Banking Journal*, February 1987.

Stone, Bernell K., "Cash Cycle Management and the ANSI X12 Committee," *Journal of Cash Management*, August/September 1983, pp. 37-38.

White, G., "U.S. Treasury's 'Vendor Express' Is Key 1980's ACH Development," *Journal of Cash Management*, July/August 1987.

Zachary, James A., "Viewpoint: Financial Service Products in the 1990s," *Journal of Cash Management*, May/June 1987, pp. 28-30.

Business and Products

"ACS Brings Out EDI Software," *MIS Week*, May 18, 1987.

"ACS Joins Marketing Program," *Knitting Times*, November 1987.

"ACS Software Allows 3rd-Party Networks," *California Apparel News*, July 30, 1987.

"APL Lands Auto Contract With a Computer System," *Traffic World*, July 20, 1987. [American President Lines]

"Are You Ready for EDI?" *PurchasingWorld*, November 1986, p. 52. [Electronic Cash Management, now named EDI Strategies]

Babcock, Charles, "M&D Builds Onto Line," *Computerworld*, January 11, 1988.

Bairstow, Jeffrey, "EDI May Force E-Mail Standards," *PC Week*, October 20, 1987. [X.400]

Beer, Stan, "Telecom, ACI Strike EDI Deal," *Pacific Computer Weekly*, December 18, 1987.

Betts, Mitch, "EDI Apple of Pentagon, IBM, Fortune 500's Eyes," *Computerworld*, December 7, 1987, p. 4.

------. "GEISCO Service Aids Processing of Trade Documents," *Computerworld*, June 30, 1986.

Bonney, Joseph, "Starcom Narrows Database Service," *The Journal of Commerce*, February 5, 1987, pp. 14A, 22B.

Bozman, Jean S., "McDonnell Douglas Shifts Mainframe Gears," *Computerworld*, October 12, 1987.

Bradford, Laurie, "Swedish Software Group Joins GE Global Network; New EDI Service Planned," *Traffic World*, October 19, 1987.

Brown, Jim, "Software Turns S/36-, S/38-Type Files to EDI," *Network World*, May 11, 1987.

Calvo, Melissa, "Trade Data Put On-Line by Service," *Info World*, July 14, 1986.

Canna, Elizabeth, "Access APL Over Any Touch Tone," *American Shipper*, December 1987, p. 22.

"Caterpillar Now Licensed to Distribute Supply Tech System," *Michigan Industry*, November 1986.

"CDC Enhances EDI Services for Business Communications," *Computerworld*, January 5, 1987.

"Computers/Data Collection: 301. American Custom Software Inc.," *Bobbin Magazine*, November 1987.

Cortino, Juli, "Telenet to Offer EDI Service," *InformationWEEK*, July 27, 1987, p. 15.

Crockett, Barton, "IBM Sets Up Nationwide EDI-UPC Network," *InformationWEEK*, January 18, 1988, p. 17.

"Data View," *Computerworld*, June 22, 1987.

Dooley, Bill, "M&D in Geisco, Aion Accords to Shape, Vend EDI, Al Tech," *MIS Week*, January 11, 1988.

Dreyfuss, Joel, "Networking: Japan's Latest Computer Craze," *Fortune*, July 7, 1986, pp. 94-96.

Drizen, Ruth, "National Computer Net Debuts," *Apparel Industry Magazine*, September 1986, pp. 98 f. [Apparel Computer Systems]

"EDI: A $1.9 Billion Market By 1992," *Computer Age EDP Weekly*, June 22, 1987.

"E.D.I. Capability," *Apparel Industry*, August 1987. [Compu Soft Inc.]

"EDI Communications Growing in Europe," *Software News*, May 1987.

"EDI Customers Use Muscle to Forge INS/Istel Link, IBM Next," *IDB*, October 26, 1987.

"EDI Market Takes Off With A Bang," *Computer Age EDP Weekly*, April 20, 1987.

"EDI Market to Soar," *Interface*, October 1987.

"EDI Provider Creates Cost-Cutting Programs," *The Journal of Commerce*, October 6, 1987. [TranSettlements]

"EDI Services Enhanced by SP Transportation Co.," *Traffic World*, January 25, 1988, p. 48.

"EDI Software Links Carrier, Shipper Data," *Transport Topics*, February 23, 1987, p. 23.

"EDI Software Package Offered by Supply Tech," *Traffic World*, July 13, 1987.

"EDI System Built to Link Carriers With Small Shippers," *Transport Topics*, February 23, 1987, p. 19.

"EDI System for Small Shippers," *Heavy Duty Trucking*, April 1987. [P-I-E]

"EDI Tied Into Telenet: Fortune 500 Is Target Market for Services," *Business Software Review*, November 1987.

"EDI Use on Rise," *Communications News*, October 1987.

"Electronic Data Interchange Market Poised for Exponential Growth," *Telemarketing*, March 1986.

"Electronic Date Interchange Saves Time and Money," *Manufacturing Systems*, September 1987, p. 8.

"Electronic Order Entry," *Healthcare Computing*, August 1987.

"Electronic-to-Paper Conversion Service Available," *Do-It- Yourself Retailing*, April 1987.

"Facts On FAX and REDINET," *ID*, August 1987, pp. 38-41, 43.

"Forms Handling and Transmission," *What's New In Computing*, November 1987.

"GE and Transtema Offer Communications Support," *Florida Shipper*, November 9, 1987.

"GE Information Service Endorsed by Industry," *Canadian Printer and Publisher*, June 1986. [Also reported in *New England Printer & GCA Perspective*, May/June 1986.]

"GE Information, Transtema to Provide Communications for Shipping Companies," *Daily Commercial News & Shipping Guide*, November 2, 1987.

"GE Trade Express Pilot is Underway," *Brandon's Shipper & Forwarder*, October 7, 1985.

"GEISCO and ICL Form International Network Services Ltd and Swipe Financial Pilot Contract From IBM," *Telegram*, London, England, January 23, 1987, pp. 1-2.

"GEISCO Appoints First EDI Sales Agent,"*PurchasingWorld*, November 1986, p. 52.

"GEISCO Hits UK With Reformat Service," *Computer Weekly*, June 19, 1986.

"GEISCO Looks for EDI Link-Up With Nokia," *International Businessgram*, October 24, 1987.

"GEISCO Service to Exchange Companies' Data Electronically," *Computerworld*, December 23, 1985.

Goldstein, Michael, "EDI Network Use Grows," *The Journal of Commerce*, December 2, 1987.

------. "Software for EDI Versatile," *The Journal of Commerce*, December 2, 1987.

Green-Armytage, J., "EDI Groups Opt to Sail One Way," *Computer Weekly, London, England, December 11, 1986.*

Greenstein, Irwin, "GEISCO Offers Generic EDI On Its Network," *MIS Week*, January 20, 1986, p. 32.

------. "Wave of the Future: EDI Growth Balloons," *MIS Week*, January 20, 1986, p. 32.

"Growing Market for Electronic Document Interchange," *Information & Software Technology*, August 1987, p. 342.

Hall, Daniel, "UCC Is Now Administering Warehouse Data Standard," *Supermarket News*, December 7, 1987.

Harrington, L., "Joint Venture Promises One-Stop Shopping," *Traffic Management*, February 1987, p. 19.

Hayes, Dawn, "Why ICL & GEISCO Are Looking for Very Big Things From Their Network Venture," *Computergram International*, London, England, February 20, 1987, p. 2.

Helliwell, John, "Firms Forge Closer Ties via Electronic Data Interchange," *PC Week*, June 16, 1987, pp. C/1 ff.

"Hey Buffalo! Here's an EDI Network Just for You," *PurchasingWorld*, November 1986, p. 52. [IBC]

Heydt, Bruce, "More Than One Way to Pay a Bill," *Distribution*, March 1987, pp. 72 f.

Hill, Thomas, "Saving Time and Labor with Electronic Data Interchange," *PC Week*, August 4, 1987.

Hoffmann, R. D. R., "IBM Information Network: Looking to Connect 'Anything to Anything,'" *InformationWEEK*, December 22-29, 1986, pp. 20-25.

Hoffman, Susan S., "DEC Announcements Stress Integration Theme," *InformationWEEK*, September 21, 1987.

Horowitz, Rose A., and Porter, Janet, "Global EDI Services on Horizon," *The Journal of Commerce*, May 20, 1986.

Horwitt, Elisabeth, "EDI Formats Ease Information Exchange," *Computerworld*, May 4, 1987. [ACS]

------. "Telenet Staking Claim to EDI Market," *Computerworld*, July 27, 1987.

------. "Vendors Gear Up to Provide Document Interchange Options," *Computerworld*, December 8, 1986.

"The Hot Markets," *Government Data Systems*, February 1987.

"How to Select the Right Computer System," *Modern Bulk Transporter, November 1986, p. 120 f.*

"IBM: EDI + Information Network = Inter-User Link," *Telecommunications Alert*, September 1987.

"ICL and EDI," *New Zealand Interface*, August 1986.

"INS Upsets Car Giants by Trying to Change Gear," *Computing*, London, England, April 23, 1987.

"Integration Next Step for Computer and Supplier Firms," *Knitting Times*, November 1987, pp. 46, 48, 50.

Jackson, Kelly, "Japanese Firm Will Sell GEISCO Services in U.S.," *MIS Week*, August 10, 1987, p. 18.

Jacobs, Jon, "'ACROSS'Computer System Speeds Clearance Time," *International Trade & Transport*, March 1987, p. B-38.

------. "GEISCO's 'Trade-Express' Breaks New Groundin Document Automation," *Brandon's Shipper & Forwarder*, February 10, 1986.

Korzeniowski, Paul, "Users Detail Net Plans," *Network World*, May 18, 1987, pp. 2, 48.

Kutler, Jeffrey, "Electronic Data Interchange Market Finally Rolls Out," *American Banker*, April 29, 1987.

LiCalzi, Pamela, "CompuServe Plans to Offer EDI," *Communications Week*, January 11, 1988.

------. "IBM Brings Information Network Into VAN Limelight," *Communications Week*, September 7, 1987.

------. "Telenet Joins EDI Fray With Ordernet Deal," *Computer Systems News*, August 10, 1987.

------. "Telenet Signs Second Data Interchange Pact," *Computer Systems News*, October 26, 1987.

------. "Telenet Teams With Ordernet for EDI Transmissions," *Communications Week*, August 3, 1987.

------. "Western Union Debuts EasyLink Upgrades," *Computer Systems News*, October 19, 1987, p. 56.

Little, Trevor, "Apparelnet Apparel Computer System," *America's Textiles*, December 1986, p. 72.

Mannis, Larry, "Extending the Reach Toward CIM," *Manufacturing Systems*, November 1986, pp. 32 ff.

"Market for EDI Will Double This Year, Study Predicts," *Transport Topics*, April 27, 1987.

"Marketers Exploring New Channels of Distribution," *Adweek's Marketing Week*, November 24, 1986.

McCune, Jenny, "Electronic Document Market Bursting," *Computer Systems News*, April 20, 1987.

McGee, Marianne Kolbasuk, "McCormack & Dodge Signs Tech Deals," *Computer Systems News*, January 11, 1988.

Miles, J.B., "EasyLink to Ease Transfer of Electronic Messages," *Government Computer News*, November 10, 1987.

------. "EDI, E-Mail Destined to Share Desktop," *Government Computer News*, September 25, 1987.

Moran, Nuala, "Duo Aims to Drive Vans Round the Globe," *Computer Weekly*, January 22, 1987.

------. "Tate Spurns EDI Network Scheme," *Computer Weekly*, London, England, April 2, 1987.

"Motor Firms Set Up Direct Line," *Systems International*, October 1987.

"MSA, GEISCO Deal Increases EDI Software," *The Journal of Commerce,* December 8, 1987.

"MSA, GEISCO Undertake Joint Marketing Deal," *Computer Systems News*, January 12, 1987.

"MSA Signs Marketing Accord for TranSettlements Package," *Computer Systems News*, December 8, 1986.

"MSA Teams Up With GEISCO for EDI," *EMMS*, February 16, 1987, pp. 12-13.

"New Study: EDI Transactions, to 1990-2000," *Stores*, May 1987. p. 48.

North, Mark, "EDI at the Leading 'Edge,'" *Cargo Systems*, August 1987, p. 53.

"Paperless Banking Comes of Age," *Bankers Monthly*, December 1987.

"Paperless Payables," *Business Software Review*, August 1986, pp. 16-17.

Perry, Adrienne, "Field Shortens In EDI Stakes," *Pacific Computer Weekly,* October 16, 1987.

Porter, Janet, "New Software to Aid Trade," *The Journal of Commerce*, July 15, 1987. [SITPRO]

"REDINET--A Year of Progress," *Industrial Distribution*, August 1986.

"REDINET Endorsed by Distributor Associations," *Industrial Distribution*, November 1985, p. 41.

Reich, Caroline, "Users Keen on EDI, Look for More Applications," *PurchasingWorld*, November 1986, pp. 50-51. [Sterling Software]

Rimkus, Algis, "EDI Seeks Wider Role in Business," *Canadian Data Systems*, Toronto, Ontario, April 1987, pp. 61, 63.

Russo, Kathy, "Apparel Adds EDI Software for ANSI X.12," *Computer Systems News*, May 11, 1987.

"S/36/38 EDI Software," *Systems/3X World*, December 1987.

"S/3X Gains EDI Entree," *MIS Week*, December 7, 1987.

Sandberg-Diment, Erik, "Data Interchange Gets a Test Spin," *The New York Times*, March 29, 1987. [APL]

Sauers, Janine, "Linkage Furthered Through EDI Feature," *Bobbin Magazine*, February 1987, p. 30.

Seideman, Tony, "Abundance of Networks Confusing and Costly," *The Journal of Commerce*, December 18, 1987.

------. "Electronic Data Interchange Poised for Sharp Growth," *The Journal of Commerce*, October 8, 1987.

------. "GE Unit to Market New ACS Software," *The Journal of Commerce*, September 4, 1987.

------. "IBM, GE Information Offer New Technology," *The Journal of Commerce,* January 13, 1988.

-------. "McDonnell Douglas Promotion Masks EDI Costs, Suppliers Say," *The Journal of Commerce*, December 4, 1987.

------. "What Do the People...Think Will Happen...in 1988?" *The Journal of Commerce*, January 7, 1988.

Shorrock, Tim, "Starcom Ends Tariff Retrieval Service," *International Trade & Transport*, March 1987, p. 23.

Slofstra, Martin, "EDI Tidal Wave Yet to Come," *Computing Canada*, June 25, 1987.

"So You Want to Do Business With the Big Three?" *PurchasingWorld*, November 1986, p. 52. [ACS/Systore]

"Software Package Allows Industry-Wide Fund Transfers," *Commercial West*, April 4, 1987, p. 33. [Supply Tech]

Spiegelman, Lisa L., "Three Products Enable Electronic Data Interchange," *Infoworld*, January 12, 1987.

"The Spotlight Is On At Yankee Group," *Business Electronics Dealer*, May 1987, p. 58.

"SP's Liberator: A Rail Locator," *Purchasing*, January 15, 1987, p. 37.

Stix, Gary, "A New Player In the EDI Game," *Computer & Communications*, August 1987. [Ameritech]

"SUPERTRACS Helps Ore-Ida Move the Spuds," *Software Times*, Summer 1987.

Taff, Anita, "GE Service Eases EDI System Set-up," *MIS Week*.

"Technology Supplier Going Out of Business," *The Journal of Commerce*, January 15, 1988. [Crowntek]

"Telecom Deal Over EDI," *Computerworld Australia*, September 18, 1987.

"Telecom, GEISCO's INS Ask Vanguard to Fund Study on EDIFact-To-X400," *Computergram International*, October 30, 1987.

"Telecom Offers Document Exchange Service," *Canadian Data Systems*, October 1986.

"Telenet Enters EDI Ring," *Systems 3X World*, October 1987.

"Telenet Offers Ordernet Business Transaction Service," *Telecommunications Alert*, August 1987.

"Telenet, Sterling In Pact," *Computer Systems News*, August 3, 1987.

"Telenet Taps Software Firms for EDI Catch-Up," *Telecommunications Alert*, November 1987.

"Telenet To Market TranSlate Software," *Modern Bulk Transporter*, December 1987. [Also appeared in *Refrigerated Transporter*, December 1987.]

"TFL's Computer Service To Give Shippers Access to Reports," *World Wide Shipping*, June 1985.

Thompson, Don, "Hard Talk," *Executive Report*, June 1987, pp. 49 f. [Can/Am Tech]

Thompson, Kevin D., "GEISCO Computer System Facilitates Trade Data Transfer," *The Journal of Commerce*, June 18, 1986. [Also reported in *Payment Systems Newsletter*.]

------. "P-I-E Computerizes Bill of Lading," *The Journal of Commerce*, November 28, 1986.

------. "Ships Data System Plying Way to US," *The Journal of Commerce,* September 11, 1986.

------. "Upsurge In Market for EDI Foreseen," *The Journal of Commerce*, April 16, 1987.

------. "Young Firm Benefits from Shipper Drive for EDI," *The Journal of Commerce,* October 20, 1986. [APL Group]

"Translate EDI Software Now Marketed by Telenet," *Traffic World*, November 2, 1987.

Unsworth, Edwin, "GEISCO, ICL Form Company," *The Journal of Commerce*, January 15, 1987.

"Videotex," *Computer Marketing Newsletter*, October 1987.

Vizachero, Rick, "EDI Market Looking Good," *Government Computer News*, October 23, 1987.

Wallace, Bob, "GEISCO Will Sell ASC Ware," *Network World*, August 31, 1987.

------. "IBM Entices EDI Users to Information Network," *Network World*, August 17, 1987.

Watson, Lloyd, "Adaptable Software--From Apparel to Airplanes," *San Francisco Chronicle*, April 27, 1987.

Watson, Neil, "EDI Software Now Supports 7 Services," *Communications Week*, December 14, 1987, p. 24. [ACS Network Systems]

Weart, Wally, "'Vans' Hinge on Your Every Word," *Distribution*, October 1986, pp. 108, 110.

Werff, Jan, "Electronic Interchange Usage Gaining Acceptance," *Cincinnati Business Courier*, November 23, 1987.

"What's Ahead for Fax?" *Canadian Data Systems*, August 1987.

Wheatman, Victor S., "Competitive Directions in Electronic Data Interchange," *Business Communications Review*, July-August 1987, pp. 36-40.

"Winged Foothold for Mercury," *Infomatics*, August 1986. [ICL]
"Wright EDI," *Computerworld*, September 21, 1987.

"Wright Has EDI Package for Minis and Micros," *InformationWEEK*, June 8, 1987.

Zane, Connie, "Transportation Speeds Up With Data Communications Software," *Telemarketing*, June 1986. [Sterling Software]

Chemical Industry

"Chemical Industry Plunges Into EDI," *Materials Management and Distribution*, December 1987.

"Chemical Shipments Data to Speed Up," *Chemical & Engineering News*, September 28, 1987.

"Data Handling To Go Electronic," *Manufacturing Chemist*, London, England, May 1987.

"EDI Breakthrough In European Market," *Spectrum*, GE Information Services, January 1988, p. 11.

Freedman, David H., "IS Outsiders," *Infosystems*, April 1987.

Introducing ... The Hoechst Electronic Materials Acquisition Network, American Hoechst Corporation, Somerville, NJ, November 25, 1985.

"Is The End of the Paper Trail In Sight?" *Chemical Business*, July 1987, p. 7.

Jacobs, Jon, "DuPont Readies Overseas EDI Network," *International Trade & Transport*, March 1987, pp. 27, 41.

Paustian, Chuck, "6 Chemical Companies Try Trade Program," *Pensions & Investment Age*, May 18, 1987, pp. 30-31.

Unsworth, Edwin, "Europe Testing EDI Network," *The Journal of Commerce*, October 13, 1987.

"Where the Action Is Now," *Chemical Week*, April 22, 1987.

Drugs

"Behrens Inc. Shows that Regional Strategy Works for Independents," *Wholesale Drugs Magazine*, June/July 1986.

Cardinale, Val, "EDI Offers New Bottom-Line Hopes to Businesses," *Drug Topics*, January 19, 1987, pp. 40, 45.

"Drug Wholesalers Sharpen Tools," *American Druggist*, November 1987.

Fillon, Michael, "EDI Now In Corner Drugstore," *InformationWEEK*, October 26, 1987.

Hoffman, Susan S., "Conference Spreads the Gospel of EDI," *InformationWEEK*, June 22, 1987.

The Meaning, Impact and Implementation of Electronic Data Interchange (EDI) in the Drug Distribution Industry, National Wholesale Druggists Association, 1985.

"NWDA Task Force on Electronic Data Interchange Holds First Meeting," *NWDA Executive Newsletter*, March 3, 1986, p. 1.

"NWDA's Pioneering Work in EDI Proves Its Worth for a Decade," *Wholesale Drugs*, December 1986/January 1987, pp. 18, 20.

Rosendahl, Iris, "Electronic Shopping--A Danger to Drugstores?" *Drug Topics*, December 14, 1987, p. 94.

Siecker, Bruce R., Ph.D., "Managing Information is Prime Challenge for American Business, *Wholesale Drugs*, August/September 1986, pp. 12, 13, 15.

EDI Yellow Pages

"Data Bases and Directories: Reach Out and Find Something," *New England Purchaser*, August 1987.

"Directory of EDI Services," *Traffic Management*, November 1987.

"EDI Bibliography Offered," *Traffic World*, August 24, 1987.

"EDI Directory Locates Customers," *Industrial Distribution*, June 1987.

"EDI Directory Provides Resources," *Apparel Industry Magazine*, April 1987.

"EDI Directory Tells Who's Using It," *PurchasingWorld*, June 1987.

"EDI Having Impact on Other U. S. Sectors," *Materials Management and Distribution*, May 1987.

"EDI Yellow Pages," *Geyer's Office Dealer*, June 1987.

"EDI Yellow Pages," *Ohio Banker*, January 1987.

"EDI Yellow Pages," *Electronic Shipping News*, January 1987. [Also reported in *International Trade & Transport.*]

"EDI: 'Yellow Pages,'" *Software News*, May 1987.

"The EDI Yellow Pages Inaugural Edition," *Apparel Industry*, November 1987.

"The EDI Yellow Pages Inaugural Edition, a resource...," *Software News*, December 1987.

"The EDI Yellow Pages is a new resource . . . ," *Business Credit*, December 1987.

"EDI Yellow Pages Now Being Offered," *Transport Topics*, January 18, 1988.

"EDI Yellow Pages Out Soon," *Traffic World*, March 23, 1987.

"An Excellent Source Guide...," *Distribution*, October 1987.

"Expanded Directory Scheduled for Print," *Transportation & Distribution*, December 1987.

"The Inaugural Edition of the EDI Yellow Pages Directory," *NITL Notice*, August 14, 1987.

"Information. Electronic Data Interchange," *Bobbin Magazine*, November 1987.

"Let Your Computer Do the Walking," *PurchasingWorld*, January 1988.

Sarkissian, Richard, "Wholesalers Are Coming of Age In Electronic Data Interchange," *United States Tobacco and Candy Journal*, August 24-September 14, 1987, pp. 24, 27.

Seideman, Tony, "Phone Book Covers EDI Network Users," *The Journal of Commerce*, August 31, 1987.

"Shipper Fingers Do Walking Through EDI Yellow Pages," *Materials Management and Distribution*, October 1987, p. 33.

"Two EDI Directories Now Available," *Business Credit*, December 1987, p. 26.

"Who's Who in EDI," *PurchasingWorld*, May 1987.

"Yellow Pages Directory Is Available," *Office Products Industry Report*, August 14, 1987.

"Yellow Pages for EDI in the Works," *Materials Management and Distribution*, February 1987.

Electrical

"EDX Fully On-Line, Marketing Committee Says," *The Electrical Distributor*, October 1987.

"EDX Moves Ahead With Two New Standards," *The Electrical Distributor*, Norwalk, CT, July 1986, pp. 35-38.

Government

"Defense Dept. Has Big Plans to Use Electronic Data Interchange Systems," *Transport Topics*, January 4, 1988, p. 31.

"DPSC Pushes Back Deadline for Product Codes," *Military Market*, December 1987.

"EDI: Pet Project for AAFES," *Military Market*, January 1987.

"EDI Proves Successful for DOD Transportation, Says Civilian Official," *Traffic World*, March 30, 1987, p. 66.

"EDI Use by DOD," *Computer Daily*, January 6, 1988.

Evans, Sandy, "Electronic Data Interchange: Moving Into the 21st Century," *Interservice*, Fall 1985, pp. 58-61.

Gibson, Stanley, "Magnetic Tape Attracts Banking Industry, IRS," *Computerworld*, June 8, 1987.

Goldstein, Michael, "Big Step Ahead For Military," *The Journal of Commerce,* December 7, 1987.

Gonze, Josh, "X.12 Gains Momentum With DOD Endorsement," *Network World*, December 14, 1987.

Hoffman, Susan S., "Federal Government Ready to Put Its Stamp On EDI," *InformationWEEK*, August 31, 1987, p. 16.

Jackson, Kelly, "DoD Opts for ANSI X12 Standard On Heels of Successful EDI Pilot," *Communications Week*, December 7, 1987.

Kantrow, Yvette, "Government Blazes Electronic Trail," *American Banker*, November 17, 1987, p. 31.

Pompili, Tony, "Defense Department Tests EDI System," *PC Week*, July 14, 1987.

Seideman, Tony, "Department of Defense: Bill Us Via Computer," *The Journal of Commerce*, December 24, 1987.

Wheatman, Victor S., "Business Returns Go High-Tech," *Computerworld*, May 11, 1987. [IRS]

Grocery Industry

Batt, Robert, "Network Pilots Could Save Grocers $500,000 Annually," *Computerworld*, April 30, 1984.

Blackburn, Marsh H., "UCS: A Giant Step Forward," *Progressive Grocer Executive Report, The Total System*, July 1985, pp. 52-54.

Boodman, D. M., and Norris, Richard C., "Progress and Distribution: Computer to Computer Ordering," *Handling & Shipping Management, Presidential Issue*, September 1985.

Calderwood, Lynne, "EDI Reduces Paperwork," *Canadian Grocer*, June 1987, pp. 46, 50 f.

"Canadian UCS Test Near End," *Supermarket News*, July 15, 1985, p. 23.

Cobb, Holly A., "Microcomputers Handling Long-Term UCS Needs," *Supermarket News*, September 29, 1986, p. 22

Cohn, Cathy, "Jewel Moving Steadily Into UCS," *Supermarket News*, September 17, 1984.

"Computer-to-Computer Era in Wings," *GPMC Newsletter*, December 1984.

"Computer-to-Computer Ordering Passes Test by Wholesale Grocers Association," *Marketing News*, November 9, 1984, p. 36.

Davis, D., "A General Marches to EDI's Beat," *Distribution*, August 1985, pp. 112-113. [General Foods]

"DEX/UCS: Acronym for Supplier/Retailer Data Interchange through Direct EXchange Methods with Data in the Uniform Communications Standard," *Milling & Baking News*, September 8, 1987.

"EDICC Seminar A Sellout," *GPMC Newsletter*, February 1985.

Gatty, Bob, "The Spreading Computer Revolution," *Nation's Business*, February 1983.

"General Foods Winning Warehouse Productivity Edge" (WINS), *Quick Frozen Foods*, June 1985, p. 26.

Goss, Eileen, "Food Industry Gets the Message from UCS," *Shelby Report of the Southeast*, October 1984.

Hall, Daniel, "UCS Can Dramatically Cut Order Lead Times," *Supermarket News*, December 14, 1987.

------. "Vendor Participation Is Needed for UCS Success," *Supermarket News*, December 1987.

Hampson, Robert D., "UCS Benefits for Brach," *The Manufacturing Confectioner*, September 1986, p. 34.

"In the Trade - Benefits of UCS Begin to Spread," *Progressive Grocer*, March 1986.

"Kroger, Topco UCS Through EDI With ORDERNET Agreements," *Food Industry Advisor*, March 1987.

Lydecker, Toni H., "Electronic Data Interchange: The Fast Paperless Way to Do Business," *ALA Journal*, Spring 1985, pp. 24-29.

"Major Advantages of UCS Seen Coming Into Focus as System Is Refined," *Frozen Food Age*, July 1986.

O'Neill, Robert E., "A Better Way To Do Business," *Progressive Grocer*, August 1984, pp. 71, 72, 74.

Ostroff, Jim, "Uniform Communications System Slated to Enter Full-Scale, Industry-Wide Use," *Supermarket News*, August 9, 1982.

Plumb, William D., "Electronic Data Interchange: Don't Lose in the Translation," *Progressive Grocer*, May 1986, pp. 14-15.

Sandler, Susan, "Calif. CG Cites Benefits of UCS," *Supermarket News*, March 11, 1985.

"Smaller Wholesalers Can Benefit From Uniform Communications Standards," *Grocers Spotlight*, July 5, 1986.

Tanner, Ronald, "Computerization: The Future is Now," *Progressive Grocer*, January 1987, pp. 40-42, 44.

"UCS: Perfecting Communications," *Food Broker Quarterly*, Summer 1986, pp. 29-32.

"UCS Takes a Giant Electronic Step," *Progressive Grocer*, May 1982, pp. 87-88.

"The UCS/DSD Task Force Report: What Impact Will It Have on Your DSD Program?" *Supermarket Business*, April 1987, pp. 19-20.

The UCS Video, Uniform Code Council, Inc., 1986. [Videotape]

"The Uniform Communications Standard," *Institutional Distribution*, April 1987, pp. 113-117.

U.S. Grocery Industry Uniform Communication Standard-Phase III Report on Pilot Implementation, Transportation Data Coordinating Committee, April 30, 1982.

Uniform Communication Standard (UCS) and the Food Broker, National Food Brokers Association.

"Will Grocers Go High Tech All the Way?" (UCS), *Advertising Age*, October 10, 1983, p. M50.

Zimmerman, Susan, "UCS Ordering Shaves Lead Time, Inventory," *Supermarket News*, April 13, 1987, p. 26.

------. "UCS Test of DSD Pairs Vendors, Distributors," *Supermarket News*, June 1, 1987. pp. 30, 32.

Hardlines

Plumb, William D., "Merits of Eagle System Explained," *National Home Center News*, November 30, 1987.

"Productivity Up With Computers," *Sporting Goods Dealer*, December 1987.

"Usage of Eagle Sets Standard in Industry," *National Home Center News*, December 14, 1987, p. 48.

Health Care Purchasing

"Abbott, 3M Officials Say Alliance to Focus on Logistics," *Hospital Purchasing News*, December 1987, pp. 1, 32-36.

"All-Vendor Ordering System to be Offered," *Hospital Purchasing News*, September 1987.

"And From the Folks Who Brought You Bar Coding . . . ," *Hospitals*, May 20, 1986.

Anthony, M., "The Next Step in Computerized Purchasing," *Hospital Materials Management News*, May-June 1985.

"Automated Ordering System Marketed to Major Group," *Hospital Purchasing News*, January 1988, pp. 1, 26.

"Baxter Wants a Cut ASAP," *S&MM*, September 1987.

"EDI May Topple Tower of Babel," *Hospital Purchasing News*, June 1987.

"Electronic Data Group Makes Recommendations," *Hospital Purchasing News*, July 1986.

"Electronic Networks Focus On Hospitals," *Hospital Purchasing News*, August 1987.

"Foxmeyer and Harris Join HIDA's COMM-NET," *MPS*, March 1987.

"From Producer to Patient: A New Study of Healthcare Product Distribution," *Health Industry Today*, November-December 1987, pp. 40-45.

"Healthcare Computer Standardization Efforts Continue," *Journal of Health Care Materials Management*, May-June 1986, p. 19.

"HIBCC Considers Data Transmission Standards," *Medical Products Sales*, June 1986.

"HIBCC to Coordinate Data Standardization Effort for Health Care Industry," *Bar Code News*, June 1986.

"HIDA Committee Makes Sense of Alphabet Soup," *Medical Products Sales*, January 1988.

Hoffman, Susan S., "The Humana Touch: A Dose of High-Tech," *InformationWEEK*, October 5, 1987, pp. 34 f.

Horwitt, Elisabeth, "Supply Firm Offers Access to Proprietary Purchasing Net," *Computerworld*, May 18, 1987.

Janis, Pamela R., "Prescription for Rising Healthcare Costs," *Healthcare Computing & Communications*, June 1987, p. 46.

Ludlum, David A., "Prescription for a New Service," *Computerworld*, June 8, 1987.

"Reducing Paperwork to Save Money is Goal of New Health Industry Task Force," *Journal of Health Care Materials Management*, Nov-Dec 1985.

"Standardized Electronic Data Interchange for the Health-Care Industry," *American Journal of Hospital Pharmacy*, November 1986, pp. 27-32.

Watts, Susan, "Health Battle End Is In Sight," *Computer Weekly*, London, England, June 11, 1987.

------. "NHS Worries Over the Right System," *Computer Weekly*, London, England, June 18, 1987.

Wilkinson, R., "Automated Ordering Standard on the Way," *Hospitals*, February 5, 1986, p. 68.

Implementation

ANSI X12 Implementation Guide, ANSI X12 Committee, September 9, 1986. [Draft]

Barrett, Colin, "EDIA: Complicated Path Toward Simple, Straight-Forward Idea," *Traffic World*, December 14, 1987, p. 63.

------. "Thoughts On Ways and Means of Electronic Data Interchange," *Traffic World*, December 28, 1987, p. 42.

Carley, Joseph, "Circumstances Dictate Choice," *InformationWEEK*, October 5, 1987, p. 32.

Carter, Joseph R.; Monczka, Robert M.; Clauson, Keith S.; Zelinski, Thomas P., "Education and Training for Successful EDI Implementation," *Journal of Purchasing & Materials Management*, Summer 1987.

EDINet(tm) Implementation Guide, McDonnell Douglas Electronic Data Interchange Systems Company, 1987.

EDI Workbook, Transportation Data Coordinating Committee, Washington, D. C., 1983.

Foster, David F., "EDI Translation Options," *InformationWEEK*, October 5, 1987, p. 47.

Hagen, Jane, and Sanderson, Tom, "Tips for Success With EDI," *Transport Topics*, February 23, 1987, p. 22.

Harding, Peter W., "How to Get Started in Quick Response," *Textile World*, February 1987, pp. 39-40, 43.

Heard, Thomas W., "Some Observations on Implementing Electronic Data Interchange," *Transport Topics*.

"How A Vendor-Support System Begins," *Bobbin Magazine*, January 1987. p. 60.

Humphreys, Doug, "EDI: Issues and Implementation," *Computing Canada*, April 2, 1987, pp. 14-15.

Implementing ACH Corporate Payments, NACHA, 1987.

Locke, James L., *The Roles of the Trade Association and Third Party Vendors in Electronic Data Interchange Implementation*, General Electric Information Services Company, Rockville, MD, December 13, 1983.

McDonald, Hal, "A Guideline for Getting Started With X-12 Electronic Business Data Interchange," *Utility Purchasing & Stores*, February 1986.

Pinkerton, Jeff, "It's What Is At the Other End of EDI That Counts," *PurchasingWorld*, May 1986, pp. 86-89.

Reich, Caroline, "How to Get Started in EDI," *PurchasingWorld*, June 1985, pp. 72-74.

Rimkus, Al, "Exploring the Other Side of EDI," *Computing Canada*, Willowdale, Ontario, December 29, 1986.

Robinson, Connie, "EDI: Improving the Rate of Data Exchange," *Metal Center News*, September 1987, pp. 51, 53, 55.

Seideman, Tony, "Installation Seen Easier Than Implementation," *The Journal of Commerce*, December 18, 1987.

Tinley, James Patrick, "The Time Is Now to Implement EDI," *InformationWEEK*, August 31, 1987, p. 48.

"What's Needed to Make EDI Work," *Purchasing*, June 26, 1986.

Wintrob, Suzanne, "Provigo Chief Cites EDI Inhibitors," *Computing Canada*, November 26, 1987.

Wintrode, Lee, "When Applying EDI, Plan Big, Start Small," *Transport Topics*, February 23, 1987, p. 22.

Industry Standards and Guidelines

Convention for the Electronic Transmission of Releases for Production Material, Automotive Industry Action Group (AIAG), May 1985. [Other volumes provide standards for other documents.]

EDI Conventions Applicable to CIDX Chemical Industry Applications, Transportation Data Coordinating Committee, March 1987.

EDI Conventions Applicable to TAMCS, Textile-Apparel Manufacturing Common Standard, Transportation Data Coordinating Committee, August 1987.

Electronic Data Interchange Implementation Guidelines, Automotive Industry Action Group, 1987.

Implementation Guidelines for Automotive Industry Action Group (AIAG), July 1987.

Metals Industry Implementation Guidelines, American Iron and Steel Institute, Washington, DC, 1986.

Specification EMBARC: Electronic Manifesting and Bar Coding of Paper Stock Shipments, Graphic Communications Association, 1985.

VICS Retail Industry Conventions & Implementation Guidelines for EDI, Voluntary Interindustry Communications Standards, 1987.

Inter-industry Standards

The Business Data Interchange Standards, American National Standards Institute Committee X12, 1983, 1984, 1986. 1987.

Computers in International Trade and Transport-Data Standards, Simplification of International Trade Procedures Board, London, England, 1978. [SITPRO]

Draft American National Standard-Electronic Business Data Interchange-Common U.S. Data Dictionary, X12B86-005, American National Standards Institute, 1986. [JEDI Dictionary]

EDI for Administration, Commerce & Trade (EDIFACT), 1987.

Trade Data Interchange Directory, United Nations Economic Commission for Europe, Geneva, Switzerland, 1981, 1983, 1984. [TDI]

United States Electronic Data Interchange (EDI) Standards, Transportation Data Coordinating Committee. [In addition to transportation standards, these standards include EDX, UCS, and WINS.]

International and Transportation - General

Barrett, Colin, "Computer Software for Transportation," *Traffic World*, January 26, 1987, pp. 51-53.

Bender, Paul S., "The International Dimension of Physical Distribution Management," *The Distribution Handbook*, ed. James F. Robeson and Robert G. House, The Free Press, 1985.

Borsellino, Matt, "Spreading the Gospel of EDI Around the World," *Materials Management and Distribution*, October 1987, pp. 32-33.

Calderwood, Lynne, "Customs' New Code Is Here!" *Materials Management and Distribution*, January 1988, pp. 30, 32.

"Can EDI Break Out From Underneath the Red Tape," *Computing*, London, England, February 26, 1987.

"Can We Talk? Computer-to-Computer, That Is?" *American Import Export Management*, February 1985, p. 34. [Name changed to *Global Trade Executive*, May 1985.]

Chapman, Stan, "Getting ANSI Over EDI," *Distribution*, September 1986.

"Chase Trade Programs Speed Transactions," *Global Trade Executive*, November 1987.

"Copacino, William C., "Logistics Strategy," *Traffic Management*, p. 31.

"Data Protocol Being 'Bulldozed Thorough,'" *The Australian*, May 1, 1987.

Drabble, Alan, "Exchange for Marts," *Computer Weekly*, London, England, September 24, 1987.

"EDI Progress," *Containerisation International*, February 1987.

"EDI Software Links Carrier, Shipper Data," *American Sailings*, March 2, 1987.

"Electronic Data Focus of Paris Conference," *The Journal of Commerce*, September 11, 1986.

"Enormous Savings Seen in Switch to EDI," *The Journal of Commerce*, September 15, 1986.

"Export Expeditors," *Business Computer Systems*, July 1986.

"FIATA World Congress Held," *Air Cargo World*, December 1987.

Freeman, Kirby V., "Electronic Interchange Aids Carriers," *The Journal of Commerce*, November 15, 1983.

"Global Meeting Opens On Computerized Data," *The Journal of Commerce*, June 29, 1987.

Guilbert, Edward A., "EDI Should Be Part of Your Business Plan TDCC Says, Join the Fleets That Are Going Electronic," *Transport Topics*.

Hart, Charles, "EDI Relatively Untried By Air Carriers," *Jet Cargo News*, December 1986, pp. 19-20.

Heydt, Bruce, "A Better Way to Pay," *Distribution*, March 1987, pp. 22, 24, 26.

------. "Telephone Tag, Aussie Style," *Distribution*, October 1987, pp. 104 f.

Hoffman, Susan S., "EDI Making Great Strides In Europe," *InformationWEEK*, November 2, 1987.

"In Sickness and In Health? [Electronic Data Interchange for the NHS]," *IT Focus*, November 1987.

"ITOFCA Consolidators Restructures Operations to Emphasize Time-Sensitive Shipping, Control," *Weekly Commercial News*, November 30, 1987.

Jacobs, Jon, "EDI, Facilitation Bring Challenges and Opportunities for World's Forwarders," *International Trade & Transport*, October 1987, pp. 43 ff.

Kallman, Ernie, "Electronic Billing: Paperless Billing," *Commercial Carrier Journal*, July 1983.

Kuzela, Lad, "Users Control Price/Service Elevator Ride," *Handling & Shipping Management*, June 1987, pp. 26-27.

Levine, Stephen I., "Global Economic Trends Spur Movement to Automate Logistics Management," *American Sailings*, January 1987, pp. 29, 30, 69.

Mann, John M., "Opportunities Through Electronic Data Interchange," *Florida Shipper*, October 19, 1987.

Maraschiello, Bill, "EDI: An End to the Paper Chase," *Handling & Shipping Management*, October 1985, pp. 48-52.

Mongelluzzo, Bill, "Customs Urges Brokers to Go Electronic," *The Journal of Commerce*, March 9, 1987.

Moran, Nuala, "UK Heads EDI World," *Computer Weekly*, October 22, 1987.

Moser, Vic, "Is Electronic Data Interchange in Your Future?" *Transportation Outlook*, September 1987.

"Paperless Trading Is Something to Declare," *Computing*, November 12, 1987, pp. 40 ff.

Porter, Janet, "UK Companies Seek EDI Edge," *The Journal of Commerce* (European Edition), November 23, 1987.

------. "UK Exporters Push Electronic Trading," *The Journal of Commerce*, November 9, 1987.

------. "UK Set to Pass US in Data Interchange," *The Journal of Commerce*, October 22, 1987.

------. "UK Shippers Push for Electronic Trading," *The Journal of Commerce*, October 7, 1987.

Reines, Maria, "We Have Met the Enemy and It is Paper; Conference Hails the Age of Automation," *Shipping Digest*, July 13, 1987.

Schwartz, Herbert, "UN Seeks Unified Documentation," *The Journal of Commerce*, June 29, 1987, pp. 12A f.

Seideman, Tony, "Global Shipping Invoices Help Break Communication Barriers," *The Journal of Commerce*, December 4, 1987.

------. "Management Awareness Held Vital for Success," *The Journal of Commerce, December 18, 1987.*

Solomon, Mark B., "Transport Warming Up to EDI Following a Chilly Interlude," *Traffic World*, December 14, 1987.

"A Special Summary and Forecast of Scientific Developments Affecting Business," *The Wall Street Journal*, Europe Edition, Brussels, Belgium, March 10, 1987.

Tausz, Andrew, "Computerized Rating Takes Off," *The Journal of Commerce*, December 3, 1987.

Thompson, Kevin D., "Data Systems Expected to Ease Import Process," *The Journal of Commerce*, February 4, 1987.

------. "EDI Expected to 'Byte' Into Courier Business," *The Journal of Commerce*, April 20, 1987.

------. "On-Line Systems Become Old Hat," *The Journal of Commerce*, December 30, 1986.

"UK Leads Europe In EDI Race," *Electronics Weekly*, December 16, 1987, pp. 19 f.

Wing, John F., "Technology Talking Electronic Language," *Handling & Shipping Management, Presidential Issue*, September 1985, pp. 68-74.

Legal Aspects

"NIT League Has Antitrust Guidelines on EDI," *Transport Topics*, January 4, 1988.

Manufacturing/Diversified Corporations

"Bearings Inc's Electronic Data Interchange for Speeding Up Orders," *Purchasing*, March 26, 1987, pp. 81 f.

"British Coal Opts for Electronic Buying," *Procurement Weekly*, August 6, 1987.

"Computer Links Contractor With Major Local Suppliers," *Electrical Contractor*, June 1986.

"Computers Touch Distribution's Heart," *Electronics Times*, London, England, October 9, 1986. [Motorola Europe]

Corporate Electronic Information and Payment Program Vendor Conference, First National Bank of Chicago, 1986.

Cottee, Joanne, and Green-Armytage, J., "Lloyds Tries IBM for Broker Link," *Computer Weekly*, September 4, 1986.

Drenning, Dave, "The Westinghouse Approach to Electronic Data Interchange," *Utility Purchasing and Stores*, December 1986, pp. 1-2 f.

"Electronic Data Interchange," *America's Textiles*, December 1986, p. 34. [J. P. Stevens]

Electronic Data Interchange, GE Aircraft Engine Business Group, 1987. [Videotape]

Electronic Data Interchange Guidelines to Vendor, RCA Corporation, October 1985.

"Electronic Data Interchange System Cuts Ordering Time from Days to Hours, Increases Accuracy for Fastener Company," *Fastener Technology*, April 1987, pp. 34-35. [Multifastener Spring Division Inc]

Farrell, Paul V., "RCA Moves to Paperless Purchasing With EDI," *PurchasingWorld*, April 1985, p. 39.

Graybar NET II, Graybar Electric Company, St. Louis, MO, 1985.

"Hoechst Celanese Hooks Up With EDI," *Apparel Industry Magazine*, August 1987.

Jacobson, Gary, "Texas Instruments Unleashes System's Potential for Speed," *The Dallas Morning News*, March 29, 1986.

Kavanagh, John, "Pact Boosts Data Interchange Hopes," *Computer Weekly*, November 26, 1987.

"Kodak Purchasing Launches EDI Program With Top Suppliers," *PurchasingWorld*, September 1985, p. 64.

Krepchin, Ira P., "Videotex System Reduces Inventory Levels," *Modern Materials Handling*, October 1986, pp. 79-81. [Shelby Supply Co.]

Lloyd, Brenda, "Tropical Garment Grabs Hold of Quick Response," *Daily News Record*, August 24, 1987.

Louzoun, Michelle, "Bechtel Builds On IS In Troubled Times," *InformationWEEK*, November 2, 1987, p. 36.

"Mayflower Transit Finds 'Perfect Balance' in Communications Network," *Traffic World*, July 20, 1987, p. 74.

Minner, Frank, "EDI, Computerized Order Entry Cut Paperwork," *Modern Bulk Transporter*, May 1987, pp. 92 f. [Matlack Inc]

"RCA Purchasing Handles 17,000 Suppliers, 400,000 P.O.S./Yr.," *Purchasing*, September 12, 1985, pp. 106A30-106A31.

Shea, Kelly, "Ups and Downs of Maverick's Role," *Computerworld*, April 13, 1987, p. 53.

Seideman, Tony, "Canadian Tire Corp. Supplier Reaps Benefits of Technology," *The Journal of Commerce*, January 13, 1988.

Thompson, Kevin D., "Marten Blames Loss On Poor EDI Efforts," *The Journal of Commerce*, March 26, 1987.

------. "Procter & Gamble Clears EDI Hurdle," *The Journal of Commerce,* December 11, 1986.

Yonda, Marge, "Data Transfer to Be Business Necessity," *Democrat & Chronicle*, Rochester, NY, November 30, 1987.

Metals Industry

"AISI Throws It Weight Behind ANSI X.12," *Metal Producing*, November 1987, p. 33.

Alter, Joy, "After Babel," *Metal Center News*, March 1986, pp. 48-54.

Burr, Barry B., "Bethlehem Goes to Data System," *Pensions & Investment Age*, June 15, 1987, pp. 13-14.

Collier, Andrew, "Some Do Business the Electronic Way," *AMM-Metals Distribution*, September 12, 1986.

Electronic Trading: Productivity Partnerships With Bethlehem EDI, Bethlehem Steel Corporation, 1987.

Nellis, Tom, "The PC Solution to EDI--Software is the Key," *Metal Stamping*, November 1986, pp. 22, 24, 26.

"Steel Industry Data System for Transport and Purchasing," *Pacific Shipper*, November 30, 1987.

Thompson, Donald, "Boiling a Technology Down to PCs," *Industry Week*, April 6, 1987, p. 59.

Werber, Marilyn, "Steel Eyes Electronic Communications," *American Metal Market*, November 12, 1987.

York, Wayne, "JIT--It Won't Fly Without EDI," *Metal Stamping*, October 1986.

Motor

"The ABCs of EDI," *Distribution*, March 1987.

Abruzzese, Leo, "Shipper Says Size No Barrier to Use of EDI," *The Journal of Commerce*, December 4, 1987.

Barrett, Colin, "Computer Software for Transportation," *Traffic World*, June 23, 1986.

Cassidy, William B., "For-Hire Fleets Go Electronic With EDI to Stay Competitive," *Fleet Owner*, January 1987, pp. 79-82.

Chancellor, Andrea, "Shippers' Demands Spur Growth In the Data Interchange Market," *The Journal of Commerce*, November 25, 1987.

Crump, Robert, "Electronic Data Interchange: Let Your Computers Do the Talking," *Heavy Duty Trucking*, March 1987, p. 124.

"Designing An Efficient EDI System," *Refrigerated Transporter*, September 1987.

"Drugs Seen As Barrier to Cargo Facilitation," *American Sailings*, October 1987.

"EDI Application Remains Strong Area of Interest, According to ATA Survey," *Traffic World*, August 24, 1987, p. 57.

"EDI Invoicing Cuts P&G Error 75%," *Traffic World*, December 14, 1987, p. 62.

"EDI Makes Electronic Communication a Reality," *Transportation Business*, September 1987.

"EDI Puts Buyers in Control," *PurchasingWorld*, March 1987, pp. 46-47.

"Electronic Data Interchange Skeptics," *Traffic World*, July 6, 1987.

"Electronic Data Interchange: Taming the Paper Tiger," *Traffic Management*, February 1986, pp. 44-45.

Erickson, Stanford, "Some Shippers Wary of EDI," *The Journal of Commerce*, April 23, 1987.

Foster, Thomas, "Federated Dept. Stores: A Motor Carrier's EDI System Helps a Retailer Automate Vendor Returns," *Distribution*, November 1987, p. 28.

Guilbert, Edward A., "TDCC Gives Progress Report on Carrier/Shipper EDI," *Transport Topics*, February 23, 1987, p. 23.

Habeck, Bill, "Shippers' Agents Gearing Up for Electronic Data Interchange," *Traffic World*, March 16, 1987, pp. 31-32.

Hagen, Jane, and Sanderson, Tom, "EDI Becoming More Important as Part of Service Package," *Transport Topics*, February 23, 1987, pp. 13, 22.

Harrington, Lisa H., "Shippers and Carriers Make the EDI Connection," *Traffic Management*, October 1987, pp. 41-44.

"Intermodal Cooperation," *Traffic World*, March 16, 1987, p. 2.

"KMart's KIS," *American Import/Export Management*, November 1982, p. 16.

Moses, Jim, "EDI Boon to Truck Firms," *The Journal of Commerce*, December 2, 1987.

Nelson, Paul, "EDI Is Ready for Reefer Fleets," *Refrigerated Transporter*, June 1987, pp. 44 f.

"'Once Only' Data Entry Offered by Multi Service," *Traffic World*, November 30, 1987.

"P-I-E Nationwide Executive Vice-President Tells ATA Meeting 'Days of Paperless Business' in Transportation Has [sic] Arrived," *Weekly Commercial News*, June 16, 1986.

Seideman, Tony, "Consolidated Hopes For Quick Payoff From Data System," *The Journal of Commerce*, September 1, 1987.

------. "Technology Alters Way EDI Is Used," *The Journal of Commerce*, October 24, 1987.

------. "Truckers Favor Data Interchange," *The Journal of Commerce*, August 19, 1987.

------. "Trucking Moves Closer to Paperwork Automation," *The Journal of Commerce*, October 27, 1987.

Solomon, Mark B., "Transport Warming Up to EDI Following A Chilly Interlude," *Traffic World*, December 14, 1987.

Sparkman, David L., "Computer Systems for Carriers Replace Paper Shuffle with Paperless Shuffle," *Transport Topics*, November 10, 1986.

Sullivan-Trainor, Michael, "Truckers Roll Past EDI Fog," *Computerworld*, April 13, 1987, pp. 47, 53, 55.

"Temple, Barker & Sloane Consultants Report Electronic Data Interchange Is Not A Panacea for Motor Carriers," *Weekly Commercial News*, April 6, 1987.

Thompson, Kevin D., "Air Cargo Revise Electronic Data Interchange Standards," *Weekly Bulletin Port of New Orleans*, February 9, 1987.

------. "Bill of Lading Systems Go Electronic," *The Journal of Commerce*, January 12, 1987.

------. "P-I-E's Shipmaster Attracts Interest," *The Journal of Commerce*, May 28, 1987.

------. "Shippers Go Inside Computer System," *The Journal of Commerce*, March 1987.

------. "Small Truck Firms Lose Out in EDI," *The Journal of Commerce*, January 13, 1987.

------. "Truck Firms Hope to End Paperwork," *The Journal of Commerce, May 21, 1986.*

"Trucking Execs Cite New Programs For EDI," *Stores*, May 1987.

"Victor Marsh, P-I-E Develop EDI System: Better Service Cited," *Traffic World*, April 21, 1986.

Newsletters Providing Substantial EDI Coverage

EDI Executive, EDI Executive Publications, Inc., Marietta, GA, November 1986 to present.

EDI News, Phillips Publishing, Inc., Potomac, Maryland, September 1987.

EDI Reporter, INPUT, Mountain View, CA, 1986 to present.

Electronic Shipping News, International Thomson Transport Press, 1985 to present.

Industry ActionLine, Automotive Industry Action Group, Southfield, Michigan, February 1982 to present.

Interchange, Electronic Data Interchange Council of Canada, Don Mills, Ontario.

Interchange: The Newsletter of SITPRO, Simplification of International Trade Procedures Board, London, 1986.

Simprofrance la gazette, Comite Francais Pour La Simplification Des Procedures Du Commerce International, Paris, France, No. 3/Hiver 87-88.

TDCC Reports, Transportation Data Coordinating Committee, Washington, D. C.

Trade Facilitation: Journal on Paperless Trade and Transport, Elsevier Science Publishers B.V., The Netherlands, Vol. 1, No. 1, 1987.

Trade-Flash: The Electronic Data Interchange News Briefs, Eurotech Forum, Brussels, Belgium, 1986.

UCS Bulletin, Uniform Code Council, Dayton, Ohio, 1984 to present.

Ocean

Bell, Stephen, "Factions Threaten Cargo System," *Computerworld*, October 19, 1987.

Carey, Ben, "Customs' Paperless Entry Test Scaled Back," *American Shipper*, August 1987, p. 52.

------. "VPA Computer Link to Customs," *American Shipper*, November 1986, p. 70.

"Conference Explores Electronic Data Use," *Marine Digest*, August 23, 1986.

Cooke, James Aaron, "Should Ports Provide the Electronic Links to Customs?" *Traffic Management*, May 1987, pp. 74-77.

Dupin, Chris, "Data Interchange Systems Vital to Maritime Industry," *The Journal of Commerce*, December 2, 1987.

------. "Sea-Land Weighs Mart Potential of Cargo Tracking System," *The Journal of Commerce*, January 4, 1988.

------. "Standardization Necessary, US Ports Claim," *The Journal of Commerce*, December 2, 1987.

"EDI Vital to Ship Industry," *The Journal of Commerce*, June 29, 1987, pp. 11A f.

"Electronic Data Interchange of Cargo Manifests," *Weekly Bulletin Port of New Orleans*, February 9, 1987.

Feldman, Joan M., "Be Prepared for the Electronic Dam to Burst," *Handling & Shipping Management*, October 1986, pp. 54-55 ff.

Goldstein, Michael, "ACES Program A Joint Effort," *The Journal of Commerce,* December 7, 1987.

Graziani, Joseph M., "Business Is Booming at Southern Pacific's ICTF," *American Sailings*, August 1987, pp. 39, 40, 62.

Horowitz, Rose A., "Customs Will Require Uniform Bill of Lading," *The Journal of Commerce*, September 18, 1987.

Illingworth, Montieth M., "Intermodal Global Village Close at Hand," *The Journal of Commerce*, June 22, 1987.

Jacobs, Jon, "'Across' Computer System Speeds Clearance Time," *Port of Baltimore*, 1987, p. B-38.

------. "New ACS Chief Discusses Automation In Customs and Industry," *Port of Baltimore*, March 1987, pp. 17, 42.

------. "New York Freight Forwarders: Shippers May Access Sea-Land's Computer," *Brandon's Shipper & Forwarder*, December 1, 1986, p. 20.

Johnson, Gregory S., "Sea-Land Puts EDI System to Work," *The Journal of Commerce*, November 25, 1986.

Joseph, Gloria, "Customs Pushes Automation," *The Journal of Commerce*, October 20, 1987.

------. "Tacoma to Use Customs System," *The Journal of Commerce*, March 26, 1987.

Knee, Richard, "APL Tests Electronic BL," *American Shipper*, October 1986, pp. 28, 30.

MacLeod, Marcia, "Freight Forwarding," *Which Computer?*, July 1987, pp. 104-110.

Maclure, Clare, "BT Aims to Link 1,000 at Ports," *Computer Weekly*, London, England, August 27, 1987.

"The Mean Green Screen: The Community Cargo Release System (CCRS)," *Boston Marine Guide*, November 27, 1987.

Mongelluzzo, Bill, "Automation Pleases Ports," *The Journal of Commerce*, March 1987.

------. "Brokers Feel Neglected In Customs Automation," *The Journal of Commerce*, June 15, 1987.

------. "Brokers Hail Customs For Its Quota System," *The Journal of Commerce*, June 10, 1987.

------. "Customs Brokers Heed Calls To Automate, Some Reluctantly," *The Journal of Commerce*, March 2, 1987, pp. 1A, 7A.

------. "Customs Does Computer Shuffle," *The Journal of Commerce*, October 23, 1987.

------. "Customs May Widen Paperless Filing Test," *The Journal of Commerce*, August 24, 1987.

Morison, Robert F., "Ports Hail Bill of Lading Plan," *The Journal of Commerce*, June 4, 1987.

"Paperless--At Last!" *American Shipper*, January 1988, pp. 42-43.

Prat, Marie, "Day One to Weed Out Poor Brokers," *The Journal of Commerce*, May 6, 1987.

"Sea-Trac Shows Sea-Land's Instant Report Card To Shippers for Better Service," *Global Trade*, November 1987.

Seideman, Tony, "GE Subsidiary Develops EDI System for Ports," *The Journal of Commerce*, December 2, 1987, pp. 1A, 14A.

------. "Global Invoice System Enacted," *The Journal of Commerce,* January 4, 1988.

------. "Shipping Industry Slow in Adoption of Computerization," *The Journal of Commerce*, September 16, 1987.

Selwitz, Robert, "Paper Era Fading Out as EDI Takes Hold," *The Journal of Commerce*, May 20, 1986.

"Seminar to Explain Computer Network for Transportation," *Port of Houston*, November 1987.

"Slaying the 'Paper Dragon,'" *Via Port of New York-New Jersey*, New York, N.Y., May 1986, pp. 14-15.

Steinberg, Don, "Shipper Offers On-Line Cargo Tracking," *PC Week*, December 8, 1987.

Swartz, Herbert, "Tariff Data Reporting Has New Approach," *The Journal of Commerce*, June 29, 1987.

Thompson, Kevin D., "Customs Official Notes Billing System Progress," *The Journal of Commerce*, July 8, 1987.

------. "Popularity of EDI Growing: Freight Forwarders, Brokers Recognize Automation Benefits," *The Journal of Commerce*, July 1, 1987.

Willmott, Kevin, "Deep-Sea Exporters Try Data Transfer," *Materials Management and Distribution*, December 1986.

Office Products Industry

Brisebois, Diane J., "The Challenge of EDI," *Canadian Office Products & Stationery*, Don Mills, Ontario, April 1987, p. 70.

"Computer-to-Computer Orders Score Again" (Industry Committee on Office Productivity Standards), *SM&M*, September 10, 1984. [Name changed to *Sales and Marketing Management* 10-7-85.]

"Electronic Data Interchange: A Look at What It Means for the Industry," *Office Products Industry Report*, July 19, 1986, pp. 4-5.

"First PO Sent as Part of ICOPS Pilot Test," *Office Products Industry Report*, June 21, 1985, pp. 1, 6.

"ICOPS Publishes Draft Standards for Computer-Based Industry Communications," *Office Products Industry Report*, June 1, 1984, pp. 1, 8.

"Industry Begins to Take on EDI," *Office Products Dealer*, August 1986.

"May Start-up Set for ICOPS Pilot," *Geyer's Office Dealer*, May 1985.

"NOPA Plans Electronic Communications Seminar," *Southern Office Dealer*, May 1986.

Powell, Gil, "Ready or Not, Here Comes EDI," *Office Products Dealer*, October 1986, pp. 259-260, 262.

Questions and Answers About Electronic Data Interchange and the Office Products Industry, Industry Committee on Office Products Standards (ICOPS), June 1986.

"Spectrum Office Products, Eastman Kodak Test the EDI Concept," *Office Products Industry Report*, May 23, 1986.

"WSA Conference Includes ICOPS Update," *Office Products Industry Report*, May 24, 1985, pp. 1, 13.

Paper & Publishing Industries

Clarke, R. L., "Computer Technology: A Focus on Customer Service," *Pulp & Paper Canada*, July 1987, pp. 56, 57 f.

Cullen, Dan, "Electronic Ordering - The Future Arrives," *American Bookseller*, September 1986. pp. 47-48, 50-52.

Hutchison, James L., "Paper Industry Should Brace for Growth of EDI Systems in Business," *Pulp & Paper*, San Francisco, CA, August 1986, pp. 89-91.

"Paper Makers, Buyers Get Assist from Electronic Data Interchange," *Printing News*, June 7, 1986.

"Proponents Claim All Can Benefit from Electronic Data Interchange," *Printing News*, May 31, 1986.

Rath, Bernie, "The International Scene - Telecommunication Systems in Use," *American Bookseller*, September 1986, pp. 53-54.

Slatin, Dr. Benjamin, "The Paper Industry - Supplier and User of Naval Stores," *Naval Stores Review*, November-December 1986, pp. 3-9.

Petroleum

Petree, Dale L. and Robertson, Ken, "EDI--Cost Cutting Applications for Petroleum Accountants," *Journal of Petroleum Accounting*, Spring 1987, pp. 27-35.

Sedgwick, Fred, "Data Processing Services for E&P Operations," *Petroleum Management*, November 1987, pp. 14 ff.

Thomas, Gerald P., and Steen, Michael, "Profits Through Technology," *Petroleum Management*, February 1987, pp. 40-45.

Rail

"Conrail to Volume Shippers: Use EDI Instead of Paper," *International Trade & Transport*, February 1987.

Davies, John, "SP's Computerized Link Eases Booking Logjams," *The Journal of Commerce*, June 8, 1987.

"The Electronic Connection," *Traffic Management*, September 1986, pp. 58-61, 65.

"Electronic Data Interchange," *Electronic Business Network*, Burlington Northern Railroad, August 1986.

"An End to the Car-Tracing Blues," *Traffic Management*, April 1986.

Freeman, Annette, "Bohemia Inc.," *Distribution*, September 1987. pp. 32 f.

Keeney, Kathleen R., "RAILINC Head Tells Club EDI Will Go Beyond Role As Current Catch Phrase," *Traffic World*, March 23, 1987.

Kursar, Robert J., "Conrail Sets Timetable for Agent Implementation of EDI Communications," *Traffic World*, November 30, 1987.

-----. "Shippers' Agents Are Poised to Link Up With Rails Via EDI," *Traffic World*, July 6, 1987.

Lemay, Stephen, "Rails Eager to Get Shippers On Line With EDI," *The Journal of Commerce*, December 2, 1987.

"Presenting 'Streamliner,' Union Pacific's EDI Solution: Better Ways to Move Information--and Freight," *Union Pacific Railroad, 1987.*

"Railway Computers Now Help Shippers," *Materials Management and Distribution*, September 1987, p. 40.

Seideman, Tony, "Conrail Eases Demands of Customer Automation," *The Journal of Commerce*, December 15, 1987.

------. "Rail Committee to Engineer Industry Into Computer Age," *The Journal of Commerce*, December 14, 1987.

------. "Rails Take Gentle Route to Encourage EDI Use," *The Journal of Commerce*, December 11, 1987.

Swartz, Herbert, "EDI Right Track for Rail Industry," *The Journal of Commerce*, June 29, 1987.

Thompson, Kevin D., "Carriers, Shippers Find EDI Talks Productive," *The Journal of Commerce*, May 1987.

------. "Conrail's Mandate on EDI," *The Journal of Commerce*, February 4, 1987.

------. "EDI Demand Has Rails Hopping," *The Journal of Commerce*, December 10, 1986.

------. "Rails, Shippers Work Together On EDI Issue," *The Journal of Commerce*, May 1, 1987.

------. "UP Revamps Computer System," *The Journal of Commerce*, February 12, 1987.

Standards Organizations

"AIAG Promotes Standards," *Automation News*, August 1986.

Barrett, Colin, "Toward A Universal Standard In Electronic Data Interchange," *Traffic World*, January 25, 1988, p. 46.

Benning, Karen M., "TALC Sets Defect Flagging Standards," *Apparel Industry Magazine*, July 1987, pp. 64 f.

"Booklet Describes Status of EDI," *Heavy Duty Trucking*, October 1987.

Canna, Elizabeth, "EDIFACT," *American Shipper*, January 1988, pp. 38, 40.

"Clash of EDI Standards," *Computerworld*, August 1, 1987.

Clune, Ray, "Nonwoven Industry Divides Duties for Its Task Forces on Standards," *Daily News Record*, October 13, 1987.

------. "TALC Calls for More Unity Between Textile, Apparel Cos.," *Daily News Record*, June 8, 1987.

"Code Council Will Regulate Electronic Data," *Women's Wear Daily*, December 2, 1987.

Cribbs, Gillian, "SITPRO Closes Gap On Paperless Trade," *Computer Weekly*, July 23, 1987.

Dallas, Daniel B., "The AIAG: What It Is and What It Does," *DE Technology*, January 1985.

"David v. Goliath on Standards," *Computerworld*, August 1, 1987.

Direct Store Delivery Store-level Study, Arthur D. Little, Inc., April 1987.

"EDI Movers Try to Lull Users' Fears," *Computerworld*, November 30, 1987.

"EDI Services Gets Standards Boost," *IDB*, London, England, February 4, 1987.

"EDI To Make C.P.M. Exam Debut," *Pacific Purchasor*, December 1987.

"EDI Training Sessions," *Traffic World*, November 2, 1987.

Fahey, Michael, "Airlines Go On-line for Supplies: Specification 2000 Cuts Paperwork," *Network World*, October 26, 1987.

Freedman, David H., "Intercompany Network Vendors Look Forward to Standards," *High Technology*, September 1986, p. 34.

Gerus, Michael W., *International EDI: A Comment and Advisory*, AIAG, June 1987.

Gonze, Josh, "EDI Users Anticipate X.12 Boost," *Network World*, November 30, 1987.

"Groups Try to Keep Up With Growth," *The Journal of Commerce*, December 17, 1987.

"Guilbert to Move On," *Traffic World*, December 14, 1987, p. 61.

"Here's the Ticket to the Bottom Line," *Home Textiles Today*, April 6, 1987, p. 9. [VICS]

Hoffman, Susan S., "The EDI Big Leagues: Pick A Winner," *InformationWEEK*, June 29, 1987, p. 4.

Hogsett, Don, "Throughout Industry, a 'Common Language,'" *Home Textiles Today*, April 6, 1987, p. 8. [VICS]

Hunter, Philip, "Europe: U.S. EDI Users Must Get Together," *InformationWEEK*, October 12, 1987.

"Improving Customer Service Through Partnerships," *Bobbin Magazine*, April 1987, p. 96. [VICS]

"International Data Exchange Association," *Journal of Cash Management*, May/June 1987.

"International EDI Seminar to Take Place in New York," *American Sailings*, November 16, 1987.

Jones, Stephen, "Group Seeks to Soothe User EDI Fears," *Networking*, November 30, 1987.

Joseph, Gloria, "Conference to Explore Trade Role of Electronic Communications," *The Journal of Commerce*, January 15, 1988.

Kilbane, Doris E., "FACT Crosses Industry Lines With New Standards," *Automatic I.D. News*, September 1987, pp. 50, 66.

"A Major Step...," *Mass Market Retailers*, December 14, 1987.

"Mills Link With Suppliers," *Apparel Industry Magazine*, April 1987. [FASLINC]

"The Nature of Language," *Earnshaw's*, November 1987, p. 59.

"New EDIA President," *Traffic World*, December 28, 1987.

"Nonwoven Group Wants Standards," *Apparel Industry Magazine*, September 1987.

"The ODETTE File: EDI to the Rescue," *Transport Topics*, January 4, 1988.

Powers, Pam, "Standards Chaos Haunts Users," *Computerworld*, November 19, 1987. [Also reported in *Computerworld New Zealand, November 30, 1987.]*

Robinson, Teri, "EDI Builds Clan of Supporters," *MIS Week*, December 7, 1987.

Santora, Joyce E., "TALC Sets the Standard," *Bobbin Magazine*, January 1987. pp. 68, 70-72, 74, 76 f.

Seideman, Tony, "Administrative Changes Give EDI Boost in Retailing," *The Journal of Commerce*, December 9, 1987.

------. "Bar Codes, Data Interchange Facilitate Tracking of Goods," *The Journal of Commerce*, November 23, 1987, pp. 1A, 11B.

------. "Data Technology Comes of Age As Action Supersedes Theory," *The Journal of Commerce*, December 3, 1987, pp. 1A, 2A.

------. "EDI Exchange," *The Journal of Commerce*, December 31, 1987. [Jerome L. Dreyer]

------. "EDI Group Names Dreyer President," *The Journal of Commerce*, December 24, 1987.

------. "EDI Suppliers Gearing Up for Convention," *The Journal of Commerce*, November 19, 1987.

------. "Shipping Seeks to Set Standard for Its Data," *The Journal of Commerce*, November 27, 1987.

"Six Associations Develop EDI Standard 'Embarc,'" *Fibre Market News*, April 22, 1986.

Smarr, Susan L., "The Latest Link is SAFLINC," *Bobbin Magazine*, May 1987, pp. 134 ff.

------. "The TALC Talks," *Bobbin Magazine*, July 1987, pp. 98, 100.

Stix, G., "EDI Standards: A Crucial Juncture," *Computer Decisions*, April 22, 1986.

Swank, Gary, "The TALC Mission," *Bobbin Magazine*, January 1987, pp. 78 f.

"TDCC Changes Name to Meet Electronic Data Interchange Surge," *Handling & Shipping Management*, February 1986, p. 27.

"Technical Advisory Group Recommends Positive U.S. Vote On Int'l Syntax," *NITL Notice*, August 21, 1987.

Thome, Judy Thompson, "TALC: A New Way of Doing Business," *Apparel Industry Magazine*, January 1987, pp. 24, 26.

Thompson, Kevin D., "EDI Standard for N. America, Europe Nears," *The Journal of Commerce*, June 2, 1987.

------. "Multiple EDI Rules Big Obstacle," *The Journal of Commerce*, September 19, 1986.

"Tower of Babel," *Hardware Merchandiser*, September 1987.

"UNJEDI Group Works on Int'l Messages," *NITL Notice*, October 23, 1987, p. 371.

Unsworth, Edwin, "Greater Standardization Urged for Input Data in EDI Systems," *The Journal of Commerce* (European Edition), October 15, 1987.

------. "Standards Urged for EDI Input," *The Journal of Commerce* (European Edition), November 23, 1987.

"Update On the Retail EDI Users Group," *Stores*, May 1987, p. 53.

"VICS Working to Support UPC for General Merchandise," *Apparel Industry Magazine*, March 1987.

Watson, Terry, "Call for an EDI Council," *Computerworld Australia*, November 13, 1987.

Weiss, Julian, "Worldwide Standards Are Closer," *The Journal of Commerce*, December 2, 1987.

"What Is the Difference Between VICS and GMAIC?" *Women's Wear Daily*, September 1987, p. 15.

Strategic Information Systems

Cash, James I., Jr., and Konsynski, Benn R., "IS Redraws Competitive Boundaries," *Harvard Business Review*, March-April 1985, p. 134.

Clemons, Eric K., and McFarlan, F. Warren, "Telecom: Hook Up or Lose Out," *Harvard Business Review*, July-August 1986, pp. 91-97.

Feldman, Robert, "IBM Pitches Plan for Business Links," *MIS Week*, August 10, 1987, pp. 1, 8.

Porter, Michael E. and Millar, Victor E., "How Information Gives You Competitive Advantage," *Harvard Business Review*, July-August 1985, pp. 149-160.

Stenger, Alan J., "Information Systems in Logistics Management: Past, Present, and Future," *Transportation Journal*, Fall 1986, pp. 65-81.

Studies and Surveys

"Booming Growth in EDI Expected to Triple in Next 5 Years," *Sales & Marketing Digest*, December 1987.

Bosomworth, Ken, *Electronic Document Interchange Markets: U.S. and International*, Report Number 732, International Resource Development, Norwalk, CT, April 1987.

"EDI In Australia," *Yankee Group*, September 1987.

Electronic Data Interchange: Intra-Industry Networking, LINK Resources, New York, NY, 1986.

Electronic Data Interchange Software Markets 1987-1992, INPUT, December 1987.

Meyer, David, "Survey: EDI Use to Double Yearly," *Communications Week*, September 28, 1987, pp. 20, 26.

Telecommunications Industry

Nelson-Rowe, Laurel, "NYNEX Proposes Standards Group," *Communications Week*, April 21, 1986.

"Purchasing Standards at NYNEX," *Utility Purchasing & Stores*, May 1986.

Warehousing

"EDI Making Major Inroads in Public Space But Total Computerization Is Still Far Off," *Frozen Food Age*, July 1987, pp. 36 f.

Leatham, Jerry, "Living in Interesting Times: Warehousing in the 1980's," *Transportation, 1985*, Myasthenia Foundation, White Plains, New York, 1985, pp. 32-36.

"Warehouse Software: Ready When You Are," *Material Handling Engineering*, March 1987, pp. 79-82.

"Warehouses Embracing New Computer Standards," *Traffic Management*, January 1987, p. 17 f.

Bibliography Acknowledgments

For contributing references: Charles Biddle of Milliken, Susan Crocker formerly with the National Association of Purchasing Management, Chris Frapwell of the Uniform Code Council, Harriet Rusk of the Data Interchange Standards Association. Also the authors are grateful to Ms. Sheryl Stilwell for editorial assistance.

Recommended Reading

EDI Yellow Pages. Find partners, customers, services and products FAST! in the comprehensive directory of EDI users and vendors with over 5000 listings. Listings are FREE to users. The directory, published semi-annually, is international, inter- network, and inter-industry. The reference section includes The EDI Glossary, implementation tips and an EDI international calendar.

TRADE-FLASH International. The original EDI Newsletter. Guides the reader through all aspects of EDI and advises on the optimal approach to EDI implementation. Broad coverage of international news on EDI and the EDIFACT standard. (In association with Eurotech Forum.)

Electronic Data Interchange: Making Business More Efficient. Comprehensive guide on the basics of EDI and its value as a strategic tool in business by Ben Milbrandt. Includes a detailed analysis of standards in non-technical language and real, quanti- tative success stories from major corporations. For those already familiar with EDI, the book provides steps to follow in implemen- tation. 79 pages. (In association with EDI in Business.)

Electronic Data Interchange and Paperless Trade: The Implementation Guide. Geared to the needs of businessmen in general and to those who have not had time to explore EDI in depth but need to know the concepts. Written in plain language, the book covers costs and benefits, EDI in International Trade, developments in Europe and the EDIFACT Standard. 100 pages. (In association with Euromatica S.A.)

The EDI Eye (tm). "EDI, spread the standards!" A series of rapid-access "help screens" for your PC. As an adjunct to the standards manuals themselves, "The Eye" moves quickly from a transaction set standard to details of the data segments, data elements and code lists. Includes "used by" queries. All TDCC and X12 transaction sets. The EDI Eye is a trademark of National Systems Corporation.

EDI, spread the word!
Publications-Recruiting-Consulting
13805 Wooded Creek #100
Dallas, Texas 75244-4754
1-214-243-3456

Glossary of Terms

accounts payable — business area within a company that receives supplier invoices and makes payments.

accounts receivable — business area within a company that generates customer invoices and receives payments.

ACK — In communication, when an error detecting scheme is used, some means must be provided for retransmission of a block of data in error. The receiver may signal the sender with an acknowledgment (ACK) of data receipt or a negative acknowledgment (NAK) of error detection.

advance shipping notice — a transaction set that is transmitted from a supplier to a customer to give details of a pending shipment.

AIAG — Automobile industry action group — group formed to coordinate EDI activities for the automobile industry.

AISI — American Steel Institute.

ANSI ASC X12 — American National Standards Institute, X12 Committee — committee within the ANSI organization charged with developing data formats for standard business documents with cross-industry application.

ANSI X12 data element dictionary — ANSI document that contains definitions and attributes of all data elements of ANSI X12 transaction sets plus code list values for all elements requiring them.

ANSI X12 segment directory — ANSI document that contains definition and layouts of all segments used in the ANSI X12 transaction sets.

API — American Paper Institute.

application format — the specific file format generated by a computer program or expected as input to a computer program.

application link software — program developed to act as a link between an application program and a pre-defined data format. The data format may be a fixed field format or a public or industry data format.

application-to-application — transference of data generated by a computer program directly to another computer program. In EDI, these programs would be housed in systems at trading partner sites.

asynchronous transmission — a method of transmitting data in which each character is preceded by a start bit and followed by a stop bit. Intervals between characters vary.

audit trail — record of transactions created as a by-product of data processing runs or mechanized operations.

authentication — Procedure to insure that data cannot be tampered with without being detectable by the receiver. Using the original data, a macro authentication code (MAC) is computed through a series of complex calculations beginning with a secret key (authentication key). The MAC is appended to the data and transmitted to the receiver. Upon receipt, the identical calculations are performed, starting with the same authentication key. If the data has been changed in any way, the MAC computed at the receiving site will be different than that sent.

authentication key — a group of characters which is used to initiate the authentication process. Each partner of a trading partner pair must have possession of the same key.

automated environment — functions handled by computer programs with no need for human intervention except on an exception basis.

award bid notification — a transaction set sent by a manufacturer in the pharmaceutical industry to a distributor, to describe details of a contract between the manufacturer and a hospital.

back-end processor — a small computer attached to a larger computer as a standard data processor for some processing after the main application processing.

barcode — UPC printed on a product permitting electronic scanning equipment to read it. Bars provide key to the product identification, price, and such other information as manufacturer, stock number, and product category.

baud rate — transmission rate, used as a measure of serial data flow between computers or between communication equipment devices.

billing transaction — data stream containing information relating to payment for products or services received.

bill of lading (BOL) — a transaction that is sent by a supplier to a carrier that describes shipment content and delivery details of an order awaiting pickup, from which the carrier BOL can be generated.

bisynchronous protocol — set of conventions controlling synchronous transmission which defines the controlling start and end characters and the error checking performed.

bits/second — the number of bits that pass a given point in a communication line per second.

CAD — computer aided design. Capability of a computer to be used for industrial design through visual devices.

carbon copy routing — transmission of a duplicate data stream to another receiving location or trading partner.

cash management — process of controlling cash by keeping track of accounts payable and receivable and making financial decisions based on maximizing interest earned by accelerating receipts and holding disbursements until due date.

cash position — comparison of a company's payables and receivables dollar amounts.

central bank — a banker's bank, accepting deposits by, making payments to, and extending loans to commerical banks.

centralized processing — A system of handling data concentrated at a single location or by a single computer application.

chargeback debit memo — ORDERNET/NWDA standard data format transaction set that is sent from a pharmaceutical distributor to manufacturer containing information related to sale of product to a hospital that has a special contract of sale with the manufacturer.

chargeback reconciliation — ORDERNET/NWDA standard data format transaction set sent by a pharmaceutical manufacturer to a distributor in response to a chargeback debit memo. It contains corrections to the chargeback debit memo generated out of a reconciliation with the hospital/manufacturer contract terms.

CIDX — Chemical Industry Data Exchange — group formed to coordinate EDI activities for the chemical industry.

codify — generate a code to identify a narrative message or parameter.

COMMNET — An EDI standard data format used by distributors and manufacturers in the medical/surgical industry.

communication board — an electrical panel which allows a computer to perform communications via telephone line.

communication capability — protocol and line speed at which the communication device component of a computer system is able to transfer data to another computer or communication device.

communication medium — the basis in which data is communicated. EDI provides the message format, communication software provides the communication procedures.

communication protocol — see protocol.

communication software — computer instructions for monitoring communication activities.

compatibility — the characteristic of computers, communication devices, and software to accept and process data prepared by another computer system or another component of one computer system without conversion or code modification.

competitive edge — anything that gives a company a favorable position over its competitors.

computer application — computer program or programs which solves a problem or performs a function. Example, the order/entry application handles incoming purchase orders.

computer memory — storage facilities in which all data are accessible to the computer.

computer operator — the person who actually manipulates computer controls.

computer pad — a device attached to a computer on which graphical information can be drawn. For example, a signature. And which can transmit that data into a computer application. It provides a means to identify the authorized signature of a user of the system.

computer memory — storage facilities in which all data are accessible to the computer.

computer program — set of instructions for solving a problem on a computer.

computer storage — device capable of receiving data, retaining them for an indefinite period of time and supplying them upon command.

computer-to-computer — transference of data generated by one computer to another computer.

conditional usage designator — see usage designator.

control envelope — the beginning and ending segments of an interchange or functional group in a standard data format. Used by the receiver to validate that the complete group has been received and that it contains the correct number of units as counted by the sender.

control number/ reference number — number used to identify an entity. For example, a segment identifier identifies a standard segment; a data element identifier identifies a standard data element.

CPU — central processing unit. Central processor of the computer system, containing the main storage and arithmetic computation unit.

cross-industry standard — A data standard that has cross- industry application. ANSI X12 is such a standard, with broad participation from many industries and a requirement of public review prior to becoming a standard.

CRT — cathode ray tube. Computer terminal that may be for display only or may be fully programmable.

CTX — Corporate trade exchange. Process of effecting electronic funds transfer by use of EDI transaction sets.

data — a general term to denote the basic elements of information which can be processed or produced by a computer.

data availability — describes those data elements accessible to a computer application for purposes of generating an EDI data transmission.

data base — vast and continuously updatable file of information on a particular subject. Usually can be randomly accessed on predefined key words or values.

data communication — transmission of information from one point to another.

data element — a group of characters that specify an item at or near the basic level. The smallest unit of data defined in a standard data format.

data element delimiter character — a character that marks the end of information contained in a variable length data field.

data element number — see data element reference number.

data element reference number — The number which identifies each element found in a standard segment with its corresponding definition in the data element dictionary.

data element usage indicator — see usage designator.

data flow path — the route taken by data at each step in the procedures of a system or business area.

data integrity — maintenance of identical data stream as transmitted by sending party.

data requirements — describes those data elements needed by a computer application in order to process a specified business transaction.

data stream — all data transmitted through a channel in a single transmission.

data type — the characteristic of a data element that describes whether it is numeric, alphabetic, or alphanumeric.

de-authentication — perform the same authentication process at the receiving site of a transmission as that performed at the sending site. Process must be initiated using the identical authentication key. If the same MAC is computed, the data can be assumed to be identical to that sent; if different, the data has been altered during transmission.

debug — locate and correct any errors in a computer program.

decryption — a procedure for the interpretation or deciphering of coded data specifically, the reversal of an encryption process (data scrambling) to insure data privacy.

DEX/UCS — direct exchange of UCS data; standard data transactions to be used by the direct store delivery segment of the grocery industry, specifically those transactions carried by the supplier agent (route driver) to the back door receiving computer of the retailer.

direct benefits — Benefits attributable to EDI that happen as a result of reducing or eliminating costs associated with handling or processing paper transactions.

discount terms — identification of the time to pay an invoice and any discounts offered by the vendor.

disk — circular metal plate connected to a computer that is continually rotated for reading or writing of data.

distributed processing — having multiple sites/computers within a company, performing processing of similar transactions. For example: each division of a company performs its own purchasing through a different application program or at a different data center.

DOE — direct order entry, a standard data format used by rack jobbers.

download — transfer of data from a large computer to a front- end processor (smaller computer).

down time — the period during which a omputer is malfunctioning or not operating correctly due to machine failures.

DSD/UCS — direct store delivery of UCS data; standard data transactions to be used by the direct store delivery segment of the grocery industry, specifically those transactions having to do with a particular transaction used at the receiving location (back door) of the retailer.

EAGLE — Standard data format used by the wholesalers and manufacturers in the hardware/houseware industry.

EDIFACT — EDI for administration, commerce, and trade. The acronym for the international data standard of business transactions.

EDI — Electronic data interchange — Intercompany, computer to computer communication of data which permits the receiver to perform the function of a standard business transaction and is in a standard data format.

EDIA — EDI Association — formerly TDCC.

EDI "gateway" — logical location of entry or exit of EDI data into/out of your company. A device having output and input channels through which EDI communication of EDI data is effected.

EDI potential — an indicator of potential payoff attainable through implementing EDI; derived by subtracting setup and ongoing costs of implementing and performing EDI from potential short and long term benefits such as satifying market factors.

EDI readiness — an indicator to determine a firm's ability to physically accomplish and attain benefits from EDI based on the presence of computer and communication hardware and application software.

EDX — Electrical Industry Data Exchange — group formed to coordinate EDI activities for the electrical industry.

EFT — electronic funds transfer. Computerized systems that process financial transactions and information about financial transactions, or that effect an exhange of value between two parties.

EIDX — electronics industry data exchange — group formed to coordinate EDI activities for the electronics industry.

elastic demand — demand that changes in relatively large volume as prices increase or decrease.

electronic mail — system which provides the ability to deliver user-generated messages to any and all defined locations (addresses) on the system. Usually, intra-company capability in people readable format.

electronic mailbox — see mailbox.

electronic invoice — invoice transaction in standard data format.

electronic trade — electronic transmission and receipt of transaction sets for the purpose of transacting business.

E-MAIL — see electronic mail.

encryption — Procedure of scrambling data through a series of calculations starting with a secret key, that makes it indecipherable to the outside observer. The receiver of such data must perform the same calculations to get the data back to its original form.

encryption key — a group of characters which is used to initiate the encryption process. Each partner of a trading partner pair, must have possession of the same key.

error detecting protocol — protocol having a procedure in place to detect when data received is not identical to that sent.

evaluated receipts settlement — procedure for authorizing payment for good based on comparing anticipated receipts to actual receipts, when price has already been negotiated. Used extensively in the automotive industry.

express mail — refers to a mail service offered by a third party service provider in which EDI data is transformed into print format and mailed to a trading partner recipient..

FAX, facsimile — transmission of text, pictures, maps, diagrams, etc. by radio waves. The image is scanned at the transmitter and reconstructed at the receiving station.

feasibility stage — the stage during which the possible benefits and costs of implementing EDI are evaluated. Deliverable of this stage is a feasibility study.

feasibility study — a document generated out of investigation into the economic environment, internal and external pressures, systems, procedures, and communication capability in a business area within a firm. A deliverable to help corporate managers to evaluate possible benefits of implementing EDI in the business area and is an integral part of a corporate implementation plan.

financial institution — private or governmental organization which serves the purpose of accumulating funds from savers, channeling them to individuals, households, and businesses needing credit.

financial transaction — data stream containing information relating to payment or any other financial application within a company.

first tier supplier — first tier supplier of a manufacturer or assembler organization.

format syntax rules — see standard syntax rules.

freight bill — a bill generated by a carrier to cover the costs of carrying a shipment.

front-end processor — a small computer attached to a larger computer that serves as a standard data processor for some processing preceding the main application processing.

functional acknowledgment (FA) — an ANSI X12 transaction set generated by the receiver of EDI data and transmitted to the sender. The transaction set acknowledges receipt of the data and reports the results of validation edits on the functional group, transaction set, or data element level.

functional business manager — manager of a functional business area within a company.

functional group — A group of like EDI transaction sets being sent from one party to another.

functional group — a group of like standard data format transaction sets.

functional group header segment — a standard data format segment defined as the start of a functional group. It contains group type, group identifier, sender and receiver codes and version of the standard used.

functional group level — refers to receiving, sending, or processing a full functional group of data.

function group level acknowledgment — a functional acknowledgement which acknowledges receipt of data and reports back to the sender on the completeness of the functional group.

functional group trailer segment — a standard data format segment defined as the end of a functional group. It contains the group identifier and the number of transaction sets contained in the group.

gateway application — a computer program or group of programs which receives EDI data directly after being translated from the standard data format or which sends data directly to be translated into the standard data format. The first internal application that EDI data enters at the receiving site; the last internal application that EDI data exits at the sending site. Example order/entry application receives purchase orders from the customer; purchasing application sends purchase orders to the supplier.

generic standard — a data standard with cross-industry application such as ANSI X12.

group level acknowledgment — see functional group level acknowledgment.

guidelines for usage — a document usually developed by an industry, sometimes by a company, which describes the selected subset of a standard and the way data will be used by the industry or company EDI trading community.

hand-held data entry device — a portable piece of hardware on which data can be entered. It can be attached to other pieces of hardware such as a computer.

handshaking — the required sequence of signals for communication between system devices.

hardware — the electric, electronic, and processing equipment used for processing data; any piece of automatic data processing equipment, such as computer, communication device, printer or other computer peripheral.

homogeneous data requirements — the uniformity of data elements required to transact business across company, industry, and country boundaries.

indirect benefits — benefits attributable to EDI that happen as a result of making effective use of data received.

industry specific standard — A data format containing transaction sets and data elements that are designed to specifically fill the business needs of a particular industry group. Examples are UCS for the grocery industry, EAGLE for the hardlines industry, and ORDERNET/NWDA for the pharmaceutical industry.

integrated applications — a series of applications designed as output of one application can be automatically fed into the next application with no modifications or human intervention.

interchange — all data coming from one party and going to one party in a single transmission. In a standard data format, an interchange begins with an interchange header segment and ends with an interchange trailer segment.

interchange header — a standard segment defined as the start of an interchange group. It contains the interchange identifier, sender and receiver codes, and other data fields needed to interpret the incoming interchange.

interchange level — Examination of EDI data received for a full interchange.

interchange trailer — a standard data segment defined as the end of an interchange group. It contains the interchange identifier and the number of functional groups contained within the interchange.

inter-company — pertaining to transactions crossing company boundaries.

interconnection — transferring of data from one third party service to another via communication link.

internal edits — validation of data elements as found within computer application programs.

internal format — see application format.

internal order — an order generated within a company and sent to the manufacturing or assembly location ordering product required to fulfill incoming purchase orders or to maintain inventory levels.

internal staging order — based on an incoming purchase order, a document describing the requirements for staging a shipment based on a customer purchase order.

internal systems — see application program.

interpretation — refers to reading and understand the meaning of EDI data that has been received from a trading partner.

intra-company — pertaining to transactions within a company.

inventory availability inquiry — a transaction set containing information requesting availability information on a particular product or products.

inventory — a supply of various goods kept on hand by a firm in order to meet needs promptly as they arise, and thus assure uninterrupted operation of the business and/or ability to fulfill customer orders.

invoice — document containing a record of the transaction between buyer and seller (a bill for merchandise) prepared by the seller.

invoicing application — a computer program or group of programs that generates an invoice.

item authorization transaction — a transaction set containing information on terms of sale and delivery schedule of product used in the direct store delivery segment of the grocery industry.

Just-in-time (JIT) — manufacturing philosophy of receiving parts from suppliers at the manufacturing site just in time to be used in a manufacturing process. This requires very fast turn around of orders and shipment of goods on a pre-determined schedule.

JIT manufacturing schedules — schedule of manufacturing tasks such that each task is dependent on conclusion of the previous task toward development/assembly of a complete product.

key-entry — entry of data into a computer by typing it onto a keyboard of a computer terminal.

key management — pertaining to authentication and encryption, the procurement and control of the keys required to perform the procedures.

labor-intensive — any production process requiring a large proportion of human effort relative to capital investment.

labor rates — level of wages.

levels of security — various degrees of access to data in order to assure protection of computer-stored data.

linespeed — see bits/second.

lockbox — a post office box in which customer payments are deposited. The box is accessible by local bank who passes the payments to the company's main bank. A lockbox serves the purpose of reducing float for the receiver company.

logon — a procedure for user access to a system involving identification, access control, and exchange of information between user and system.

logon ID — the personally generated identification code used when logging on to a system, which permits the system to recognize the user. May be associated with varying levels of security.

looping — repetition of a group of segments in a standard data format transaction set.

MAC — Macro Authentication code — a character string computed as a result of an authentication of an EDI data stream. The MAC is appended to the original stream and transmitted along with the data. After performing the identical computations at the receiving location, the receiver must verify that his computed MAC is identical to that sent. If not, he knows that the data has been tampered with during transmission.

machine readable data — data contained in pre-defined locations (fields) within a data stream. This data can be interpreted by a computer program.

Mailbox — A logical partition of disk data storage in which all data sent to a particular recipient is stored until retrieved by that recipient. Mailboxes are provided as a service by third party EDI service providers.

mainframe — technically, the fundamental portion of a computer, i.e., the portion that contains the CPU and control elements; commonly refers to any large computer.

mainframe computer — generally characterized as being faster, more expensive, and having a larger set of capabilities and instruction sets than mini or micro computers.

mandatory data element/segment — a data element or segment within a standard data format in which information must be contained.

manufacturing requirements — those components required to manufacture or assemble a product.

map — the logical association of one set of values with values in another set. In EDI, moving data element values in an EDI data stream from one format to another.

market factors — those situations outside of a company that influence its decision to implement EDI. For example, pressure from a major customer.

mass merchandiser — a large, low level retailer, carrying a large variety of merchandise and competing for consumers mainly on the basis of price.

material release — a transaction set used by the automotive industry which acts as a release for product against an annually negotiated purchase order.

material requirements planning (MRP) — a production scheduling process, usually computer-based, which arranges for the placement of materials and components where and when they are needed.

menu-driven — refers to computer programs whose functionality can be accessed by a user via on-line, pre-formatted screens.

message — a transmitted series of words or symbols that are designed and intended to relay information.

micro-computer — a general term referring to a complete, tiny computing system consisting of hardware and software.

mini computer — a mid-sized computer, usually characterized by higher performance than micro computers, having instruction sets, higher price, and a proliferation of high level languages, operating systems, and network methodologies.

MODEM — Modulator/Demodulator. An interface device that enables a computer to communicate digital information over telephone lines.

multi-media EDI — passing data electronically via any combination of batch, interactive, print, and electronic mail media.

NACHA — National Clearing House Association.

NAK — see ACK.

NEX/UCS — network exchance of UCS data; standard data transactions to be used in office to office EDI transmissions in the direct store delivery segment of the grocery industry.

node — in a network, a point having both input and output circuits.

non-customer — half of the trading partner pair who sends data to its trading partner and receives data from its trading partner through a third party service provider, but is not a customer of that third party.

NOPA — National Office Products Association.

notification of shipment — a transaction set containing information describing a shipment and its delivery schedule.

NRMA — National Retail Managers Association.

OEM — original equipment manufacturer.

on-line — condition in which a user, terminal, or other device is actively connected with the facilities of a communications network or computer. As pertaining to an application, requiring input by a human.

Open network — A service provided by a third party EDI service provider which allows a customer to transmit data to or recieve data from a non- customer. Non-customers recieve the data through an auto-dial feature, having no mailbox on the network.

operational level manager — a manager responsible for the implementation of the larger goals and strategies that have been determined by the strategic manager; improving current operations and the allocation of resources through the operating budget.

Operational "window" — A pre-defined number of hours per day and days per week in which normal business can be transacted. In

EDI, those hours when data can be transmitted to a company directly.

optional data element/segment — a data element or segment within a standard transaction set in which data can, but does not need to be present.

order entry application — a computer program or group of programs, accepting data from an incoming order as input, validating its information, and usually passing it to an order processing application.

ORDERNET — An industry standard for the drug and pharmaceutical industry. Developed by the National Wholesale Druggists Association in conjunction with Informatics General.

order processing application — a computer program or group of programs accepting a validated order from an order entry application, evaluating it in terms of available inventory, and generating an internal staging order for stock items with inventory availability and an internal order to a manufacturing or assembly location for stock items with no inventory availiability.

order status inquiry — a transaction requesting information on the status of an order.

outdial — see autodial.

paper-based business document — a business document whose information is printed on a paper form. Example, a purchase order or invoice.

payment remittance transaction — a transaction to authorize payment and/or to describe payment as related to a purchase order and all its previous partial payments.

payment terms — see discount terms.

pick instructions — instructions to a warehouseman that describes what product to pick and how much, in order to stage a shipment.

planning schedule transaction — a transaction set used in the automotive industry containing information describing a customer's forecasted manufacturing requirements.

point of sale (POS) — a computer application that permits the seller to input product identification and price of a product at time of sale. Often a point of sale system will have the ability to interpret barcoded product identification.

potential payoff — see EDI potential.

pre-defined fixed file — a file defined as input or output of an application program containing records whose data elements are each of a fixed length. In EDI, this type of file may be defined by a third party service provider as input to an in- network translation capability.

pre-formatted screen — a user-friendly screen that may offer menu options or act as a data entry medium.

pre-ordering transaction — one of several transactions containing information relating to requests and responses transacted during the pre-ordering phase. For example, request for quote, responding quote.

print format — an organization of data that makes it user- friendly and easily human readable.

product code — a code uniquely identifying product. It may contain components of price, manufacturer, stock number, and product category.

production mode — in data processing, automatic job scheduling and execution; occurs after programs have been debugged during test mode.

program — see application program.

programmer — one who prepares programs for a computer; i.e., prepares problem solving procedures, flow charts, and who may also write and debug routines.

proprietary company standard — A standard data format developed and owned by a company to handle transactions between that company and its trading partners. Most often developed by a major customer company.

proprietary inquiry system — a program or group of programs developed and owned by a supplier, which is offered to its customers to handle inventory and order status inquiries. Usually, such a system is interactive.

proprietary ordering system — a group of programs developed and owned by a supplier, which is offered to its customers to handle ordering. Usually, such a system is interactive.

protocol — a set of conventions between communicating devices on the format and content of messages to be exchanged. Simple protocols define only hardware configuration, more complex protocols define timings, data formats, error detection, and correction techniques.

public warehouse — a warehouse that is privately owned and is used to store product of many manufacturers.

purchase order acknowledgment transaction — a transaction set generated as response to a purchase order, containing information from that order and disposition on availability and delivery of the product ordered.

purchase order change acknowledgment transaction — a transaction set containing original purchase order information, purchase order change information, and disposition on availability or delivery of the product ordered.

purchase order change transaction — a transaction set containing original purchase order information and changes to that original order.

purchase order transaction — a transaction set containing all of the information required by a supplier to handle an order of product or services.

purchase-pay cycle — period of time from generation of a purchase order, through receipt of ordered product, and to payment for that product.

purchasing transaction — one of many transactions containing information relating to the purchase of a product or service. For example, purchase order, purchase order change, purchase order acknowledgment.

qualifier code — a piece of information placed in a data element which is related to a second element and is used to identify how to interpret the data in the second element. Example, qualifier code = SH, related to second element NAME, means interpret name as shipper's name (code list is found in ANSI X12 data element dictionary for element number).

quote — a transaction set responding to a request for quote, containing information on price, availability, and delivery schedule of a product.

randomly accessed file — a data file whose information can be accessed by key in any and all sequences.

receiving advice transaction — a transaction set containing information on product identification, quantity, and condition received.

reconciliation procedure — a group of steps used to validate and match information from various sources in order to uncover the equalities and errors in the various data files.

relational data base — a file of information in normalized form, i.e., a flat file that has been inverted.

remote job entry — executing a program or group of programs by entering a series of commands to a computer from a remote source.

request for quote (RFQ) transaction — a transaction set containing information needed by a vendor to perform a request for price and availability quote of a product. Sometimes, this EDI transaction requires supporting documentation in the form of graphic des-signs, blue prints, and other visual aids to complete the required information.

safety stock — the amount of inventory required to fulfill expected customer orders from the time that the purchase order is sent to the supplier for replenishment of stock until shipment of product arrives.

scanning — examining stored information for a specific purpose as for content or arrangement.

scanning device/scanner — an optical scanning unit which can read documents encoded in a special barcode.

screen — see CRT.

segment — in a standard data format, a unit of a transaction set made up of related data elements.

segment delimiter character — a character that marks the end of information contained in a variable length segment.

segment diagram — as related to a standard data format, a diagramatic representation of a segment in terms of all of its data elements.

segment identifier — as related to a standard data format, the code that uniquely identifies a segment, contained in the segment as the first data field.

segment terminator — as related to a standard data format, the character that defines the end of a data segment.

sequential file — a data file organized in such a way that its information must be accessed in sequential order from first to last record.

shipment staging application — a program or group of programs designed to accept as input an internal staging order and develop pick instructions to fulfill product requirements for the order.

shipping transaction — one of several transaction sets containing information on shipment of product.

single sourcing — purchasing full quanitiy requirements of any one product from a single supplier.

SITPRO — British Simplification of International Trade Processing Board.

Smart Card — floppy disk which is used to carry EDI transactions from a direct store delivery supplier to the retailer. The disk is inserted in the retailer's back door computer to display the delivery invoice and can be updated with invoice corrections before being returned to the supplier.

SMC — Standard Maintenance Committee that handles maintenance for the UCS standard.

software — any program that runs on a computer.

Stand-alone — a micro-computer that acts as a complete unit, not attached to any other computers and containing application software.

Standard business transaction — A business procedure between trading partners which accomplishes a specific purpose, for example, relaying the intent to purchase goods. Many transactions are characterized by the paper document which was developed to communicate the data requirements to the trading partner, i.e., the purchase order. EDI transaction sets are designed to accomplish this same goal using a standard machine-readable data format.

Standard data format — A machine-readable data format, predefined and agreed to by the trading partners, which can accomplish a standard business transaction.

standard syntax rules — the rules governing structure in a standard data format.

stock items — items having pre-defined manufacturing and assembly specifications that are stocked by the vendor and can usually be ordered by a product code.

Stock Keeping Unit (SKU) — an internal number generated by a company to uniquely identify a product, as opposed to the UPS code which is a universal numbering system.

store and forward — pertaining to communication systems in which messages are received at intermediate routing points and recorded (stored). They are then transmitted to a further routing point or to the ultimate recipient.

strategic manager — a long range planner responsible for comprehensive, corporate, integrated, overall, and managerial planning.

subset of a standard — a selected group of transaction sets, segments, and data elements from a data standard such as ANSI X12 or UCS.

supplier base — vendor companies from which an organization purchases all of its production and non-production products and services.

supplier delinquencies — related to late shipments by a supplier.

TDCC (EDIA) — Transportation Data Coordinating Committee.

Electronic Data Interchange Association — company which has developed EDI standards for the transportation industry, the grocery industry, and which has acted as the coordinating body of EDI standards for EDX, CIDX, and other industry groups.

telecommunication — the transmission or reception of signals, writing, sounds, or intelligence of any nature by wire, radio, light beam or any other electromagnetic means.

telecommunication port — entry channel through which data is communicated. A port is part of a central computer system.

TERMS — a micro-based software application developed by First National Bank of Chicago which allows the user to input pertinent parameters from which it computes a range of discount terms giving benefits to both partners of a trading partner pair.

third party service provider — A company which acts as a communications intermediary between EDI trading partners, providing communications services such as line speed conversion, and protocol matching as well as electronic mailbox, translation, and other services.

trade organization — an association formed to represent the interests of an industry or industry segment.

trading partner — any company with whom an organization does business. Example, customers, suppliers, carriers, banks.

transaction level acknowledgment — a functional acknowledgment which acknowledges receipt of data and reports back on completeness of each functional group within the interchange and on the completeness of each transaction set within each group.

transaction set — A collection of information required by the receiver to perform a standard business transaction. In a standard data format, a transaction set contains a pre- defined group of segments in header, detail, and summary areas.

transaction set detail area — segments that contain information relating to the line items within the transaction set.

transaction set diagram — a diagramatic representation of the segments in a transaction in the order in which they are valid in that transacion.

transaction set header area — segments that contain information relating to the entire transaction set.

transaction set header segment — a data segment which defines the beginning of a transaction.

transaction set level — sending, receiving, or processing data for a full transaction set.

transaction set summary area — segments that contain information relating to transaction set totals.

transaction set trailer segment — a segment which defines the end of a transaction set.

translation software — A program or group of programs that maps data between an application data format or a pre-defined fixed-field data format to a standard data format.

translator — see translation software.

transmission — an electrical transfer of a signal, message, or other form of intelligence from one location to another.

transmission acknowledgement — an ANSI X12 transaction set generated by a receiver of EDI data and transmitted to the sender which acknowledges receipt of a full transmission and contains no validation of data in that transmission.

UCC — Uniform Communication Council.

UCS — The group that coordinates all EDI activity for the grocery industry.

UCS/DSD Task force — group of corporate members who participate on the direct store delivery task force, developing UCS transactions for this segment of the grocery industry.

UNIX — a multi-programming, operating system developed by Bell Laboratories that features sophisticated software and text-developing utilities.

UPC code — see barcode.

upload — to transfer data from a front-end processor to a large computer.

usage designator — see data element usage indicator.

usage rules — see guidelines for usage.

user-friendly — computer-related but easily understandable by a non-computer oriented person.

user group — an organization made up of users of a specific system, to give the users the opportunity to share knowledge thay have gained and to identify additional system needs.

VAN — Value added network — A company that provides communications services such as line speed conversion and protocol matching.

variable length file — a file containing segments whose data elements may be of varying lengths from a pre-defined minimum to maximum. Such a file requires an element delimiter character to mark the end of each element and a segment delimiter character to mark the end of each segment.

vendor management — evaluation of vendor performance on the baisis of selected vendor parameters such as quality of product and delivery on promised and requested delivery schedule.

vendor performance — statistics on actual delivery dates as compared to requested and promised dates and on product quality for a particular vendor.

VICS — Voluntary Interindustry Communication Standard committee active in EDI on behalf of the apparel sector of the retail industry.

WINS — Warehouse Information Network Standard.

WSA — Wholesale Stationers Association.

X12 — the accredited subcommittee of American National Standards Institute whose mandate is to development standard data formats for business transactions with cross-industry application.

X.400 — A series of protocol standards for international electronic-mail interexchange.

2780/3780 protocol — communication protocols that use or emulate IBM's binary synchronous protocol. 3780 can operate in unattended mode.

Index

Bibliography Credits and Availability of Additional Materials

EDI: A Selected Bibliography, Volume III, Number 1, Robert A. Payne and A. L. Payne, is reprinted with permission. First published, February, 1986.

Bibliography Acknowledgements

For contributing references:

Charles Biddle of Milliken, Susan Crocker, formerly with the National Association of Purchasing Management, Chris Frapwell of the Uniform Code Council, Harriet Rusk of the Data Interchange Standards Association. Also, the authors are grateful to Ms. Sheryl Stilwell for editorial assistance.

Recommended Reading

EDI Yellow Pages. Find partners, customers, services and products fast in the comprehensive directory of EDI users and vendors with over 5000 listings. Listings are free to users. The directory, published semi-annually, is international, inter-network, and inter-industry. The reference section includes The EDI Glossary, implementation tips, and an EDI international calendar.

TRADE-FLASH International. The original EDI Newsletter. Guides the reader through all aspects of EDI and advises on the optimal approach to EDI implementation. Broad coverage of international news on EDI and the EDIFACT standard. (In association with Eurotech Forum.)

Electronic Data Interchange: Making Business More Efficient. Comprehensive guide on the basics of EDI and its value as a strategic tool in business by Ben Milbrandt. Includes a detailed analysis of standards in non-technical language and real, quantitative success stories from major corporations. For those already familiar with EDI, the book provides steps to follow in implementation. 79 pages. (In association with EDI in Business.)

Electronic Data Interchange and Paperless Trade: The Implementation Guide. Geared to the needs of businessmen in general and to those who have not had time to explore EDI in depth but need to know the concepts. Written in plain language, the book covers costs and benefits, EDI in International Trade, developments in Europe and the EDIFACT Standards. 100 pages. (In association with Euromatica S.A.)

The EDI Eye (tm). "EDI, spread the standards!" A series of rapid-access "help screens" for your PC. As an adjunct to the standards manuals themselves, "The Eye" moves quickly from a transaction set standard to details of the data segments, data elements and code lists. Includes "used by" queries. All TDCC and X12 transaction sets. The EDI Eye is a trademark of National Systems Corporation.

For more information, contact: